UNIVERSITY OF NOTTINGHAM

WITHDRAWN

FROM THE LIBRARY

Any book which you borrow remains your responsibility until the loan
is cancelled.

D1356791

Madonnas
and Magdalens

Madonnas and Magdalens

THE ORIGINS AND DEVELOPMENT OF
VICTORIAN SEXUAL ATTITUDES

Eric Trudgill

Heinemann: London

UNIVERSITY of NOTTINGHAM
MEDICAL LIBRARY
Class HQ 18.97
Fund JACOB
Book No. 9780152/000/01

William Heinemann Ltd
15 Queen Street, Mayfair, London W1X 8BE

LONDON   MELBOURNE   TORONTO
JOHANNESBURG   AUCKLAND

First published 1976

© Eric Trudgill 1976

434 79462-7

PRINTED AND BOUND IN THE UNITED STATES

Contents

v

Part Two: The Development of Victorian Sexual Attitudes

List of Illustrations

ix

Preface

VICTORIAN SEXUALITY has been treated in numerous catch-penny works in a facetious, sensationalist or righteously indignant vein. Even the attention it has received from serious scholars has, with a few exceptions, been deficient in depth of historical sympathy, in comprehensiveness of scale, and in complexity and clarity of generalization. This book is an attempt first to explain sympathetically the sources of Victorian sexual attitudes and in particular the Victorian view of woman; and then to trace through, I hope, a complex yet cogent analytical model the gradual evolution of these attitudes from the middle of the eighteenth century to the beginning of the twentieth. Believing imaginative literature to be the best index of the inward thoughts of past societies, I shall refer extensively to the writers of the day, from the timeless genius to the long-forgotten hack, from the most facetious journalistic flotsam to the most solemn dissertations of the pulpit; but I shall attempt also to illuminate the discrepancies between literary image and sociological fact, the gap where it existed between expressed attitudes and actual behaviour.

It need hardly be said that, with such an abundance of materials, I have treated only certain kinds of sexual attitudes (homosexuality, the so-called perversions, and the huge subject of woman's view of man, for example, receive very little discussion); and I have confined myself largely to the thought and conduct of the middle classes (the London middle classes in particular), with less attention to those of the aristocracy and still less to those of the proletariat.

I am indebted to more secondary works than I can acknowledge briefly. But I must mention my heavy obligation in the area of historical sympathy to the studies of Walter E. Houghton and Maurice J. Quinlan, and in the area of chronological evolution to those of Cyril Pearl, Patricia Thomson and J. M. S. Tompkins. I have also used extensively the materials, if not the arguments, offered in the works I cite by Myron J. Brightfield and Peter T. Cominos. I should like to thank also *Victorian Studies* of Indiana University and the Research Board of Leicester University for their grants in aid of research and Michael Wolff, Steven Marcus, David Spring, Kellow Chesney, Francis Doggett, and especially Philip Collins, for their encouragement and assistance. And lastly I should like to thank Routledge and Kegan Paul for permission to reprint the material in Chapter 5 which I used in my contribution to *The Victorian City: Images and Realities*, ed. H. J. Dyos and Michael Wolff (1973).

For ease of reference I have used the following collected editions:

The Shakespeare Head Brontë ed. T. J. Wise and J. A. Symington (Oxford 1932–8)

The Illustrated Library Edition of the Works of Charles Dickens (1873–6)

The Illustrated Copyright Edition of the Works of George Eliot (1908–11)

The Life and Works of Charles Kingsley (1901–3)

The Memorial Edition of the Works of George Meredith (1909–11)

The Biographical Edition of the Works of William Makepeace Thackeray (1898–9)

For my mother and father

I

The Origins of
Victorian Sexual Attitudes

1

Bumble and the Nude

'FOR THE BUMBLE WHO RULES OVER US,' wrote James Thomson in 1866, 'the naked beauty is obscene, and the naked truth is blasphemous, he thinks that the Venus de Milo came out of Holywell Street.'[1] One need not look far for evidence of the Victorian horror of the nude. In the same year Edward Dowden, writing for the *Contemporary Review* on 'French Aesthetics', found that even the word 'nude' itself was open to objection and was forced by the editor to change it to 'unclothed'; it was 'an indecent, or rather, a *nice* word.' [1] In the previous year the rejection of a nude Cupid and Psyche vignette for an edition of *The Angel in the House* had led Coventry Patmore to say, 'The more I know of English chastity the more it reminds me of that of a saint of whom I was reading, the other day, in Butler's *Lives*, that he was so chaste that he could never remain in a room alone with his mother.' [2]

Art galleries throughout the century provided opportunities for just this kind of over-sensitive purity. Female visitors especially were distinguished by embarrassed, averted looks, by blushing sidelong glances, and often by feelings of intense shame and outrage. Drusilla Way, for example, the nineteen-year-old daughter of an Evangelical clergyman, was greatly troubled in Florence in 1823 by the sight of the Venus de

---

[1] *National Reformer* 23 Dec. 1866, p. 404 (cf. Thomson's poem 'The Naked Goddess', written at this time). Holywell Street was notorious for its dealers in pornography.

3

Medici and the Apollo Belvedere: 'As to the Venus she looks just like what she *is*, and ought to be. *A naked woman thoroughly ashamed of herself!! Perfect nudity* I never saw before, and how ladies can stand *looking* and *staring* and *admiring* with *gentlemen* at it, I can not conceive and *hope I never shall*.' [3] The gentlemen indeed were often equally troubled. Even Thackeray, for all his many attacks on prudish cant (and for all his training as a painter), protested against Etty's nudes: a Sleeping Nymph he found 'so naked, as to be unfit for appearance among respectable people at an exhibition'. [4] In May 1859 a great to-do erupted in Glasgow and elsewhere with the discovery that public money was being spent in art schools in London, Edinburgh and Dublin to procure nude models for the students. [5] And in March 1872 John Ruskin, in his capacity as Slade Professor of Fine Arts at the University of Oxford, claimed that the nude meant degradation for the artist, 'and further yet, that even the study of the external form of the human body, more exposed than it may be healthily and decently in daily life, has been essentially destructive to every school of art in which it has been practised'. [6]

The extent to which the body might healthily and decently be exposed in daily life was of course very narrowly circumscribed. Married people often never saw each other nude, the husband either using a separate dressing room or, where none was available, waiting downstairs until his wife's discreet signal told him that all was now clear in the bedroom. A correspondent of Havelock Ellis told him of an old lady, the mother of three sons, who confessed that she had never even looked at her own nakedness in the whole course of her life, because 'it frightened her'. [7] Bathing, especially at the seaside, presented problems for the Victorian prude, since until the adoption of swimming costumes in the 1870s bathing machines were the only protection for outraged modesty; and the correspondence columns of the press each summer were full of bitter complaints about the shameless seaside cavortings of loose women and unblushing men. How a gentleman was expected to react to the inadvertent exposure of female nudity is nicely shown in a passage from Lady Lennard's *Constance Rivers* 1867, where a young Englishman in India espies through his telescope a native girl on the point of disrobing by a bathing pool: 'Eustace dropped his glass—to continue to observe her would have been profanation. He turned away and tried to think of the landscape.' (I, 300)

It is tempting to make broad generalizations from all this about the Victorian horror of the nude, to equate the Victorian view of nudity with that of 'the Bumble who rules over us', to ascribe it simply to priggish narrow-mindedness and timorous conformity. It is tempting; but it is misleading, it is inaccurate, and it is historically insensitive.

It is misleading to begin with, because English Bumbledom was by no means uniquely Victorian, and one of the fundamental concerns of this study will be to trace the evolution of nineteenth century sexual attitudes from their antecedent sources. In Wycherley's *Country Wife*, for example, Lady Fidget answers her husband's innocent 'Faith, to tell you the naked truth' with the crushing rejoinder 'Fye, Sir Jasper, do not use that word naked' (II, i, 420–1); and this is almost two hundred years before Dowden's trouble with the *Contemporary*. In 1780 the Royal Academy's exhibition of casts from famous statues on the staircases and in the Antique Room at Somerset House, produced a violent storm of disapproval; [8] and among these casts, 'the terror of every decent woman', were ones of the Venus de Medici and the Apollo Belvedere—forty-three years before they outraged Drusilla Way. In February 1778 the *Critical Review* showed a more than Victorian fastidiousness on the subject of nude bathing. In a review of Richard Cumberland's *Battle of Hastings* it protested that the lines 'I saw your hero dart into the fight/As a train'd swimmer springs into the flood' were too indelicate for 'even a princess of those rude days' to use: 'we do not doubt, that if Matilda's eyes had ever, *by accident*, been gratified with the sight of a swimmer springing into the flood, the young lady had more judgement than to use it in her common conversation, *by the way of simile'*. (XLV, 154-5)

To ascribe the Victorian view of nudity simply to Victorian Bumbledom is historically misleading. It is also historically inaccurate, making no allowance for the enormous variety of nineteenth century sexual attitudes. A great many Victorians, for example, though prudish by our standards, regarded the nude with unembarrassed common sense. Queen Victoria, for one, went to an exhibition at Gore House in 1853 and by accident saw some Mulready nude drawings hidden from her by anxious officialdom: far from being shocked she admired them immensely, summoned her children to enjoy them too, and offered to purchase some. [9] And Robert Browning, for all his prudish scruples in some respects, was for much of his writing life an energetic champion of the nude:

> God's best of beauteous and magnificent
> Revealed to earth—the naked female form. [10]

Browning, it is true, was almost morbidly self-conscious about his own personal nudity. [11] But not Francis Kilvert, the chaste, young West country clergyman. In his diary for the seventies he is both lyrical about the delights of nude sea-bathing and indignant about 'the detestable custom of bathing in drawers' that was becoming *de rigueur*. At Seaton in 1873, he notes with scant embarrassment, he scandalized the beach by being unaware of the new convention. But in fact he did not scandalize everyone: 'the young ladies who were strolling near seemed to have no objection'. [12] And this was, or rather had been before the adoption of bathing drawers, one of the mysteries of the age, that ladies at the seaside seemed to throw off all prudish apprehensions as they did their shawls and wrappers. [13] In all the major resorts, crowds of perfectly respectable women thronged the gentlemen's part of the beach, within a few yards of the bathing machines, quite unconcerned by the sights before them. 'There they sit,' commented the *Saturday Review*, happy, innocent, undisturbed—placidly and immovably gazing at hundreds of males in the costume of Adam. There does not seem to be a notion that there is anything improper—there are no averted looks, no sidelong glances, no blushes or shame. Naked men are treated as one of the products of the place, like lobsters, or soles, or pebbles. Hundreds of highly respectable and modest women . . . their artificial modesty blunted by custom look on the living statues so close to them as complacently and stedfastly as they would on the marble images in the Crystal Palace. [14]

Common sense here, as in the case of nudity in the fine arts, could often quite displace the influence of Bumble.

Coexisting with this common sense lack of embarrassment and this aesthetic appreciation of the nude there was also a great deal of moral apathy and furtive prurience—as the *Saturday Review*'s allusion to 'living statues' reminds us. Living statues, *poses plastiques* or *tableaux vivants*, were an early and rather gentle form of striptease: the exhibition of theatrical artistes, especially young women, in classical poses and scanty dresses. The gentlemen who in summer lined the ladies' beaches opera glass in hands, exchanging their opinions of the view, might in winter apply their critical judgements to *poses plastiques* in theatrical burlesques and extravaganzas.[1] On 13 September 1841 the short-lived *Daily Dispatch* raged about the moral pollution of Drury Lane: 'Where, we ask, in the name of common decency are these things to end? Are we to calmly suffer our mothers and sisters to sit and witness human figures —but one remove from nudity—standing in positions which, if represented by the artist's skill, would justly call down a prosecution from the Society for the Suppression of Vice?' (p. 3). Where were these things to end? A question asked, in a different way, by many an appreciative patron of their pleasures:

[1] Even the chaste Mr Kilvert hardly came up to the scrupulous standards of Lady Lennard's Eustace. See, for example, his frank enjoyment of the sight of a nude young girl at the seaside in 1875—*op. cit.*, III, 208.

Since every day they're less inclined to clothes;
Group follows group, each *tableau* has its brother
Trying, the wags say, to outstrip the other. [15]

The *Daily Dispatch* claimed that these exhibitions owed their survival to the 'prurient feelings and esoteric ideas of the aristocracy', but the success a few years later of the Naked Lady, the American actress Adah Menken, suggests such prurience was diffused throughout society. Her appearance at Astley's in 1864 as the hero in an adaptation of Byron's *Mazeppa* was fanfared with posters all over London showing her semi-nude and bound to the back of a galloping horse. All seats for the first four weeks of the run were sold prior to the opening, and after the first night when she received twenty curtain calls long queues formed outside the box-office. Afterwards she enjoyed a hugely prosperous national tour, despite the competition of a crop of plagiarizing rivals, and she repeated her success in London in 1865 and 1867. Her success with the public, with poets, playwrights and novelists, Dickens among them, and her generally favourable reviews (*Punch* was a furious exception) were not wholly due to her 'nakedness'—in fact tight fleshings and a short white tunic left only her limbs uncovered—but this was clearly the principal factor.

By the late 1860s the costumes of female ballet dancers, a source of complaint from the beginning of the century, became increasingly abbreviated as theatre managers discovered that the size of their audience was often in inverse proportion to the length of their dancers' skirts. On 30 January 1869 we find the *Saturday Review* complaining that 'the manager relies for his effects on the female form, tastefully disposed in every conceivable combination; its nudity just sufficiently relieved by dress and veiled by drapery to leave it fascinatingly suggestive instead of repellently coarse. "Startling effects", indeed, as the play-bills advertise them, would they have been to the last generation. Nowadays these things are taken as matter of course. . . .' (XXVII, 140) Six months later, with the first thoroughgoing cancan performed in England, in Offenbach's *Orpheus in the Underworld*, at the St James's Theatre, there was further evidence of the public's toleration, or rather enthusiastic approval of feminine undress. *The Times* 15 July sardonically advised 'all fastidious persons to take leave of *Orphée* at the end of the third *tableau*, though we are perfectly aware that by this very advice we are only recommending a large majority of the audience to remain in the theatre till the final descent of the curtain'. (p. 10) *The Times* recognized, as we must too, the variety and discordance of Victorian attitudes to nudity. To ascribe them simply to Victorian Bumbledom is not only historically misleading in view of Bumbledom's antecedents, but patently inaccurate in view of their diversity.

It might be thought perhaps that the Victorian view of nudity corresponds less to the narrowminded prudery of Thomson's Bumble than the smug, canting, hypocritical Bumble of Charles Dickens. Certainly the prurient titillation of partially clothed *tableaux vivants*, equestrienne actresses, ballerinas and cancan dancers is very much part of an age that prided itself on the purity of its literature— a literature that would not bring a blush to a virgin's cheek—and yet allowed sexual innuendo, salacious advertisement and prurient law court reports in its daily newspapers. Even its family literature was not as pure as it liked to think. Kingsley, for example, an Anglican clergyman, had a predilection for indulging erotic fantasy in his writings. It is remarkable how often his heroines turn up naked: Argemone in *Yeast* is the subject of a nude drawing by the hero; St Maura in the poem of that name tells how she underwent public stripping and flagellation; Rose Salterne in *Westward Ho!* takes a nude sea-bathe at night; and the heroine of *Hypatia* is twice seen naked, on the second occasion, like St Maura, being subjected to public stripping. It is remarkable too how all these women meet agonizing deaths as if to expiate their exhibitionism: Argemone dies disfigured and in great pain from typhus fever, St Maura is crucified, Rose is tortured and immolated by the Spanish Inquisition, and the naked Hypatia is stoned to death by a vicious mob. Kingsley's blend of prurience and moral sadism is admittedly extreme. [16] But there is a good deal of covert salaciousness in mid- and late-Victorian literature. In April 1862 we are presented with the irony of a prudish Evangelical magazine, the *Christian Observer*, in accents similar to the *Saturday Review*'s charge against ballerinas, preferring the blatant indecencies of Pope and Swift to the furtive prurience of modern writers: 'Our primitive nakedness is not half so dangerous to our moral sense as a tricked out and enticing pudicity. The filthiness of nineteenth-century decency may pollute more, because it offends less, than the plain-spoken honesty of our forefathers in calling things by their right names.' (LXII, 281–2).

Bland hypocrisy would seem the charge for the Victorians to face: preaching purity whilst condoning lubricity; canting about the blush on a virgin's cheek whilst turning a Nelson eye to the prurient in their literature; fussing about with fig leaves for statues and drapes for piano legs, whilst drawing a veil over the sordid facts of English life—the existence of a double standard of morality, the prostitutes in streets and public places, the figures of venereal disease, illegitimacy, infanticide, and abortion. 'England is a prude among nations,' charged the *Monthly Repository* in 1833, 'As long as she preserves external propriety, she plumes herself on the possession of superior virtue.' (n.s. VII, 784) Detailed consideration of this question of hypocrisy would be premature at this juncture. For the moment I wish only to anticipate the discussion in later chapters by suggesting once again how easy it is to oversimplify. For one thing, the belief in England's possession of superior virtue was by no means an English monopoly: foreign observers rarely questioned the superior chastity of her literature, and many—Von Raumer, for example, in the 1830s and Taine in the 1860s—were impressed, despite the evidence of the streets, by the superior chastity of her morals. [17] For another, many Victorians, as we shall see later, were anything but complacent about their country's sexual virtues. But more important, to accuse Victorian England of complacent humbug on the subject of her own morality, to see her as Dickensian Bumbledom writ large, is historically very insensitive. 'So far as we pretend to social purity as a nation,' wrote Walter Besant in 1890, 'we are indeed hypocrites. But to set up a standard of purity and to advocate it is not hypocrisy.' [18] The Victorians may have been prudish to set up such a standard of purity, but it is unjust to dismiss them as simple humbugs.

In the same way, a horror of the naked truth should not always be dismissed as hypocritical Bumbledom. Drawing a veil over the sordid features of English life was not necessarily evidence of humbug, of evading, or even conniving at, the facts of social immorality. It could mean very often, as we shall see, a helpless appreciation of the intractability of the problem, and a concern that undue exposure might prove only an aggravation. Focussing society's attention on a standard of purity might prove a better solution than recognizing openly the extent of its infraction. In the first place it would avoid making vice seem almost respectable in view of its unofficial social acceptance: it is interesting to see Thackeray in *The Times* 2 September 1840 contrasting nineteenth-century decency, like the *Christian Observer*, with the primitive nakedness of our forefathers, and yet arguing that 'it is good to pretend to the virtue of chastity even though we do not possess it; nay, the very restraint which the hypocrisy lays on a man is not unapt in some circumstances to profit him'. (p. 6) But more than this, exposure of social immorality might serve only to debase the standard of purity, making society unduly preoccupied with the existence of impurity. Hence Tennyson's objection to what he considered the degrading morbidity and materialism of realistic fiction analysing man's sexual functions:

Rip your brothers' vices open, strip your own foul passions bare;
Down with Reticence, down with Reverence—forward—naked—
—let them stare. [19]

'Reverence' is the key. To focus on immorality, as French writers did, rather than on purity, was to see 'the most secret and sacred recesses of the soul explored and mastered, not for reverential contemplation of their beauties and their mysteries, but in order to expose them, with a hideous grin—naked, sensitive, and shrinking—to the desecrating sneers of a misbelieving and mocking world'. [20]

This writer and Tennyson may have been misguided and over-sensitive in their attitudes, in demanding reticence and reverence. But they were very far from hypocritical humbugs. Neither, if they were prudes, were they Bumbles to whom 'the naked beauty is obscene, and the naked truth is blasphemous'. To equate the Victorian view of nudity with Victorian Bumbledom is finally misleading, inaccurate and insensitive because of the varieties of Victorian prudery. The lineaments of Thomson's Bumble, timorous conformity and narrow-mindedness, and the lineaments of Dickens' Bumble, affected gentility, ignorant bigotry, economic self-interest and phari-saical cant—these are all to be found there. But there is also a good deal else, as we shall see. Victorian prudery is not always a sign of moral shallowness and cowardice, but very often the reverse; and this is a vital distinction. The lineaments of the Bumbles are not to be found in Tennyson's brand of prudery but in the smooth self-righteousness and smug, narrow-minded conventionalism of one of Tennyson's own creations, and in one of his bitterest enemies, the 'British Goddess Sleek Respectability'. [21] And yet perhaps, when we have examined the contours of this creature in some detail, unlike Tennyson we may with historical hindsight feel a certain sympathy even for her and for the Bumbles.

2

The British Goddess
Sleek Respectability

I ASCETICISM

IN 1894 GRANT ALLEN, an anti-Victorian prophet of 'The
New Hedonism', fulminated against the spirit of asceticism,
the repression of natural and especially sexual pleasure, that
he claimed was crippling English society. Not surprisingly
Allen equated asceticism, the hatred of 'painting and sculpture,
nude limbs of classic nymphs . . . innocent love, innocent
pleasure', [22] effectively with Bumbledom, or the smug self-
righteousness, the timid, narrow-minded conventionalism of
the British Goddess Sleek Respectability. Asceticism in short
was a synonym for psalm-singing cant. Allen's picture was by
no means wholly inaccurate: the oily sleekness of Dickens'
Mr Chadband was doubtless a feature of Victorian religious
life. But whilst recognizing the amount of pharisaism and
hypocrisy in Victorian asceticism, we should recognize also the
genuine moral seriousness at its base.

It was Evangelicalism that did most to establish the anti-
pleasure principle. But the whole spectrum of Victorian
religion, from the austere puritanism of Methodism and the
Nonconformist sects, through the Established Church, to the
moral earnestness of the Oxford Movement, showed a similar
asceticism. The asceticism, for example, of the great schoolman
Dr Arnold: 'Life, in his view of it,' wrote a contemporary,
'was no pilgrimage of pleasure, but a scene of toil, of effort, of

13

appointed work—of grand purposes to be striven for—of vast ends to be achieved—of fearful evils to be uprooted or trampled down—of sacred and mighty principles to be asserted and carried out.' [23] The reward for strenuous toil was eternal bliss, the penalty for a life of pleasure was everlasting hell. Often the austerity was so strict that even the smallest indulgence was taboo. The Evangelical Sir James Stephen, for example, was so inexorably suspicious of pleasure that when he asked himself once why he continued to take snuff and could find no satisfactory answer, he ceremoniously emptied the box out of the window; 'he once smoked a cigar', wrote his son, 'and found it so delicious that he never smoked again.' [24] The extreme punctiliousness of this self-denial was partly a reflection of the seriousness of life's mission, of the need for unceasing dedication and the danger of petty indiscipline and distractions. The Evangelical mind in this respect, as in others, was identical to that of the early Puritans.[1] But the extreme punctiliousness was also, with the Evangelicals as with the early Puritans, a reflection of a very over-developed sense of sin.

The Evangelical mind was obsessed with sin, by its fearful consequences and by the sway it yet enjoyed in the human heart; mankind was innately corrupt. The obsession was frequently planted in early childhood: anxious parents, believing that their young were the children not of innocence but of sin, tried to frighten them into sanctity with grim catalogues of their failings, with vivid pictures of a ubiquitous Satan working ever to damn them, with gruesome descriptions of Judgement Day and Hellfire. How many Victorian children, one wonders, shared the agonies of Kingsley's Alton Locke: 'Now and then, believing, in obedience to my mother's assurances, and the solemn prayers of the ministers about me,

[1] Cf. R. H. Tawney's vivid analysis of the Puritan mentality in *Religion and the Rise of Capitalism* (1926): 'like an engineer, who, to canalize the rush of the oncoming tide, dams all channels save that through which it is to pour, like a painter who makes light visible by plunging all that is not light in gloom, the Puritan attunes his heart to the voice from Heaven by an immense effort of concentration and abnegation'. (p. 228)

that I was a child of hell, and a lost and miserable sinner, I used to have accesses of terror, and fancy that I should surely wake next morning in everlasting flames.' [25] Part of this morbidity and the stringent moral punctiliousness came from the doctrine of 'little by little': the slightest indiscretion, if left unchecked, prepared the mind for error, error for laxity, and laxity for insensible depravity. Hence the brutal punishment of trivial crimes in much of the fiction designed for children: the model father, for example, in Margaret Sherwood's *The Fairchild Family*, which went through fourteen editions between 1818 and its extension in 1842, takes his children, as a warning to them for quarrelling over a doll, to see the gibbetted corpse of a fratricidal murderer; Mrs Randolph in *Melbourne House* by Elizabeth Wetherill whips her little daughter till the blood comes, to punish her for not saying grace before eating.

The only safeguard against Satan and his insidious, 'little by little' wiles was persistent vigilance, persistent self-examination, of the most scrupulous and most censorious kind. In no area of morality was this more true than in the sexual. The slightest deviation from the strictest rectitude could be the beginning of disaster; to listen to even a mildly equivocal joke, to look at even a mildly suggestive picture was to flirt with spiritual suicide. The Methodist *Eclectic Review* in October 1806 warned its readers of the dangers lurking in a collection of love poems by Thomas Moore:

If then, in the perusal of these voluptuous volumes, he finds himself fascinated with their beauty, let him tremble, let him fly; it is the beauty, it is the fascination of the serpent, of the Old Serpent, which ought to inspire terror and repugnance, while it is tempting, attracting, delighting him into destruction. . . . The danger lies in dallying with sin, and with sensual sin above all other: it works, it winds, it wins its way with imperceptible, with irresistible insinuation, through all the passages of the mind, into the innermost recesses of the heart; while it is softening the bosom, it is hardening the conscience; while, by its exhilaration, it seems to be spiritualizing the body, it is brutalizing the soul, and, by mingling with its eternal essence, it is giving *immortality* to impotent unappeasable desires, it is engendering 'the worm that dieth not', it is kindling 'the fire that is not quenched'. (II, Pt 2, 813–14)

'Painting and sculpture, nude limbs of classic nymphs', indeed every form of sensual enjoyment, were inevitably highly suspect. But such prudish suspicion arose from understandable, if misguided, spiritual fears, not merely from the smug psalm-singing of the British Goddess Sleek Respectability.

If Grant Allen was insensitive about the spiritual side of Victorian asceticism, he was over-simple too in his attack on its materialistic, 'money-grubbing' aspects. It is true that society's sponsorship of an ascetic sexual principle was under-written by prudential considerations. The premium on femi-nine purity, for example, had arisen long before the Victorian period, in large measure from the property mentality of the emergent middle-class. There was first the economic factor, given classic formulation by Dr Johnson: 'Consider of what importance to society the chastity of woman is. Upon that all property in the world depends. They who forfeit it should not have any possibility of being restored to good character; nor should the children of an illicit connection attain the full right of lawful children.' [26] And then there was the psychological factor, the tendency of the proprietorial mind to see women as properties, whose values were determined by their purity: the sex reformer Edward Carpenter in 1896 argued that the stress on feminine purity was partly the historical product of com-mercialism, in that the sense of Private Property had 'turned Woman more and more—especially of course among the possessing classes—into an emblem of possession—a mere doll, an empty idol, a brag of a man's exclusive right in the sex'. [27] Woman was not only the hereditary custodian of man's treasure, she was a treasure herself, an ornament of his material acquisitions, a kind of status symbol and a treasure secure from loss or theft by her immaculate sexual purity. The prudential, proprietorial motive is undeniable. But it would be ungenerous not to recognize that it was often very understandable. Pride in one's possessions and the desire to protect them from improper inheritance are very natural human foibles; and they were the more natural for an emergent class gaining its wealth not through birth, like the aristocracy, but through hard work and self-sacrifice. The aristocrat too could practise primogeniture and therefore insist on only a legitimate first born. But the middle-class capitalist required the legitimacy of all his children: not only to protect his hard won possessions from being enjoyed by the offspring of other men, but to ensure the loyalty of his sons, who might be business partners, and of his daughters, who might make valuable marriages.

There were material advantages too from masculine asceticism as well as feminine. But here again it is easy for an anti-Victorian like Grant Allen to be unduly censorious. Asceticism, he claimed, taught 'the money-grubbing and narrow-minded middle-class, in its bald Ebenezers, that love is a thing to be got over once for all in early life, and relegated thenceforth to the back parlour of existence in the most business-like way, so that the mind may be free for the serious affairs of alternating psalm-singing and retail trading. No romance must interfere with the solid worship of Mammon.' [28] Clearly there was some connection between economic prudence and the denial of sexual indulgence. It is unnecessary to make rash analogies, as some writers have done, between the Victorian's financial prudence and his reluctance to waste his precious semen,[1] to see that there is something in Allen's claim. Even those Victorians blissfully ignorant of Malthusian economics would appreciate that unchecked sexual indulgence in a largely pre-contraceptive age could lead to financial embarrassment, and make the family more of a millstone than a springboard in the pursuit of wealth

[1] Till the end of the nineteenth century the chief English colloquialism for the orgasm was 'to spend'. For a detailed working out of the analogy I refer to see Peter T. Cominos, 'Late-Victorian Respectability and the Social System', *International Review of Social History* (1963), VIII, 18–48, 216–50.

and station. Even those Victorians unmoved by Evangelical warnings about the wages of sexual sin would appreciate that unchecked sexual indulgence could lead to dissipation and extravagance when the need was for thrifty husbandry. But we should beware of accepting too readily Allen's glib ascription of bourgeois morality to the solid worship of Mammon. Some Victorians doubtless believed in the incompatibility of sexual indulgence and devotion to work: one recalls the poet Dowson's bitter complaint that 'Passion is waste—takes away from a man's stability, his self-centralization. . . . It fastens on life like a cancer.' [29] But one has only to consider that modern businessmen are not remarkably monastic in their habits to question the general applicability of Allen's financial-sexual equation. We should note moreover, *pace* Allen, that where asceticism did have an undoubted prudential value this was often a collateral benefit rather than primary incentive: like the early Puritans, the Evangelical middle class found that industry and temperance were not only spiritual necessities but economic blessings, just as idleness and dissipation spelt economic ruin as well as spiritual damnation. 'To be serious,' writes G. M. Young, 'to redeem the time, to abstain from gambling, to remember the Sabbath day to keep it holy, to limit the gratification of the senses to the pleasures of a table lawfully earned and the embraces of a wife lawfully wedded, are virtues for which the reward is not laid up in heaven only.' [30]

It is better to talk of the prudential side of Victorian asceticism in these terms than to speak of the mind being free for the solid worship of Mammon. And it is better, while recognizing the psalm-singing, money-grubbing aspects of the Victorian fear of sex, to do justice to the sincerity of Victorian religion: to see, in short, the moral seriousness of a Puritan revival as well as the pharisaism and hypocrisy of the British Goddess Sleek Respectability.

II AFFECTATION

After his remarks about the economic rewards of asceticism G. M. Young passes on to another important collateral benefit: 'The world is very evil. An unguarded look, a word, a gesture, a picture, or a novel, might plant a seed of corruption in the most innocent heart, and the same word or gesture might betray a lingering affinity with the class below.' Again his tone is very temperate. Other modern writers, and many Victorians too, have launched indignant attacks upon the genteel affectation, the censorious snobbish cant that formed a central and quite amoral constituent of Victorian respectability and prudery—an area governed not by deference to God but by the fear of Mrs Grundy. 'We must pass over,' mocked Thackeray in *Vanity Fair*, 'a part of Mrs Rebecca Crawley's biography with that lightness and delicacy which the world demands—the moral world, that has, perhaps, no particular objection to vice, but an insuperable repugnance to hearing vice called by its proper name.' (p. 624) Even Mrs General's propriety, gibed Dickens in *Little Dorrit*, 'could not dispute that there was impropriety in the world; but Mrs General's way of getting rid of it was to put it out of sight, and make believe that there was no such thing'. (II, 25)

Clearly there was a great deal of hypocritical fastidiousness in the Victorian repression of sex, a great deal of moral display and moral censure that were quite independent of religious considerations. Indeed the prudery of class-consciousness had taken a hold on England long before the Evangelical revival. It had grown progressively with the rise of the bourgeoisie to the point that in the second half of the eighteenth century it was a frequent subject for satirical remark. In December 1791 the *Gentleman's Magazine* commented ironically on the progressive bowdlerization of the plays of Shakespeare:

It is well known that, for some time past, neither man, woman, nor child, in Great Britain or Ireland, of any rank or fashion, has been subject to that gross kind of exudation which was formerly known as *sweat*; and that now every mortal, except carters, coal-heavers, and Irish chairmen . . . merely *perspires*. . . . All our mothers and grandmothers used in due course of time to become *with-child*, or, as Shakespeare has it, *round-wombed* . . . but it is very well known, that no female, above the degree of a chambermaid or laundress, has been *with-child* these ten years past: every decent married woman now becomes *pregnant*; nor is she ever *brought-to-bed* or *delivered*, but merely, at the end of nine months, has an *accouchement*; antecedent to which, she always informs her friends that at a certain time she shall be *confined*. (LXI, 1099–1100)

But if genteel affectation was not a Victorian invention, in the nineteenth century it became much more marked and universal because of the increase in class fragmentation. In the eighteenth century the social hierarchy consisted of the aristocracy and gentry; the upper middle-class of, for example, bankers, army officers and the higher clergy; below them the professional and commercial classes; then the lower middle-class of shopkeepers, farmers, skilled craftsmen, clerks and so forth; and last the proletariat. In the nineteenth century it is still possible, and I think preferable, to think in terms of these divisions, but one must recognize the increasing complexity of social stratification. Not only were the middle classes drawing away from the poor, but each stratum within the bourgeoisie was drawing away from the stratum next below it. In a sense this seems somewhat paradoxical in view of the natural overlap, the uncertainty of demarcation, between a merchant, say, and a lesser banker on the one hand and a prosperous shopkeeper on the other. But the possible blurring of stratification only stimulated each class section to heighten the distinction, to accentuate its refinements and to view with severity the standards of its inferiors. Genteel affectation and censorious cant were an indispensable part of the class struggle. In Frances Trollope's *Uncle Walter* of 1852 the unworldly old gentleman of its title is instructed that 'all the denizens of this our mighty Babylon are ever and always engaged in a vehement twofold struggle, consisting on the one hand of a constant effort to get pulled up into the social level just above them by a sort of moral clinging to the skirts of their superiors in the great hierarchy, and on the other by an equally increasing endeavour to shake off, and kick down, those who from below are striving to cling to them.' (I, 206)

The competition in gentility increased progressively throughout the century, especially with the expanding numbers, wealth, and social self-assertiveness of the lower middle-classes and of the upper working classes, the 'aristocracy of labour', from whom they were virtually indistinguishable. It was this area of society that was the principal target of late-Victorian attacks on the cult of respectability. Geoffrey Mortimer in a book called *The Blight of Respectability* (1900) described a typical respectable man: 'He lives at Brixton or Clapham in a continuous struggle to keep up a "decent" appearance among the neighbours. His wife "takes in paying guests", and his daughters spend most of their time in blocking the pavement in front of drapers' shops. Mamma and the girls are gangrened with respectability and snobbishness.' (p. 5) A vivid sketch of suburban, lower middle-class gentility is given in George Gissing's *In the Year of Jubilee* (1894). Mrs Peachey and her two sisters fill their lives with second-hand notions of refinement culled from penny novelettes and the gossip columns and fashion pages of the illustrated weeklies. 'They spoke a peculiar tongue, the product of sham education and mock refinement grafted upon a stock of robust vulgarity. One and all would have been moved to indignant surprise if accused of ignorance or defective breeding. Ada had frequented an "establishment for young ladies" up to the close of her seventeenth year; the other two had pursued culture at a still more pretentious institute until they were eighteen.' (I, 14)

These attitudes may seem to typify the British Goddess Sleek Respectability at her worst, the fossilization of bourgeois false refinement. But we should hesitate before condemning the

Victorian middle-classes out of hand. Much of its moral affectation, seen in historical context, was in fact very understandable. Long before the Victorian period an excessive attention to formal propriety had been the natural concomitant of an emergent class unwilling to be regarded as outsiders or social upstarts. The newly arrived bourgeois lacking in social assurance and self-confidence, sensitive to slights from above and to sneers from below, anxious to establish parity with his equals, to feel the solidarity of class with him and not against him, was inevitably concerned to conceal deficiencies in his breeding. This concern, when conjoint with ignorance of the conventions, often led to an undue preoccupation with the niceties of conduct. It was here that Evangelicalism, as in other ways, provided its adherent with a bonus. Because of its 'little by little' suspicion of the smallest sin Evangelicalism formulated rules to govern the smallest acts of daily life, including matters that pertained more to etiquette than to ethics. 'With its taboos and proscriptions,' writes Maurice Quinlan, 'its pronouncements upon the minutest acts of the individual, Evangelicalism provided believers with a set of rules to guide them in almost every social situation.' [31]

Genteel affectations, then, were not necessarily the product of pompous cant: they could often be an indication of insecurity and uncertainty. This was the more likely to be the case where education was defective. Consider the following: 'We can scarcely hope to describe adequately the beauty, the gentleness, the earnest sweet simplicity of Matilda Rashleigh's character. She was one of those few beautiful beings who are only to be found in the middle classes of society in this country; and, somehow or another, are not to be found in any other country at all.' This is not, as it might seem, a sop to canting bourgeois readers. It comes in fact from a working class penny weekly of 1844. [32] The working classes exhibited the same kind of intra-stratification as their betters and, in their upper reaches, an attention to propriety that was frequently more excessive.

With their defective education it is hard to blame them. Indeed the correspondence columns of the penny weeklies are often touching in their innocent solemnity: one finds letters, for example, from shop girls asking the editor if they may accept presents from male admirers or if they may address a gentleman correspondent as 'My Dear Sir'. In the same way one feels a certain sympathy for the ignorant genteel posturing of lower middle-class snobs like Mrs Peachey and her sisters; and in a different way for those other notorious snobs, placed ambiguously between the lower middle-class and the proletariat, the clerks, national school teachers, commercial travellers and superior servants, whose exaggerated middle-class refinement was in large measure compensation and cover for the insecurity of their position.

But an assiduous cultivation of propriety could do more than form a substitute for social self-assurance: it could offer moral as well as social protection to those who needed it. Just as status was dependent upon respectable morality, so morality could be dependent upon respectable status. As Charlotte Brontë very shrewdly observes in *Villette*, 'There are people whom a lowered position degrades morally, to whom loss of connection costs loss of self-respect: are not these justified in placing the highest value on that station and association which is their safeguard from debasement?' (II, 74–5) Self-respect was a particularly vital property in the nether regions of the working class and hence the increase, not diminution, of snobbery at the base of the social pyramid. Peter T. Cominos remarks in an interesting section of his unpublished doctoral dissertation that 'Coming down the social ladder self-respect, which depended upon the degree of respectability attained, diminished while status consciousness intensified, until reaching rock bottom, then both disappeared. The undeserving poor faced the world without a character.' [33] In the brutalized conditions of much of working-class life the assiduous cultivation of propriety could act as a moral lifeline. In *The Other Victorians* (1966) Steven Marcus comments penetratingly on a poor girl's rejection of the bribes and cajolery of the author of *My Secret Life*:

> It is not usual nowadays to regard such values as chastity, propriety, modesty, even rigid prudery as positive moral values, but it is difficult to doubt that in the situation of the urban lower social classes they operated with positive force. The discipline and self-restraint which the exercise of such virtues required could not but be a giant step towards the humanization of a class of persons who had been traditionally regarded as almost of another species. Indeed, the whole question of 'respectability' stands revealed in a new light when we consider it from this point of view. One of the chief components of respectability is self-respect, and when we see this young girl resisting all that money, class, privilege, and power, we understand how vital an importance the moral idea of respectability could have for persons in her circumstances. (p. 146)

It is possible, then, to see more in Mrs Grundy than the mere embodiment of genteel affectation and censorious snobbish cant.

III ALARMISM

'Respectability,' wrote Grant Allen in 1891, 'is a peculiarly British vice. It means an utter lack of moral and intellectual courage.' [34] This kind of charge was very prevalent in the late-Victorian era. The moral seriousness of Evangelical asceticism was still common, but so too was a superficial, conformist kind of austerity in which religion meant a reverence for received ideas rather than a fervent, vital faith: ' "A most respectable man". We all know him—a sort of factory-made cheap line in humanity, with a few prim, precise, little superstitions, no reasoned morals, and no intellectual or aesthetic needs. He is a big man of a petty sect, and on Sunday he troops a stout, silk-dressed wife and seven or eight children to hear Boanerges hold forth at the tin Bethel at the end of the street.' [35] The genteel affectation issuing from social, and even moral, insecurity was perhaps more common than ever, but so too was the lazy, philistine smugness of the comfortably arrived, the complacent materialism of Villadom where the battle for self-respect had become simply a competitive obsession with the quality of the neighbours' curtains and carpets. In a social climate such as this the charge of moral and intellectual cowardice was all too easily sustained. Conventional, lazy minds were quickly alarmed by new ideas upsetting traditional notions of decency, quickly outraged by the dangers to society represented by such things as socialism, 'decadent' modern literature and a liberated womanhood. But it is important not to get this kind of alarmism out of perspective. Tennyson had painted scornfully the moral cowardice of the British Goddess Sleek Respectability:

> Poor soul! behold her: what decorous calm!
> She, with her week-day worldliness sufficed;
> Stands in her pew and hums her decent psalm
> With decent dippings at the name of Christ! (*loc. cit.*)

But Tennyson too was quick to take alarm at notions he thought threatening society's stability; and an examination of Victorian moral conservatism will distinguish sharply the fears of men like Tennyson from the conformist cowardice of sleek respectability.

One needs, to begin with, to contrast the shallowness of 'decent dippings at the name of Christ' with the profound spiritual agonies of many Victorian believers and non-believers, the terrors of doubt as religious certainty crumbled under the assaults of rationalists, scientists and scriptural theologians. As early as 1836 Carlyle was describing the age as 'at once destitute of faith and terrified of scepticism'. [36] Already, the rumblings of the geologists and the German Higher Critics were beginning to be heard. And in the coming years troubled minds were battered by a succession of new blows: between 1842 and 1846 alone they saw the publication of Blanco White's _Life_, F. W. Newman's _Phases of Faith_, Mill's _Logic_, Chambers' _Vestiges of Creation_, and George Eliot's translation of Strauss. Professor Houghton quotes a poignant passage from F. W. Robertson to illustrate the torments that religious doubts could bring:

> It is an awful moment when the soul begins to find that the props on which it has blindly rested so long are, many of them, rotten, and begins to suspect them all; when it begins to feel the nothingness of many of the traditionary opinions which have been received with implicit confidence, and in that horrible insecurity begins also to doubt whether there be anything to believe at all. It is an awful hour—let him who has passed through it say how awful—when this life has lost its meaning, and seems shrivelled into a span; when the grave appears to be the end of all, human goodness nothing but a name, and the sky above this universe a dead expanse, black with the void from which God himself has disappeared. (_op. cit._, p. 73)

After 1859, when the bombshell of Darwinism burst, the skies were blacker than ever.[1] Evolution to many seemed incompatible with faith. The mechanistic Darwinian universe, ruled by blind chance, made the Bible unfactual, prayer illogical, man a mere animal or human automaton. Far from being the centre of the universe man was merely the last link in an enormous evolutionary chain. He had lost his hope of heaven, his assurance of immortality, his spiritual uniqueness over the animal kingdom. Without a soul, without free will, virtue was mere expediency, conscience disguised egotism, love the development of an animal's gregarious instincts. And yet, paradoxically, this apparent undermining of God and religious sanctions against immorality, this apparent demonstration of the animality of man, served often to increase, not diminish,

---

[1] Again one should note the rapid succession of fresh blows: _Essays and Reviews_ (1860), Colenso's _Pentateuch_ (1862), Renan's _Vie de Jésus_ (1863) and the anonymous _Ecce Homo_ (1866). For a detailed study of the impact of _The Origin of Species_ see Alvar Ellegard, _Darwin and the General Reader_ (Göteborg 1958).

the doubting or lapsed Christian's faith in sexual purity and his alarm at possible dangers to its welfare.

The retention of Christian morality despite the rejection of Christian faith is a characteristic of Victorian agnosticism. Leslie Stephen took a fairly typical position. 'I now believe in nothing, to put it shortly; but I do not the less believe in morality, etc. . . . I mean to live and die like a gentleman if possible.' Frequently the belief in gentlemanly decency was expressed more fervently than this. One thinks of the occasion when Frederic Harrison was asked by his son what a man should do if he fell in love but could not marry. His first response was simple indignation. ' "Do!" he cried, "Do what every gentleman does in such circumstances." ' But when the son persisted with his questions Harrison fairly exploded: ' "A man who cannot learn self-control is a cad. . . . A loose man is a foul man. He is anti-social. He is a beast. . . . It is not a subject I can discuss. It is not a subject that decent men do discuss." ' [37] Harrison's prudish emotionalism looks like moral and intellectual cowardice, timorous moral conservatism of the very worst kind. But to judge it so would be quite insensitive to the psychic difficulties of Victorian unbelief. The retention of Christian morality by agnostics was usually because of, not in spite of, their rejection of Christian faith. For one thing, the unbeliever might find relief in moral earnestness from the naggings of a residual Puritan conscience, perhaps from a sense of guilt at deserting the God of his fathers; and the earnestness might well be intensified by the agnostic's necessary internalization of moral judgement—there was now no objective measurement for his sin and no objective vehicle for his atonement. But, more important, an intensified morality could bring reassurance to minds troubled by the black, empty skies from which God had disappeared and by the scientists' picture of man as a mere animal or human automaton. Strict morality could give the security of belief to unbelievers, bring shape and meaning to life, fill the void of spiritual desolation. Strict morality too could attest to the dignity of man, restore his self-esteem, his sense of uniqueness over the brute creation.

Sexual morality especially, the purity of connubial love, could act as a substitute for faith. In *Adam Bede* George Eliot gives an agnostic's description of a young man's passion: 'He was but three-and-twenty, and had only just learned what it is to love—to love with that adoration which a young man gives to a woman whom he feels to be greater and better than himself. Love of this sort is hardly distinguishable from religious feeling. What deep and worthy love is so?' (p. 51) It was just this kind of love that Leslie Stephen felt for Julia Duckworth. What he sought in marriage, as Noel Annan remarks, was 'a living image before whom he could pour out the flood of devotion that could find no outlet in religion. He idealised her and longed to sacrifice himself for her.' In one of his letters to her he wrote: 'You must let me tell you that I do and always shall feel for you something which I can only call reverence as well as love. *Think* me silly if you please. . . . You see, I have not got any saints and you must not be angry if I put you in the place where my saints ought to be.' [38]

For lapsed Christians the purity of love could be a substitute for faith. For orthodox Christians, on the other hand, it could be a much needed buttress for belief, an existential proof of the reality of God. The pure woman, the Angel in the House, was for men like Patmore, Browning, Kingsley and Tennyson not only an outlet for quasi-religious emotion, not only an assurance of the spirituality of man, but a symbolic confirmation of the truth of Christian faith, a foretaste and guarantee of heavenly love and peace:

> The best things that the best believe
> Are in her face so kindly writ
> The faithless, seeing her, conceive
> Not only heaven, but hope of it. [39]

Hence the significance of Tennyson's comment about his wife: 'The peace of God came into my life before the altar when I wedded her.' [40] Tennyson said more than once that without a belief in the spiritual reality of the universe, in the immortality of man, he could not go on living. The angelic woman therefore, as R. W. Rader points out, 'was in a real sense for Tennyson a saviour, a means of grace; in the fact of his love for her untouched by the baser affections, man, he thought, could find existential evidence of the ultimate spirituality of himself and the universe. Upon that evidence he could build a positive faith adequate to personal affirmation and action.' [41] Tennyson's prudery then, his quickness to alarm at any threat to society's sexual decency, was of a quite different order from the conformist moral cowardice of sleek respectability: it was a direct response to the Victorian crisis of faith.

It was a direct response too to the crisis of social order, the fear of society's collapse, that was inextricably connected with the problem of religion. Throughout the eighteenth century there had been scattered warnings about the dangers posed by irreligion and immorality to England's prosperity as a nation. History, it was claimed, taught that moral corruption was the cause of the decline and fall of empires. Rome inevitably was a frequent *exemplum horrendum*, and so it continued throughout the nineteenth century. [42] But in the nineteenth century the warnings were far more frequent and the alarm far more universal and consistent. For not only was religion, the guardian of morality, under greater and greater pressure, but new and sinister allies of immorality had arisen. To appreciate this fully we must first consider the political and economic structure of nineteenth century society. In doing so we shall discover that moral conservatism, prim respectability, even an hysterical fear of change, are not necessarily to be stigmatized with the charge of intellectual and moral cowardice.

Religion, as I have said, was the guardian of morality. As such it was also the guardian of social stability, with the power to command obedience, duty, industry, and patience under suffering from potentially anarchic forces. Ironically at the very time when its foundations were being shaken by new discoveries its role as social stabilizer had never been more crucial. For in the first half of the century the foundations of society were also being shaken. They were being shaken by the fear of revolution, by the haunting prospect of an insurrection of the masses, by the danger of England's suffering the chaos and carnage of post-revólution France. Anxious minds were quickly alarmed by any suggestion of the imminence of revolution and in their fears sex played a prominent part. A correspondent to the *Public Ledger* 17 January 1816, gratified by the imprisonment of a vendor of indecent prints, expressed a not uncommon view: 'That the French Revolution, with all its consequent horrors, was preceded by a total revolution of decency and morality, the virtuous qualities of the mind being sapped and undermined by the baneful exhibition of pictures, representing vice in the most alluring and varied forms, to a depraved mind, is a truth that unfortunately will not admit of a doubt.' (p. 3) This kind of alarm about pornographic prints looks very much like the small-minded suburban primness that Grant Allen found so objectionable. But if we examine more closely the impact in England of the French Revolution we shall see that the writer's thinking was historically natural and not wholly stupid.

It was not wholly stupid because in some measure there was a logical connection between sexual decency and social stability. The upper classes of the 1790s were quick to see the benefits of a pious proletariat: 'The French Revolution', reported the *Annual Register* in 1798, 'illustrated the connection between good morals and the order and peace of society more than all the eloquence of the pulpit and the disquisitions of moral philosophers had done for many centuries. . . . It was a wonder to the lower orders, throughout all parts of England, to see the avenues of the churches filled with carriages.' (p. 229) Political fear meant religious revival, an enormous boost to the growth of Evangelicalism and its ascetic view of sex. [43] But just as setting a pious example to the masses involved the adoption of Evangelical sexual standards, so the masses' adoption of Evangelical piety would require their observance of sexual decency, their cultivation of a stable home background in which piety might be nourished. The stability of family life on which society depended was as much the prerequisite as the consequence of a stabilizing faith. 'The grand spring and cement of society', claimed the *Annual Register*, 'is the divine principle of love, branching forth from conjugal into parental, fraternal, and filial affection, an attachment to kindred, neighbours, countrymen, and all, in some degree, who partake with us in the same common nature.' (pp. 229–30) But if the family was the answer to the danger of revolution, 1798 saw the emergence of another threat to its security. It was in this year that Malthus published his famous book on population; and if population, as he argued, tended to outstrip the means of feeding it when sexual self-restraint was not applied, then the masses' sexual immorality meant the economic, as well as moral, dissolution of the family.

So much was rational. But there was much in the moral conservatism of the 1790s that was purely irrational; nor was this in the light of the circumstances at all surprising. From the time of the September Massacres of 1792 the bloody events in France and the seething unrest at home produced a condition of panic that was to last for more than a decade. In 1794 it reached its first climax with the State Trials of prominent radicals; in 1795 it flared up again with the attacks on the king in his coach at the opening of Parliament; and in 1797 it burst out once more with fears of a French invasion, a rebellion in Ireland, and fleet mutinies at Spithead, the Nore and Great Yarmouth. In this very emotional atmosphere the fear of England's decline and fall was easily inflamed; indeed there was alarm for the whole of Western civilization. In the panic of 1797 a rumour grew apace (and not only in England—in Europe and in America too) that the French Revolution was only the first act of an infernal international plot, a conspiracy aimed at the destruction of organized religions and governments throughout the world by means of subversion and insidious demoralization.[1] A book by John Robison, *Proof of a Conspiracy Against All Religions and Governments of Europe*, first published in Scotland, went through three London editions in a year. Both he and a Frenchman, Barruel, writing independently, explained that the events in France were due to a threefold interacting conspiracy of French philosophes, international freemasons and Bavarian anarchists. Extracts from their two works were printed in periodicals and the substance of their arguments given in various pamphlets. In the prevailing atmosphere they found many believers: a reviewer of their books in the *British Critic* even suggested that any sceptics were probably in league with the conspirators. Anxious men sought simple explanations for frightening problems.

But anxious men too made frightening problems from simple things. In 1798 the Bishop of Durham warned the Lords that 'The French rulers, while they despaired of making any impression on us, by the force of arms, attempted a more subtle and alarming warfare, by endeavouring to enforce the influence of their example, in order to taint and undermine the morals of our youth. They sent amongst us a number of female dancers, who, by the allurements of the most indecent attitudes, and most wanton theatrical exhibitions, succeeded but too effectually in loosening and corrupting the morals of the people.' [44] This lack of proportion, this projection of sexual and political danger into fairly innocuous places had become a natural part of the moral conservatives' vision. Fear of sex, fear of conspiracy lurking in every corner, fear of the masses who were both morally and politically inflammable were forming a nexus of anxiety that was to last for several decades. In this nexus the middle-class fear of the masses and of the revolutionaries trying to subvert them was strikingly similar to the traditional moral conservatism of the American white

[1] The Russian Revolution stimulated a similar conspiracy mania: the plotters now were Jews, but their methods the same—organized international demoralization and subversion. See Norman Cohn, *Warrant for Genocide: the Myth of the Jewish World-conspiracy* (1967).

south. In each case the fear of a loss in social status, of a threat to wealth and power—perhaps the total collapse of the status quo—finds expression in a triangular sexual myth. On one corner we find the middle classes' privileged position embodied, like the white southerner's, in a saintly feminine purity; on the next the imagined ambition of the masses embodied, like the 'buck nigger's', in a rampant sexuality; and on the other the threatening plots of the revolutionary embodied, like those of the Communist subverter, in a flagrant, and perhaps deviant, immorality. The mythology indeed had a basis of fact. The working classes, like the American negro, lived often in ignorance, poverty and squalor where depravity was rife. The political radicals, like the Communist agitator, were usually radicals too in morals; easily associated (one remembers the vilification of the Godwins) with the advocacy of atheism and the abolition of the Church, with the advocacy of free love and the abolition of marriage and the family. But the mythology was grounded less on fact than on emotion, grounded in the political panic of the 1790s.

By the 1820s the political panic had considerably diminished; but the disturbances on the Continent prevented it from disappearing altogether, and in 1830 the fear of the mob returned in full with revolutions abroad and agitation at home, with the labourers' revolt and a frightening wave of rioting, arson and machine-breaking. The end of the thirties saw the rise of Chartism and fresh fears of violent revolution. In his *Reminiscences* Carlyle wrote of his last encounter with Southey: 'Our talk was long and earnest; topic ultimately the usual one, steady approach of democracy, with revolution (probably *explosive*) and a *finis* incomputable to man.' [45] 'It is too late for a peaceful solution,' predicted Engels in 1844, 'soon a slight impulse will suffice to set the avalanche in motion.' [46] In all these troubled years the middle classes' triangular sexual mythology reinforced their concern for society's moral standards, their anxiety to secure the purity of the home as society's moral buttress. The unruly mob was not only proof of the need for family piety, it was invested with a largely imaginary sexual rampancy that made it a threat to civilized decency: in the greater security of the 1860s Charles Kingsley looked back, with a significant choice of words, to the days of 'Luddite mobs, meal mobs, farm riots, riots everywhere; Captain Swing and his rick-burners, Peterloo "massacres", Bristol conflagrations, and all the ugly sights and rumours which made young lads, thirty or forty years ago, believe (and not so wrongly) that the masses were their natural enemies, and that they might have to fight, any year, or any day, for *the safety of their property and the honour of their sisters.*' [47] In the same way left-wing agitators were dangerous not only through their political machinations but through their subversion of morality. Even a relatively mild form of radicalism, such as feminism, was seen as an insidious threat to the family unit on which Christian society was built: an article on divorce in 1838, apparently by J. M. Kemble, a friend of Tennyson, asked

of those purblind, short-sighted legislators, who are so ready to revile and destroy the fundamental principle of the old law of England as a hideous tyranny, whether they are aware that, at this moment, in the very centre of London, exists a society, consisting principally of the working classes, numbering thousands of members, and having agents and booksellers and branch societies in almost all the great towns of England, whose professed object is entirely to revolutionize the whole social system? While Lords and Commons are disputing about insignificant forms and small amendments,—legislating for their own selfish interest,—these men are meditating, nay, already preparing, nothing less than the destruction of all Christian society,—propagating the belief of the necessity of a complete social sub-radical change; and what is more, one of the chief doctrines that they most zealously propagate in order to effect this change is this very one of THE EQUALITY OF THE SEXES. [48]

For many Victorians, then, a liberal view of sex was quite impossible. Apart from the ascetic dictates of religion, apart from the genteel requirements of social propriety, apart from the psychic constraints of a crisis of faith, there was a nagging political fear which made sex an insidious, subtle danger to society. Advocates of a more liberal morality, propagandists for birth-control or divorce reform, let alone free love, were inevitably suspect, quickly branded with atheism and revolutionary extremism; and not surprisingly when their leaders were godless radicals like Richard Carlile, Francis Place, W. J. Fox, Robert Owen, and the Saint Simonians, many of them distinguished also by scandalous private lives.[1] Political suspicion of a more liberal approach to sex persisted throughout the century:[2] it was the atheist republican Charles Bradlaugh who was at the front of the birth-control agitation of the 1870s, and socialists like Karl Pearson at the front of the free love controversy of the eighties and nineties. But the political fear had lost much of its urgency and its triangular sexual mythology. Indeed with the eclipse of Chartism, the relatively peaceful accession to power of the working class in 1867, and the steady improvement in proletarian sexual decency, the concern for society's moral standards as a defence against radical change underwent an ironic twist. Upper-class sexual decency was required now not to reform by example the morals of the masses, but to avoid giving their increasing moral consciousness grounds for reforming the dissolute prodigality of their betters. Hence Queen Victoria's alarm in January 1868 at the laxity of her heir:

> Many, many, with whom I have conversed, tell me that at no time for the last 60 or 70 years was frivolity the love of pleasure,

---

[1] See Richard K. P. Pankhurst, *The Saint Simonians* (1957), for examples of the scurrilous attacks made on radicals of this type (pp. 2–4). We should note also that at about this time the idea of sex was being further besmirched by sectarian bigotry: Roman Catholic priests were beginning to be invested with the same kind of furtive sexual indecency as the radicals—see Geoffrey Best, 'Popular Protestantism in Victorian Britain', *Ideas and Institutions of Victorian Britain*, ed. Robert Robson (1967), p. 125f.

[2] And indeed to this very day—one thinks of the political basis of the Moral Rearmament Movement.

self-indulgence, luxury, and idleness (producing ignorance) carried
to such an excess as now in the Higher Classes, and that it resembles
the time before the first French Revolution; and I must—alas!—
admit that this is *true*. Believe me! It is most *alarming*, although
you do not observe it, nor will you *hear* it; but those who do not
live *in* the gay circle of fashion, and who view it calmly, are
greatly, seriously alarmed. And in THIS lies the REAL *danger* of
the *present* time! [49]

But upper-class laxity had more than just a political significance. To many conservative minds it was agent and symptom
of a dangerous erosion of sexual standards: even as the fear of
revolution receded, a new fear had emerged of England's moral
decline and fall. The press in the late 1850s and 1860s gave
ample evidence of the extent of sexual immorality. Articles
exploring the size of the prostitution problem or the working
of the new divorce laws of 1857 forced home how much
immorality had existed under the old respectability; and
articles describing the sudden loosening of upper-class manners
suggested how much worse the situation might become.
Society, to some, seemed in danger of moral anarchy: on
18 January 1861 the pious *Record* warned its readers, 'the innate
depravity of human nature has been fanned to such a flame, that
it blazes forth with a lurid, ghastly light, and menaces society
with a general conflagration'. (p. 2) The 'innate depravity of
human nature' was a particularly sensitive topic in the sixties
as the implications of Darwinism began to be absorbed: man,
it seemed, might interpret the discoveries of science as
justifying his abdication of moral responsibility, as justifying
his acceptance of a life of heedless animalism.

> And when the man,
> The child of evolution, flings aside
> His swaddling-bands, the morals of the tribe,
> He, following his own instincts as his God,
> Will enter on the larger golden age;
> No pleasure then taboo'd . . .

These lines are spoken by Philip Edgar, the hero of Tennyson's play of 1882 *The Promise of May*. [50] Edgar is a dissolute young squire who seduces a farmer's daughter, but he is nothing like the old-fashioned melodramatic libertine. He is an atheist and a political extremist, and he is the more dangerous morally because he is an evolutionist, who justifies his immorality on the grounds that without God there is no meaning to life and one can only live for sensation; evolution means survival of the fittest and to hurt another being in the pursuit of selfish interest is merely Nature's way. His ultimate fate, his collapse into nihilism and despair, is Tennyson's prediction of the future of a society relinquishing sexual decency for a materialistic and animal amorality.

It is easy to attack the accuracy of Tennyson's prophecy, it is easy to attack the emotionalism at its source. But it is hard to convict him of 'an utter lack of moral and intellectual courage'. When we consider the psychic pressures of the age for sensitive minds like his, the terrors of a Godless universe and a meaningless life, the terrors of social decline and fall, the terrors of moral anarchy, it is hard to associate him with the sleek conformity of chapel-and-villadom. And if we consider now the Victorian view of Home, we will understand yet better the emotionalism at the source of the Victorian fear of sex.

3

Home, Sweet Home

I THE PLACE OF PEACE

> Now stir the fire, and close the shutters fast,
> Let fall the curtains, wheel the sofa round,
> And, while the bubbling and loud-hissing urn
> Throws up a steamy column, and the cups
> That cheer but not inebriate, wait on each,
> So let us welcome peaceful ev'ning in.

THE SENTIMENT APPEARS to be Victorian, a celebration of Dickensian cosy domesticity. But the passage in fact, as the diction warns us, is eighteenth century: Cowper's introduction in *The Task* 1785 to the chaste pleasures of a winter evening at home. (IV, 36–41) The eighteenth century too had its cult of domesticity, its picture of the fireside as a peaceful refuge from a bustling world of strife, sweet oblivion from the cares of day: in the bosom of the family, it was claimed, in the relaxed atmosphere of friendly discourse and household entertainments, there was a recreational power inestimably superior to the noisy dissipation of fashionable diversion. The similarities to the Victorian view of home are very striking. And yet the differences are even more so. For there is an emotional pressure behind the Victorian view of which we find no trace in the eighteenth century. Consider the tone, for example, of Thomson's definition of home in 1730:

> home is the resort
> Of love, of joy, of peace and plenty, where,
> Supporting and supported, polished friends
> And dear relations mingle into bliss. [51]

Consider now the tone of Ruskin's definition in 1865: 'This is the true nature of home—it is the place of Peace; the shelter, not only from all injury, but from all terror, doubt, and division. In so far as it is not this, it is not home. . . . But so far as it is a sacred place, a vestal temple, a temple of the hearth watched over by Household Gods . . . so far as it is this . . . so far it vindicates the name, and fulfils the praise, of Home.' [52] Home was no longer a mere retreat from the bustling world outside, but a sacred place, a quasi-religious centre to men's lives.

The religious imagery, the didactic earnestness, the dogmatic assurance of Ruskin's definition would seem to point to Evangelicalism as the source of the nineteenth century's different emphasis. And up to a point this was clearly the case. The evolution of the cult of domesticity was inevitably complementary to the development of sexual prudery. The early Puritan fathers had placed great stress on the home as microcosm of society and of the universe and therefore as a vital factor in the individual's salvation and the health of the Christian community.[1] As the influence of Puritanism became progressively attenuated, the belief in the home was consolidated by the needs of an emergent bourgeoisie: a stable home-life, as we saw in the previous chapter, secured the legitimacy and loyalty of a middle-class man's children who might be invaluable assistants in his material advancement; it provided cheaper and safer pleasures than the haunts of the extravagant upper classes or the thriftless proletariat; it testified to a man's financial and moral respectability; and it offered a sanctum from the strain of observing the perhaps unfamiliar rules of censorious propriety. But it was the Evangelical Revival that really laid the foundations of the Victorian view of home. It was Evangelicals like Wilberforce and Hannah More who convinced the middle classes of the need not only to observe domestic decency but to protect it most stringently from the

[1] There is some interesting material on the Puritan view of home in William and Malleville Haller, 'The Puritan Art of Love', *Huntington Library Quarterly* (Jan. 1942), V, 235–272.

slightest sullying contact with the world. And it was Evangelicals like James Plumptre and the Bowdlers who produced expurgated songs and literature to stimulate the growth of family entertainments. Daily prayers for the entire household, evening readings aloud for the whole family, anxious parental discipline, unstinted parental affection—these were the foundations of the Victorian cult of home. And yet Evangelicalism is not a sufficient explanation for the quasi-religious intensity with which the home came to be invested. Hannah More's description in 1783 of the 'almost sacred joys of home' [53] is remarkably reticent compared with Ruskin's panegyric. The full intensity of home-worship came, in fact, when Evangelicalism was on the wane.

It might seem that this emotionalism, Ruskin's nervous talk of outside terrors, was a product of the Victorians' political anxieties, for in these the home was very central. In the frightened years after the French Revolution the home, we have seen, was held to be the fount of civic virtues and thus the guardian of civil peace. If the middle classes could set a successful example of domestic piety to the masses, the home throughout society would be the bulwark against both political subversion and sexual impurity which seemed effectively synonymous. Not to reverence the home was tantamount to treason, as Coleridge argued in 1817:

> E'en women at the distaff hence may see,
> That bad men may rebel, but ne'er be free;
> May whisper, when the waves of faction foam,
> None love their country, but who love their home;
> For freedom can with those alone abide,
> Who wear the golden chain, with honest pride
> Of love and duty, at their own fire-side:
> While mad ambition ever doth caress
> Its own sure fate, in its own restlessness.[1]

[1] The concluding lines to his play *Zapolya*. Compare this passage with Dickens' plea in *The Old Curiosity Shop* for better home conditions for the masses on the grounds that 'In love of home, the love of country has its rise' (I, 364).

Political fears, however, are also an inadequate explanation for the Victorian cult of home. Like Evangelicalism they clearly helped to form its emotional climate. But, like Evangelicalism, their influence was on the wane when the cult was at its height. The key to Ruskin's panegyric is indeed in his nervous talk of outside terrors, of the home as 'the shelter not only from all injury, but from all terror, doubt, and division'. But the real explanation of the emotional pressure behind the Victorian view of home is that political worries, like religious fears, were but one feature of a quite general nineteenth century anxiety unlike anything known before, in which the home played a vital part.[1]

In 1833, when these anxieties were first coming into prominence, Tennyson in 'The Palace of Art' gave this description of 'an English home':

> gray twilight pour'd
> On dewy pastures, dewy trees,
> Softer than sleep—all things in order stored,
> A haunt of ancient Peace.

The soft pastoral harmony, the ordered simplicity, above all the sense of solid foundation deep in the ancient past, evoked in this short passage, are typical of the mythic qualities that the English home was now acquiring. Society was changing at an alarming speed as Britain entered the modern age, with revolutions, imminent and actual, on every front. Consider, for example, the ideological revolution from the sober, hierarchical rationalism of the eighteenth century, with its clockwork universe and its clockwork constitution.[2] By the 1830s and 1840s religious faith and political confidence had lost this kind of harmonious ease and order. Attacked from without by

---

[1] For a valuable analysis of the Victorian cult of home which complements many of the points I shall be making in this chapter and the next see Alexander Welsh, *The City of Dickens* (Oxford, 1971).

[2] For a helpful summary of the late-eighteenth century's ordered ideology in religion and politics see Asa Briggs, *The Age of Improvement 1783–1867* (1959), pp. 66–7, 8–13.

the alarming advance of science on the one hand and democracy on the other, confused from within by schism and controversy, by the discordant claims of the many religious and politico-economic sects, religion and the condition of England question were both now the source not of calm assurance but of terror, doubt, division. It is true that many early Victorians in fact were intoxicated by the speed of change, by the removal of outworn traditions, by the sensation of living in a new world of unlimited possibilities; but even the optimists were often troubled by disquietude. Fundamental ideas were in a disturbing state of flux. J. A. Froude, looking back at these times from the more settled world of the 1880s, remarked:

> To those who inquired with open minds it appeared that things which good and learned men were doubting about must be themselves doubtful. Thus, all around us, the intellectual lightships had broken from their moorings and it was then a new and trying experience. The present generation which has grown up in an open spiritual ocean, which has got used to it and has learned to swim for itself, will never know what it is to find the lights all drifting, all the compasses all awry, and nothing left to steer by except the stars. [54]

But there was one compass that was not awry. As Froude himself pointed out in *The Nemesis of Faith* (1849), religion, God and heaven might only be catchwords used to fill the void of a meaningless life: 'But there is one strong direction into which the needle of our being, when left to itself, is for ever determined, which is more than a catchword, which in the falsest heart of all remains still desperately genuine, the one last reality of which universal instinct is assured. . . . It is home. . . . Home—yes, home is the one perfectly pure earthly instinct which we have.' (pp. 101–2) As most of their traditional ideology was being questioned, the Victorians could at least rely on one traditional certitude: on home as an immemorial source of psychological stability, as a 'haunt of ancient peace'.

These ideological difficulties of course troubled most the intelligentsia, but even the most philistine and single-minded businessman might feel pressured by the speed of social change. In the 1830s and 1840s the instability of a developing capitalist system, with its rapid alternation of hectic boom and financial panic,[1] was a constant source of anxiety for the richer and poorer sections of the bourgeoisie alike: in an age when limited liability was yet unknown it could mean bankruptcy for the one and dismissal for the other, for both social ruin, perhaps even the debtors prison. With the greater and more stable affluence of mid-century came an increase in material appetite, a restless pursuit after wealth, connections and social status, which both raised the stakes of success and failure and also quickened the competitive tempo of social life. But more important than this self-induced sense of hurry was the effect of technological innovations in transport and communications, in industry and commerce. With the development of the steamship, the locomotive, the electric telegraph and the penny post, with the increasing size, complexity and sophistication of the economic system, business life became for many an exhausting daily struggle. 'Throughout the whole community,' complained W. R. Greg in 1851, 'we are all called to labour too early and compelled to labour too severely and too long. We live sadly too fast. Our existence in nearly all ranks is a crush, a struggle, and a strife.'[2] Work was much more tiring than in pre-industrial days. Fierce competition, hard bargaining, rapid decision, perhaps sharp practice and duplicity, were setting the pace at managerial level; and beneath this long hours of grinding tedium and mechanical ledgerwork were taking a similar toll. Little wonder, then, that the home as shelter from the cares of day received an emotional colouration

---

[1] As, for example, in 1825–6, 1836–7, 1839–42, and 1846–8.

[2] *Edinburgh Review* (April 1851) XCIII, 325. Cf. Arnold's remarks in 'The Scholar Gypsy', written around this time, on the intellectual's predicament: 'this strange disease of modern life,/With its sick hurry, its divided aims,/Its heads o'ertax'd, its palsied hearts'.

unknown in the eighteenth century. No matter how the world went during the day, at home there was sanctuary, peace, cheerfulness and love. Work could mean worry and humiliation, insincerity and mechanical impersonality, above all a constant sense of pressure, but 'at home', as J. A. Froude once again points out for us, 'when we come home, we lay aside our mask, and drop our tools. . . . We fall again into our most human relations . . . we cease the struggle in the race of the world, and give our hearts leave and leisure to love.' [55]

But the revolution in technology, like the undermining of traditional ideology, produced more than nervous stress; it presented society with a number of serious moral problems. In Matthew Arnold's 'Stanzas from the Grande Chartreuse' (1855) the emphasis is on the ideological desolation of modern man, lost in a void of unbelief, 'Wandering between two worlds, one dead,/The other powerless to be born.' But in James Thomson's poem of the same year, inspired by Arnold's, the emphasis extends to the moral corruption of modern man, filling the void of unbelief with a heedless, arrogant materialism:

> A proud strong Age fast losing all
> Earth has of heaven; bereft of faith;
> And living in Eternal Death
>
> And loudly boastful of such life:
> Blinded by our material might,
> Absorbed in frantic worldly strife. . . . [56]

The economic boom at mid-century brought ease and affluence. But it brought too for many a distressing sense of moral degeneration, evidence of an ever growing material greed, an hubristic pride in man's technological conquests, above all of a sacrifice of ethics to the dictates of financial expedience. Affluence, it was seen, was a product not only of technological advance but of a decline in moral standards, of a new harshness and self-interest in the business world and in society at large. Economic exploitation was visible across the whole spectrum of social life. There was the exploitation of the workers by which the middle classes prospered, the creation of 'Two Nations' as Disraeli put it, one of wealth and luxury, the other of poverty and squalor. There was the exploitation of the countryside, especially around London and the manufacturing centres of the North and Midlands, large tracts of once beautiful land being ruined by industrial development, by smoke and soot, by choked-up putrid rivers. Nowhere was the exploitation of men and land more visible than in the hugely expanded towns that were the source of Britain's wealth. Rapid industrial growth and the explosion in population increased the nervous stresses of city life, bringing with them the previously unexperienced noise, bustle and impersonal anonymity of large-scale urban living. But more important than the creation of nervous stress, they focussed the moral problems attending the technological and ideological revolutions. There in the cities, all too plain to see, were the proofs of society's ethical malaise, its crude materialism and economic exploitation: wealth for the few, but for the many ugliness, squalor, congestion, disease and crime.

To Victorians worried by these developments the home offered comfort and escape. The door could be bolted on the noise and harshness of modern city life; within the haven of domestic privacy the problems of society—so huge, complex and elusive—could be temporarily forgotten. But the home might be more than just a shelter from society's moral problems: it might be in some measure the answer to them, a means of restoring the sense of order and personal values that the modern age was losing, of reviving the better features of pre-industrial England. For all its deficiencies the eighteenth century, in nostalgic retrospect, seemed to have enjoyed an enviable stability, an acceptance of social hierarchy sanctified not only by tradition but by divinity: 'God made both high and lowly,/And ordered their estate.' It seemed to have enjoyed too, in both town and especially country, an enviable richness of personal values: a genuine sense of community of labour, identity of interest, and really personal inter-class contact between master and worker, between squire and countryman. Social stability, in short, had rested on deference and privilege; but it had rested too on an acknowledgment that deference and privilege also involved rights and obligations. By the Victorian period this sense of order and harmonious relationship seemed to have sunk in confusion and corruption, in division and exploitation. But there was still one traditional source of stability and concord. In the forms of family life, in the management of the home there was order and accepted custom: fixed hours for meals and a ritual grace beforehand; fixed hours for worship with ceremonial Sunday church-going and often daily domestic prayers; fixed patterns of evening recreation, of newspapers and needlework, frequently a progressive and systematic reading aloud from novel, poem or sermon; fixed patterns of family visiting to and from a hierarchy of grandparents, uncles, aunts, and cousins; in all this there was order and stability. And in the intimacy of household relationships, in the warmth and trust of familial affection, in the very personal contact between the privileged and dependent, the employers and their servants; in this there was a social harmony of moral responsibility, an antidote to the declining moral values, the impersonal exploitation of the cash nexus.[1] The world outside might lack order and harmonious relationship, but the rightly appointed home could both show the world its failings and help to counteract them:

> For something that abode endued
> With temple-like repose, an air

---

[1] Significantly, Carlyle, the foremost critic of the new values, was led to attack capitalism as the negation of the home. 'Call ye that a Society,' he asked in *Sartor Resartus* (1834), 'where there is no longer any social idea extant; not so much as the idea of a common Home, but only of a common over-crowded Lodging-house?' Capitalism, he claimed in *Past and Present* (1843) was 'a world alien, not your world; all a hostile camp for you; not a home at all, of hearts and faces who are yours, whose you are!' Both quotations are cited in Houghton, *op. cit.*, pp. 77–9.

Of life's kind purposes pursued
　　With order'd freedom sweet and fair.
A tent pitch'd in a world not right
　　It seem'd, whose inmates, every one
On tranquil faces bore the light
　　Of duties beautifully done. [57]

This passage comes from Patmore's 'Angel in the House', a classic statement of Victorian home idealism. By the time it was published between 1854 and 1856 the cult was at its peak, as we can see from the number of domestic magazines rushing to meet a clear demand. In those two years, for example, readers had had a choice of *The Home Circle, The Home Companion, The Home Friend, Home Thoughts* and *The Home Magazine,* of the *Family Economist,* the *Family Record,* the *Family Friend,* the *Family Treasury,* the *Family Prize Magazine and Household Miscellany,* the *Family Paper* and the *Family Mirror*—and this is a far from exhaustive list. The ideal had arisen from a combination of factors: Evangelical fears, political worries, and the nervous stresses and moral problems of technological and ideological revolution. As some of these factors receded in importance after 1850, others came to take their place. The most important of these was speed, the accelerating pace of social life. In 1851, as we saw, W. R. Greg was complaining that people lived sadly too fast. In 1875, in an article called 'Life at High Pressure', he returned to this theme: 'the most salient characteristic of life in this latter portion of the 19th century is its SPEED,—what we may call its hurry, the rate at which we move, the high pressure at which we work.' [58] In 1851 the impact of advances in transport and communications was beginning to be felt, but in 1875 the impact was far more general and far more pressing, much closer to the tempo of modern existence. Life was still leisurely by our standards, but speed is for us a commonplace. For the mid-Victorians life could seem much too fast. In April 1864 *Fraser's* looked back nostalgically at the slow pace of life in the first quarter of the century: 'People had leisure in those days. That constant sense of being driven—not precisely like "dumb" cattle, but cattle who must read, write, and talk more in twenty-four hours than twenty-four hours will permit, can never have been known to them, nor the curious sort of ache, somewhere between head, chest and stomach, which comes of such driving.' (LXIX, 482) But, for many, even more disturbing than the impact of technology was the restless swell of new ideas. In 1869 James Baldwin Brown, surveying 'The Revolution of the Last Quarter of a Century', concluded that the Revolution lay not so much in the country's vast material changes but in its continuous overthrow of traditional patterns of thought. [59] The sudden shock of scepticism that had frightened Froude and the early Victorians had become for many a sustained state of tension, a feeling that politically, spiritually, morally, sexually, intellectually and in almost every other way, Britain was 'Shooting Niagara'. 'We are living in the vortex of a great social revolution,' Brown wrote in 1871: 'Things in their present form, at their present pitch cannot endure. There is the straining of expectation of great changes everywhere. The old order of society is breaking up and vanishing. New ideas, new relations, new organisations, new principles of action, new beliefs, are constituting themselves.' [60] Some found the prospect of a New World exhilarating, others were anxious and fearful. But both optimists and pessimists were likely to be glad of home, as one sure source of continuing stability, one still-centre in the storm of change.

Home, then, as a haunt of ancient peace continued to exercise its very powerful influence. But it is time we began to examine more closely the nature of this influence. G. M. Young ascribed to the home a big role as a stabilizing force in the rapid advances of Victorian society: 'it gave to those who were in it a certain standing with themselves, and a cheerful confidence in the face of novelty, which is perhaps the clue to the Victorian paradox—the rushing swiftness of its intellectual advance, and the tranquil evolution of its social and moral ideas. The advance was in all directions outwards from a stable and fortified centre.' [61] There is a great deal of validity in this judgement. But it needs some qualification. The home as guardian of sexual morality, the home as a place of peace doubtless meant little to many Victorians stolidly unmoved by either the age's sexual fears or the age's psychic strains; and it was because the evolution of social and moral ideas was not so very 'tranquil' that these fears and strains had such an impact on the worship of the home. But most important we need to recognize that the home as shrine and shelter operated in many ways with counter-productive effect. If to some it was the answer to sexual fears and psychological instability, to others ironically it was the source of a greater sexual nervousness and a more deep-seated instability. 'The place of peace; the shelter, not only from all injury, but from all terror, doubt, and division'—this Ruskin claimed was the true nature of home. But the home in fact was often for men and women alike the cause of morbid fear, misery and torment.

II THE CONTAGION OF FEAR

In the respectable home sex was not a subject for frank discussion; and many parents, from an anxiety not to tarnish their children's innocence and perhaps more especially from their own embarrassment and repugnance, declined to offer anything in the way of sex instruction. George Eliot in *Middlemarch* talks of Lydgate being brought up with 'a general sense of secrecy and obscenity in connection with his internal structure'. (I, 217–8) This kind of evasion, as many Victorians recognized, often served to stimulate an unhealthy curiosity, drawing attention to what was being hidden: 'Isolation, mystery, obstacles, produce craving curiosity—in fact, morbid stimulus—instead of matter-of-fact acceptance and natural familiarity.' [62] And morbidity, conjoint with ignorance, could lead to great unhappiness in the years of immaturity. For the ignorant boy puberty could be a harrowing experience.

General Gordon, for example, once recalled how at fourteen he had wished he was a eunuch. [63] And Mark Rutherford's experience, it seems, was little better: 'Had I been taught when I was young a few facts about myself, which I only learned accidentally long afterwards, a good deal of misery might have been spared me.' [64] Learning the facts accidentally usually meant in smutty talk at school or in the street; and one can well appreciate how morbidity and a vague sense of secrecy and obscenity could become horror and disgust when knowledge was attained. George Moore in *Celibates* (1895) writes of a young man in whom 'ignorance of the material laws of existence had extended even into his sixteenth year, and when, bit by bit, the veil fell, and he understood, he was filled with loathing of life and mad desire to wash himself free of its stain'. (p. 367)

The conspiracy of silence might lead to a morbid fear of sex. But actual instruction might be a good deal worse, parents producing in childish minds an exaggerated form of their own anxieties and repressions. Doctors unfortunately, far from checking the contagion of fear, all too often spread it. Consider the advice given, in the case of a little boy especially fond of girls, in Dr Acton's *Functions and Disorders of the Reproductive Organs* (1857), which went through six editions in eighteen years:

Parents and friends are delighted at his gentleness and politeness, and not a little amused at the early flirtation. But if they were wise they would rather feel profound anxiety; and he would be an unfaithful or unwise medical friend who did not, if an opportunity occurred, warn them that the boy, unsuspicious and innocent as he is, should be carefully watched, and removed from every influence that could possibly excite his slumbering tendencies. . . . On the judicious treatment of a case such as has been sketched, it probably depends whether the dangerous propensity is so kept in check as to preserve the boy's health and innocence, or whether one more shattered constitution and wounded conscience is to be added to the victims of early sexual tendencies and careless training. [65]

Consider the advice given in *The Duties of Parents: Reproductive and Educational* (1872):

> Our children must be taught, from the earliest period at which their minds can grasp such teaching, the inviolable sanctity of their sexual nature—the irreparable ills which follow its abuse. They must be saturated with the conviction that impurity is a foul and hateful sin, that the perversion of these instincts through whatever agency is a plunge into a fathomless abyss of turpitude from which they will never emerge with a clean soul; that it will interpose an impassable gulf between them and the pure-minded; that it will disqualify them for virtuous parentage, and will degrade them beneath the brute. (pp. 132–3)

Consider the mentality of Elizabeth Sewell in her *Principles of Education* (1865), where after describing the worst consequences of an early flirtation with evil through unwatched school-children's chatter, she goes on to look at

> a brighter side to the subject. No one, however strict, would for a moment assert that these early offences are so ineffaceable, that the mind, once tainted, can never be restored to purity. God's grace, and an earnest will, and an incessant watchfulness, will work marvels in the way of such restoration; but even then it will never be anything but restoration. The scars will always remain; visible to the inward eye, though unseen by man, and, as we may humbly trust, blotted out by God. And they will not only be seen as scars, disfigurements, but they will be felt as wounds; they will give the pain of wounds; an ever increasing pain as the spirit longs more and more intensely for that purity of heart bestowed upon them who shall hereafter 'see God'.[1]

What such writers were most concerned about of course was masturbation, with its terrible spiritual and physical consequences. The spiritual horrors of self-abuse can be gauged from the tone of a fervent little tract called *The Secret Sin and its Consequences* (1858). The anonymous author appeals for frank-

---

[1] II, 81. Cf. the closing paragraphs of Ch. IX in that most popular of children's books, F. W. Farrar's *Eric, or Little by Little* (1858).

ness on the evil of fornication: 'shall the whispers of false
delicacy drown the loud call to exertion?' And on the same page
he then describes the secret sin as 'a *habit* too polluting to be
named—the fornicator has a companion in crime; but this is a
sin we shudder even to refer to, a crime committed in secret
and alone, and would suffuse the cheek of innocence with a
blush of shame, if uttered' (p. 9)—in the circumstances a rather
crippling authorial reticence. The physical consequences of
masturbation were equally horrifying, in this case even for the
most ungodly. For a mythology of masturbation propounded
by a few in the eighteenth century was in the nineteenth
near-universal medical dogma. According to this mythology,
largely created by defective methods of diagnosis,[1] self-abuse
could cause unimaginable physical mischief: impotence, con-
sumption, amnesia, curvature of the spine, dyspepsia, epilepsy,
blindness, insanity and death. Acton quotes from Dr Ritchie's
'able treatise' on a frequent cause of insanity the following
picture of some inmates of an asylum:

> The pale complexion, the emaciated form, the slouching gait,
> the clammy palm, the glassy or leaden eye, and the averted gaze,
> indicate the lunatic victim to this vice.
> Apathy, loss of memory, abeyance of concentrative power and
> manifestation of mind generally, combined with loss of self-
> reliance, and indisposition for or impulsiveness of action,
> irritability of temper, and incoherence of language, are the most
> characteristic mental phenomena of chronic dementia resulting
> from masturbation in young men. [66]

With medical propaganda of this nature it is easy to see how
readily sexual fears might spiral in an age so given to guilt,
nervous depression and hypochondriasis (all of which in fact
were considered symptoms of masturbation). 'Few persons,

[1] For a sympathetic explanation of the reasons for the extraordinary
medical views about self-abuse see E. H. Hare, 'Masturbatory Insanity:
the History of an Idea', *The Journal of Mental Science* (Jan. 1962) CVIII, 16–18.
Hare also gives a most helpful survey of the evolution of ideas about
masturbation from the eighteenth century onwards.

perhaps', wrote Acton, 'come into contact with so many conscience-stricken young men as I do. If a youth has abused himself, as soon as he learns the consequences, he becomes alarmed, and sets down all his subsequent ailments to the particular cause which is ever uppermost in his thoughts.' (p. 75). He might moreover in such circumstances be too ashamed to consult a doctor and have his fears aggravated further by the sensational pamphlets of unscrupulous quacks. Even those innocent of masturbation could be caught up in the spiral; for such results of continence as wet dreams, imperfect erections and premature ejaculation could readily be interpreted as symptoms of spermatorrhoea, the dread Victorian disease supposedly consequent on masturbation:

> From the painful stigma which its existence is imagined to cast on the past life of the patient, and the secrecy consequently desired, as well as from the ease with which indications absolutely harmless may be confounded—by the inexperience—with symptoms of this disorder, it has always been freely employed by unscrupulous quacks as a means of imposition. Every disease or fancied ailment which their unfortunate victim can be persuaded into believing to be Spermatorrhoea, is called Spermatorrhoea forthwith; and in his agony of terror and humiliation, the wretched and often innocent patient becomes a ready subject for the wickedest cruelty, and, I need hardly add, the most exorbitant extortion. [67]

But for those with 'genuine' spermatorrhoea doctors were of little more comfort than charlatans. The specialist J. L. Milton, whose *On Spermatorrhoea* went through twelve editions between 1854 and 1887, describes a urethral ring he prescribed to protect his patients from seminal emissions (a proper stock of semen was considered vital to bodily health): it is a leather ring with four metal points which was strapped to the penis at night; when the patient erected he was awakened by the pain from the points, untied the tape, bathed his genitals in cold water until the erection had subsided, replaced the ring and then went back to sleep.

If the patient find that he begins to untie the ring in his sleep, he should substitute for the tapes a hook and eye, secured by a small padlock. The key should be tied to a piece of bright coloured ribbon, with a view to its being easily found when wanted; it should, after locking on the ring, be placed just out of reach, so that the patient must get up to open the padlock. [68]

Such ghoulish matter-of-factness may to us seem comic, but before we smile we should consider the sufferings of young men driven to such extremities. 'Hundreds of young men,' wrote another doctor, 'are driven to suicide by the disease.' [69] For a great many Victorian men sleep each night brought torment not repose.

In this context it is doubly appropriate to quote Steven Marcus' description of Acton's *Functions and Disorders*: 'part fantasy, part nightmare, part hallucination, and part madhouse . . . Sex is thought of as a universal and virtually incurable scourge. It cannot ultimately be controlled, and serves as a kind of metaphor for death, as cancer does today' [70]—partly because it is largely accurate, but also because the antithesis of Acton's anxious puritanism could contribute just as much to the nightmare of sexual fear. A doctor with loose moral standards, like R. J. Culverwell, [71] or with thoroughgoing ambitions towards the rehabilitation of the flesh, like George Drysdale, could indeed be more frightening even than Acton—more frightening because they made perfect chastity seem as dangerous as masturbation. Drysdale's free love manual, for example, *The Elements of Social Science*, which went through twelve editions between 1854 and 1874 and another twenty-three by 1904, paints a horrifying picture of the results of self-abuse (10th edn, 1872, pp. 87–90). But it is equally horrifying about the results of sexual abstinence (*passim*, but especially pp. 80f, 496f). Even conservative opinion could be alarming in this matter, believing that prolonged celibacy might lead to permanent impotence; but Drysdale presented a truly nightmare world of spermatorrhoea and impotence in abstinent men, and chlorosis, hysteria and various menstrual disorders in celibate women. 'Chastity, or complete sexual abstinence, so far from being a virtue, is invariably a great natural sin' (p. 162); sexual intercourse, illicit if necessary, is the panacea. (pp. 90–7)

Drysdale's diagnosis was frightening enough, but his prescription, his confidence in free love as panacea, was for many Victorians, convinced of the need for sexual purity, still more alarming. They were indeed in a difficult dilemma. Continence meant false spermatorrhoea, masturbation the real thing, which left them with a choice of either marriage or fornication. Fornication normally meant commerce with a prostitute or other loose woman, which involved the fear of Hellfire for the faithful and, for the godly and ungodly alike, the fear of disease, social exposure and ruptured domestic relations. Marriage, on the other hand, would not always bring a solution to the problem. A husband forced, for whatever reason, to abstain a while from coitus with his wife was arguably worse off than a bachelor. And even the free exercise of conjugal rights brought a worrying medical hazard. For marital excess was believed to be as dangerous as masturbation: Acton thought the average middle-class town dweller should not indulge himself more than once in seven or ten days; [72] and even Drysdale thought the limit should be fixed at twice a week. (p. 84)

Ironically, such was the contagion of sexual fear, some Victorian men appear to have preferred the risks of fornication to the perils of lawful wedlock: Acton claimed that many young men were frightened from marriage by the apparent sexual appetite they saw in the whores and sluts they dealt with, by the delusion that their wives would be equally demanding. (p. 75) This indeed was a remarkable tribute to the morbid, ignorant fears of which Victorian men were capable: how remarkable will be seen when we have examined the sexual inclinations of the well-bred Victorian woman, the manner in which she herself had been infected with an even greater morbidity, ignorance and fear.

III THE NECESSARY ORDEAL

The sexual inclinations of the well-bred Victorian woman were, in the view of most contemporary analysts, far from being demanding, of a very limited nature. W. R. Greg, in a famous survey of prostitution in the *Westminster* (July 1850), argued that in women, unlike men, 'desire is dormant, if not non-existent, till excited; always till excited by undue familiarities; almost always till excited by actual intercourse.' (LIII, 457) Dr Acton's opinion was that

> There are many females who never feel any sexual excitement whatever. Others, again, immediately after each period, do become, to a limited degree, capable of experiencing it; but this capacity is often temporary, and may cease entirely till the next menstrual period. The best mothers, wives, and managers of households, know little or nothing of sexual indulgences. Love of home, children, and domestic duties, are the only passions they feel.
>
> As a general rule, a modest woman seldom desires any sexual gratification for herself. She submits to her husband, but only to please him; and, but for the desire of maternity, would far rather be relieved from his attentions. (p. 102)

Views like these seem, to us in the twentieth century, hardly consonant with reason and the blatant facts of human physiology. It seems difficult to believe that so many women over so long a period could be deceived on such a fundamental issue, that they could deny themselves so important an area of experience and pleasure, could stifle within themselves the natural promptings of their physical and emotional constitution.

Clearly to some extent the idea of the unsexed woman came about from masculine wishful thinking. Greg goes on to say, 'Women whose position and education have protected them from exciting causes, constantly pass through life without ever being cognizant of the prompting of the senses. Happy for them that it is so!' And Acton, with a similar parenthesis, remarks that 'the majority of women (happily for them) are not very much troubled with sexual feeling of any kind'. (p. 101) Medical writers unmoved by conservative moral scruples could give a very different picture of female sexuality. Culverwell and Alexander Walker, [73] for example, two doctors with a free and easy moral posture, made no bones about the healthy naturalness of strong sexual passion in a woman; and in the unprudish Bell's *Kalogynomia* (1821), still more in the free love medical treatise of George Drysdale, we find a striking reverence for the beauty of Nature's sexual arrangements. Even moral conservatives could sometimes show a remarkable discordance with the views of Greg and Acton. Dr Michael Ryan, for example, who wrote an alarmist book on prostitution in 1839, a few years earlier in his *Philosophy of Marriage* had argued quite matter-of-factly that women must receive more pleasure from sex than men:

> the other sex have the nervous system much more sensitive than ours, the skin finer and more delicate, . . . their feelings are more acute, their mammae the seat of vivid sensibility from uterine sympathy, the nipples erected during intercourse and extended through the whole economy, than in man, and . . . coition or impregnation generally excites in them a universal tremor in all parts of the body. (3rd edn., 1837, p. 153)

The supposition that wishful thinking helped to form the idea of the unsexed woman receives further support from the occasional glimpse we get of the Victorian lady unawares, the evidence that, when secure from comment, she was capable of very positive sexual pleasure. On the ladies' beaches, for example, at the seaside, in the anonymity of a stretch of sea crowded with other women bathers all dressed in similar costumes and bathing hats, she was free to enjoy a degree of sexual exhibitionism that was normally unthinkable: we find *The Observer* 24 August 1856 complaining that 'should the sea be rather rough the females do not venture beyond the surf, and lay themselves on their backs, waiting for the coming waves,

with their bathing dresses in a most *dégagée* style. The waves
come, and, in the majority of instances, not only cover the fair
bathers, but literally carry their dresses up to their necks, so
that, as far as decency is concerned, they might as well be
without any dresses at all.' (p. 5) A sizeable number of well-
bred Victorian women also enjoyed fairly erotic private fantasies it seems. 'How many a woman in "Society" ', wrote
Richard Burton, that enthusiastic chronicler of smut, 'when
stricken by insanity or puerperal fever, breaks out into language
that would shame the slums and which makes the hearers
marvel where she could have learned such vocabulary. How
many an old maid held to be as cold as virgin snow, how many
a matron upon whose fairest fame not a breath of scandal has
blown, how many a widow who proudly claims the title
univira, must relieve their pent-up feelings by what may be
called mental prostitution.' [74]

But evidence of this sort is far less damaging to the Greg and
Acton view than one might think. Private sexual pleasure in
fantasy and masturbation could easily coexist with a fastidious
distaste for conjugal relations. One reason was simple ignorance
of the nature of self-abuse: Havelock Ellis wrote of a married
lady, a leader in social-purity movements, who discovered,
through reading some pamphlet against solitary vice, that she
had herself been practising masturbation for years without
knowing it. [75] Another reason was guilt and shame: 'Women
who have exhausted themselves by secret licentiousness,' went a
commonplace opinion, 'are often so *virtuous* as to hate the sight
of a man, and abhor the idea of the holiest expression of mutual
love. They are our most censorious prudes.' [76] The idea of the
unsexed woman, then, was by no means purely mythical. A
number of well-bred women doubtless received genuine physical pleasure from their marriage-bed. A number of others were
clearly indifferent to the physical side of love, but welcomed
marital congress from love of their husbands and from appreciating the symbolic role of sex. But for many others conjugal
relations meant a distasteful, necessary duty, a painful, humili-

ating burden. Dr Ryan measured woman's sexuality in physiological terms. Greg and Acton, however, assessed it on the basis of her emotional constitution. They saw that emotionally the greater part of well-bred Victorian womanhood was debarred from sexual appetite, either frigidly indifferent or often strongly antagonistic. If we return once more to the Victorian home and family, if we examine the knowledge of sex available to young girls and even married women, it will be readily apparent why this was so.

The Victorian period was an age of nervous worry, and this was particularly true of the middle-class woman. Unlike her menfolk she would be disqualified by her limited education and submissive social role from suffering the full impact of the *Zeitgeist*. But her nervous constitution, as in the twentieth century, would be much weaker nonetheless than that of men. A poorly conditioned physique, deprived of proper exercise, of nourishing diet, and even healthy dress, by fashionable notions of female delicacy; an under-developed mind, ill-taught, inexperienced and trained to deference and dependence; an over-developed sensibility, easily excited within the narrow circle of her interests to emotional excesses; all these might combine to make her nervously susceptible, timorous and self-conscious. Victorian girls, therefore, were especially prone to fear on the delicate subject of sex, and unfortunately their fears, like their brothers', too often spiralled through the anxieties of their parents. Puberty, for example, was likely to be a trying enough experience for a nervous, delicate girl, but with parents unwilling to offer pre-instruction it could produce the most grievous emotional shocks. A mid-century doctor, from a statistical inquiry about the onset of menstruation in nearly a thousand women, learned that 'twenty-five per cent were totally unprepared for its appearance, thirteen out of the twenty-five were much frightened, screamed, or went into hysterical fits, and that six out of the thirteen thought themselves wounded, and washed with cold water'. [77] Parental reticence could cause severe emotional pain. It could cause also

severe physical hardship, as doctors frequently testified: women
and girls sometimes put up with agony rather than communi-
cate their trouble, let alone submit to examination. Nor was
this surprising in view of the conditioning they often received
in this direction. Francis Newman in the 1860s soberly
offered as a remedy for the Great Social Evil a veto on the
examination of women by male doctors: 'allowing that elder
men must *sometimes* be called in as a last resort, nevertheless in a
well-ordered community this would be exceptional, namely,
when severe suffering overpowers female bashfulness and puri-
fies the physician's heart by compassion. . . . It is difficult to
imagine how any medical man can retain delicacy, who has to
go through the ordeal of introspecting a long string of women
in the shortest possible time.' [78]

Parental reticence and primness inevitably made the facts of
sex seem furtive and disgusting. In a story by George Egerton a
young girl explains, ' "I was fourteen when I gave up the
gooseberry-bush theory as the origin of humanity; and I cried
myself ill with shame when I learnt what maternity meant." '
And this girl, we should note, had yet to learn the meaning of
sexual intercourse, believing until her wedding night ' "that
the words of the minister settled the matter" '. [79] Her bridal
ignorance was typical of thousands. Mothers were often only
too keen to leave the duty of enlightenment to the bridegroom;
and marriage manuals would tell a girl everything except the
most important.[1] As late as 1896, indeed, George Holyoake,
the belligerent radical and freethinker, made it one of his
points in indicting the Church that the marriage service
'contains things no bride could hear without a blush, if she
understood them'. [80] A blush in fact was a pretty mild reaction, for many a bride would respond with something stronger

[1] One looks in vain for information about sexual intercourse in such books
as John Morison's *Counsels to a Newly Wedded Pair* (1830); Mrs H. C.
Caddick's *The Bride's Book* (1835); Arthur Freeling's *The Young's Bride's Book*
(1839); or Clara L. Balfour's very popular *Whisper to a Newly Married Pair*,
which had gone through eight of its twenty-three editions by 1850.

than embarrassment. In the same year that Holyoake complained about the indecency of the liturgy Dora Langlois published a book called *The Child: Its Origin and Development. A Manual Enabling Mothers to Initiate their Daughters Gradually and Modestly into all the Mysteries of Life.* A laudable undertaking, one might think. But Mrs Langlois instead of offering the ignorant girl knowledge and reassurance offered only half-knowledge and nervous apprehension. She begins her chapter on sexual intercourse, for example, by remarking that a husband will not want ignorance in his bride, but then goes on to say: 'I incline to the belief that any right-thinking man would prefer to feel that his bride knew the sacrifice she must make of her person to his natural demands, and that her confidence in him was sufficient to enable her to face the necessary ordeal.' (p. 27)

The 'necessary ordeal', this for countless Victorian women was the meaning of the wedding night. 'The first sacrifice,' writes W. R. Greg, 'is made and exacted . . . in a delirium of mingled love and shame. The married woman feels shame, often even remorse, and a strange confusion of all her previous moral conceptions.' A respectable woman told him: ' "It is not a quarter-of-an-hour's ceremony in a church that can make *that* welcome or tolerable to pure and delicate feelings, which would otherwise outrage their whole previous notions, and their whole natural and moral sense." ' [81] Sometimes the wedding-night would be actually traumatic. Annie Besant had good cause to remark that many a marriage was doomed from its very beginning by the fact of 'a young girl's sensitive modesty and pride, her helpless bewilderment and fear'. [82] Mrs Besant's case, it is true, was rather exceptional: she was twenty when she married but had the sexual knowledge of a baby. But even when a bride was equipped with the relevant information, the result might be equally traumatic. If we consider the emotional strain of the wedding-day, the ceremony, the fuss, the leave-takings, above all the sense of beginning a new life, perhaps with a man not intimately known beforehand, we can appreciate how susceptible to nervous fear a Victorian bride might be. And if we consider the nervousness, the ignorance and inexperience of many Victorian bridegrooms, we can imagine how frequently these fears might be painfully realized. 'The first lamentable episode in many tragedies of marriage,' wrote Geoffrey Mortimer in *Chapters on Human Love* (1898), 'is enacted at the hour of physical consummation. Many bridegrooms, through ignorance, shyness, or ill-controlled passion inflict considerable mental and physical suffering upon their brides. The diffidence cannot always be dispelled; but the haste, the lack of physiological knowledge, and the misunderstanding of a sensitive woman's nature are avoidable offences.' (p. 214)

With some wives doubtless initial pain gave way in time to pleasure. But this in fact might only frighten the woman more, making her fear the promptings of her nature: if she had been told of sex at all, she might well have been told that only lascivious women experienced genuine physical pleasure.[1] But in general she probably never learned to enjoy sex much at all herself. Apart from her miseducation by parents, doctors, and friends, by the novels and poems she had been given to read, apart from the nervous shocks she might have suffered at puberty or marriage, there were two other important factors conspiring to keep her sexless. One of course was her husband's sexual ignorance. 'It is a fact,' writes Mortimer, 'that, through the precipitancy of some husbands, many wives do not begin to participate in the pleasure till it has reached its climax in the man. Thus, through the whole married life, a wife may be debarred from the normal and beneficial stimulus of the love act.' (p. 215) Never really experiencing the pleasures of sexual love, never really understanding the scope, power and beauty of the sexual impulse, the married woman was likely to continue viewing sex only as a satisfaction for her husband and for herself a necessary evil.

[1] One can imagine how she might react to a remark like this in *Rees'* *Cyclopaedia*: 'That a mucous fluid is sometimes formed in coition from the internal organs and vagina is undoubted; but this only happens in lascivious women, or such as live luxuriously.' Cited Ellis *op. cit.*, I, Pt. 2, 194.

The other principal reason for the wife's lack of sexual pleasure was the general ignorance of contraceptive methods, at least up to the 1880s: the consequences of sexual intercourse told so much more on woman than on man. First, there was often her revulsion against childbirth itself: Queen Victoria, who was no stranger to it, protested 'it is such a complete violence to all one's feelings of propriety (which God knows receive a shock enough in marriage alone)'. [83] Then there was the pain, discomfort and danger the married woman risked. 'Gestation,' wrote one doctor, 'is to many a long disease, and parturition a death agony.' 'From the first marriage-night,' wrote another as his opening words in a book to quell unnecessary fears, 'no woman under forty-five years of age can consider herself safe.' [84] Above all, perhaps, with infant mortality down, there was the physical and financial strain of rearing large families, especially amongst the less affluent: Mrs Besant, discussing her work for the birth control movement, talks of 'letters from thousands of poor married women—many from the wives of country clergymen and curates—thanking and blessing me for showing them how to escape from the veritable hell in which they lived'. [85] Previously their only escape had been self-induced miscarriages. [86] But contraception, if safer, was to many just as offensive to their conscience and, if doctors were to be believed, just as dangerous to their health: C. H. F. Routh lists, among *The Moral and Physical Evils likely to Follow if Practices intended to Act as Checks to Population be not strongly Discouraged and Condemned* (1879), metritis, leucorrhoea, menorrhagia and haematocele, hysteralgia and hyperaesthesia of the genital organs, galloping cancer, ovarian dropsy and ovaritis, sterility, mania leading to suicide, and nymphomania. Sex to the nervous woman, then, even with contraception could still be an ordeal.

One would expect the growth of feminism to help emancipate women from all these fears and inhibitions. And to some extent it did, as later we shall see. But often in fact the Woman's Revolt was rather from sex than towards it. Feminism, it was often remarked, drew its strength largely from women in whom the sexual and maternal instincts were rather weak, [87] and sometimes indeed its attacks on masculine sexuality took a fairly hysterical form. [88] Even the new woman who appeared to espouse revolutionary moral ideas about love and marriage was often very far from being emancipated. Olive Schreiner, for example, was famous as an advocate of free love, but in fact far from believing in free love she did not really believe in sexual love at all except on the level of a 'mental and spiritual union': 'Of course there are millions,' she wrote to W. T. Stead in 1895, 'even in the most civilised communities, for whom physical attraction, affection and fidelity must constitute marriage. But for natures more highly developed I believe such a union to be wrong.' [89] The new woman, in short, even when she had advanced ideas, was often far more frigid and unstable than the old: Hardy's Sue Bridehead in *Jude the Obscure* and the heroine of Pinero's *The Notorious Mrs Ebbsmith*, both also of 1895, are two moving illustrations. Even as she revolted against the cloistral constraints of home, even as she sought liberation from the narrow domestic role to which she had been conditioned, even as she demanded a new kind of social and psychological freedom, the Victorian woman all too frequently demonstrated how effective her conditioning had been. The home for the nineteenth century may have been a refuge, a place of peace, but it was also in many ways a prison, a place of crippling fear and suffering, that inflicted permanent damage on its inmates.

4

A Cross Between an Angel
and an Idiot

I SEPARATE BUT EQUAL

ONE OF THE PRINCIPAL GOALS of the new woman was inevitably electoral enfranchisement, for her inability to vote in
either national or municipal elections was both the symbol and
the seal of her subordinate social role. She could, it is true,
not only vote but hold office in certain limited areas, at the
level, for example, of sexton, churchwarden or parish overseer.
But her emancipation here was an indication of society's low
assessment of her capacity. 'This is a servile ministerial office
which requires neither skill nor understanding,' was the
verdict in a court case which upheld her right to act as sexton,
'But this cannot determine that women may vote for members
of Parliament as that choice requires an improved understanding.' [90] Woman's understanding of political issues was
necessarily very limited even without this constitutional dis-
incentive. Her education was often short through early
marriage and cheap through the financial priority of her
brothers. But more important, it was usually very restricted in
its scope, especially in the first half of the century: often she
would be trained in little more than domestic practicalities or
polite accomplishments like music, dancing and art-work; and
always inhibiting her development there would be the constraints of feminine delicacy.

Notions of feminine delicacy regularly meant an insulation

from all sullying contact with the sins and cruelties of the world, and a conditioning in bashful modesty, graceful passivity and dutiful self-negation. They meant too very often a lack of physical robustness that would reinforce this psychological conditioning: indeed, with little work and exercise, a meagre and indigestible diet, and certain unhealthy modes of dress, especially the pernicious custom of tight-lacing, the delicate woman could be positively feeble. The pettiness moreover of the woman's daily round could lead to a fragile state of nerves, particularly where enlivened by exaggerated sensibility, her dedicated indulgence in emotional excitement in poetry and fiction, in her children, pets, friendships and religion. She was in some measure, then, a mental and moral cripple, incapable of informed and independent judgement, timid, deferential, sometimes wilfully vacuous. She was notoriously a slave to conventional opinion, to class prejudice, and to a narrow and bigoted morality. Above all she was a slave to the great shibboleth of propriety. 'The proprieties are to a woman's life', it was claimed in 1850,

> what the unities are to the drama: the swaddling bands and prison bars of nature. . . . A girl may not look behind her, nor run, nor conduct herself with that artless purity of demeanour so natural to her sex, and which is at once its own apotheosis and defence, for no other reason than that the proprieties so command; though why or from what authority they so command, is not apparent. It is astounding with what blind obedience women conform to these same proprieties, as though they were the undeniable law of destiny itself, not to be doubted of or questioned. With what intensity they detest the women or the men who only conform to them as much as they see good to do, and ridicule and repudiate the remainder; with what tenacity these laws have interpenetrated their nature, until everything in the wide world is seen through the coloured glasses of the proprieties! [91]

This kind of intellectual and psychological debility was not only tolerated by men but often actively encouraged. For woman in some respects was little better than man's plaything.

In the eighteenth century Chesterfield was open in his cynicism: 'Women, then, are only children of a larger growth. . . . A man of sense only trifles with them, plays with them, humours and flatters them, as he does with a sprightly, forward child.' [92] In the nineteenth century men would rarely be so candid in their egotism, but they could be equally revealing nonetheless. Bella Harmon, for example, in *Our Mutual Friend* despite her aspirations to be 'something so much worthier than the doll in the doll's house' (II, 322) is really nothing more, and Dickens like her husband is clearly content for her to remain so: education on any level higher than the Complete British Family Housewife could only destroy her charm. Similarly the conventions which deprived women of healthy diet, exercise and dress were no accident of custom but the product of a widespread masculine predilection for a doll-like physical fragility in women. Again eighteenth-century men were more blatant in their egotism: Burke in 1757 noted complacently that women were very conscious of man's association of beauty with fragility, 'for which reason, they learn to lisp, to totter in their walk, to counterfeit weakness, and even sickness. In all this, they are guided by nature. Beauty in distress is much the most affecting beauty.' [93] But nineteenth-century men too, especially the earlier generations, often left the ladies in little doubt how much they risked by athletic tastes in recreation, by an undue enjoyment of fresh air and sun, or even by a hearty appetite for food: 'How disenchanting in the female character,' wrote the actor Macready of one offender in the last respect, 'is the manifestation of relish for the pleasures of the table'.[1] Some women were very cynical about this kind of masculine egotism and about the conventional notions of female delicacy. One of them, writing in 1844, was very forthright: 'Treated at one

[1] Quoted Alan S. Downer, *The Eminent Tragedian* (1966), who also notes that *Punch* in a 'Dictionary for the Ladies' defined 'Appetite' as 'A monstrous abortion, which is stifled in the kitchen, that it may not exist during dinner' (pp. 128, 366).

moment as a child, at another as a plaything, if fair as an
angel—for a while! Then wearied of as the child, thrown
away as the toy, and beauty vanished, stript of her angelic
splendour, and forced to tread the miry paths of life in the
way she best can. Such is woman now; trained from childhood
to believe that for man, and for man alone, she must live, that
marriage must be not only her highest, but her only aim on
earth, as in it is comprised the whole of her destiny.' [94]

But most women with feminist aspirations were powerless to
fulfil them. For woman was not only in some respects man's
plaything. She was also in a sense his serf and chattel. Marriage
inevitably was likely to be 'not only her highest, but her only
aim on earth' because the spinster's lot was usually a most
disagreeable alternative. The strong-minded woman might be
willing to endure for her freedom the insensitive condescension
and often ridicule to which the old maid was susceptible. But
unless she had a guaranteed source of income or a talent for
one of the few occupations open to her (like writing, dress-
making, or teaching), the humiliations of financial dependence,
still more the privations of destitution, might very well make
her dwindle into a wife. Once married her freedoms were in
some ways even more narrowly circumscribed: in return for
the security of a home, the name of wife, and the opportunity
to enjoy the privilege of motherhood, she owed her husband
almost absolute fealty. If she were disloyal to her marriage
vows, if she committed adultery, no matter what her pro-
vocation or the purity of her new attachment, her social ruin
was certain: she would be barred from her home and children,
rejected by her own family and friends; without a character she
would be in a much worse position than even the spinster, not
only totally and irredeemably ostracized but unemployable in
any respectable occupation; common prostitution might very
well offer her only possibility of survival. Her husband, on the
other hand, could expect indulgence for any infidelities he
might practise. And his claim for indulgence, his demand for a
double standard in marital misconduct, would be upheld by the

law of the land: the Divorce Act, for example, of 1857, gave a man his freedom on the mere grounds of his wife's adultery, but she was required to prove him guilty of rape, sodomy or bestiality, or of adultery coupled with incest, bigamy, cruelty or desertion.

This law in fact was by no means the most blatant example of sexual discrimination on the statute book. A generation earlier even the innocent wife of a broken marriage could be debarred from any access to her children: not only this, the husband was at perfect liberty to place them in the hands of his mistress. And though this anomaly was partly rectified by the Custody of Infants Act of 1839, many other statutes continued to make the married woman's serf-like status very plain. Her property, for example, with a few partial exceptions, became her husband's upon marriage in return for the maintenance and protection he had contracted to supply; she enjoyed no such reciprocal benefit. Even if she were driven from home by actual cruelty and the courts supported her by denying the husband restitution of his conjugal rights, her property remained nevertheless securely in his possession and control. Legal reforms in 1857 and 1870 helped to redress the situation somewhat, but it was not until the Married Woman's Property Act of 1882 that the inequity was finally abolished. Even in 1882, however, the wife's person remained effectively the chattel of her husband. Until 1852 he could enforce co-habitation, if she deserted him, by a writ of *habeas corpus* directed against anyone who offered her sanctuary. And until as late as 1891 he could kidnap her and subject her to physical imprisonment without a writ of *habeas corpus* being directed successfully against himself.

Woman's long acceptance of these indignities, her acceptance that in some respects she was little better than man's plaything, serf and chattel, requires some explanation. Psychological conditioning and economic necessity were clearly powerful factors. It was true, moreover, that a woman's egotism might enjoy subordination as a man's might enjoy domination: 'The best sort of women,' it was suggested in 1869, 'always feel a secret, unconfessed complacence in yielding themselves to the sway of one of the other sex, in acknowledging his superiority, his strange and potent influence.' [95] But the most basic explanation for women's acceptance of subordination was the profound conviction that sexual discrimination was the law of God and Nature:

> Man for the field and woman for the hearth;
> Man for the sword, and for the needle she;
> Man with the head, and woman with the heart;
> Man to command, and woman to obey;
> All else confusion. [96]

Man was meant by nature to be the hunter and the warrior, the protector and provider of the family; woman was intended to be the mother and the homemaker, to nurture and comfort. Man fulfilled his role by going out into the world, applying his resourcefulness and strength in competition with his fellows and with nature. Woman fulfilled hers by staying at home and applying her industry and warmth to her domestic pursuits and children. Man's intellect was speculative and inventive, sharp and practical, dynamic and resilient, adapted to the rigours of the world. Woman's intellect was less flexible and capacious, designed not for invention but arrangement, not for cunning but for assiduous application, adapted to the ordering and management of the comforts of the home. But if her intellect was inferior to man's, her judgement in matters of morality, taste and feeling was in general more developed: her intuition and emotions alike unblunted by man's struggle for existence, her judgement here in her special domain, the kingdom of the heart, was more perceptive, compassionate and unselfish. The sexes, in short, nature, religion and immemorial custom seemed to say, were totally distinct in aptitudes and functions, and to that extent required unequal social treatment. But these aptitudes and functions were equal in importance, and so it was, woman's subordination in certain areas guaranteed her sovereignty in others.

'Separate but equal' is in the twentieth century a familiar rationalization of suppression and exploitation, but the intelligent nineteenth-century male supremacist could defend its validity much better than the intelligent modern racist. For apart from the apparent sanction offered by tradition, the Bible and by the facts of human physiology, there were pressing reasons in the nineteenth century to narrow the role of woman to the purely domestic sphere and then to idealize her sovereignty within it. Her role through motherhood, for example, as the educator of mankind seemed more vital now than ever. Evangelicalism stressed the religious implications of good motherhood, urging the mother's duty to awaken her young to a sense of life's high purpose, to protect them devotedly from any contact with the insidious wiles of Satan. The French Revolution dramatized the political implication of good motherhood, urging the moral stability of the home as the prerequisite of a peaceful, ordered society. And the pervasive fears of sexual immorality especially, emanating from numerous other sources besides the Evangelical and political, put the seal on society's exaltation of good motherhood. So diffused and powerful was this exaltation that even the not remarkably religious, conservative or prudish George Henry Lewes offered in 1850 a typically Victorian panegyric tribute: 'The grand function of woman, it must always be recollected, is, and ever must be, *Maternity*: and this we regard not only as her distinctive characteristic, and most endearing charm, but as a high and holy office—the prolific source, not only of the best affections and virtues of which our nature is capable, but also of the wisest thoughtfulness, and most useful habits of observation, by which that nature can be elevated and adorned.' [97] When we add to woman's role as educator of her children her importance as the custodian of the home, increasingly important as a place of peace, a still-centre in the storm of revolutionary social changes, we can appreciate the more clearly her acceptance of a purely domestic function.

Woman's acceptance of adverse discrimination in the sphere

of sexual morality is also quite intelligible. The commonest explanation of society's double standard between the sexes was that nature had connived at this inequity: a wife's adultery, for example, in a largely pre-contraceptive age could have consequences for her husband that his adultery could not possibly have for her. Indeed the Bishop of Oxford reminded the Lords in 1856 that the double standard seemed sanctioned by the Bible on these grounds:

> It seemed to recognize an equality in the sexes; but the truth was, that though the sin might be equal in each—yet the social crime was different in magnitude as committed by the one or the other; and our blessed Master, while allowing a husband to put away his wife for adultery because all the highest purposes for which marriage was instituted by God would be defeated by the infidelity of the wife, never extended the same right to the other side. [98]

Here, as with woman's domestic aptitude and function, the sanctions of tradition, the scriptures and the facts of human physiology were reinforced by important features of nineteenth century life. A woman's immorality was less forgivable than a man's by the apparent law of Nature; it was especially less forgivable in the light of her accepted social role. It was less excusable for one thing because the deterrent effect of social punishment was so much stronger in her case. A divorced wife or cast-off daughter was far more vulnerable to economic hardship than her counterpart in the male sex. And even if she were financially independent she was still socially vulnerable in the way that not many men were. To ostracize men might occasion society a great deal of inconvenience—in the case, for example, of an architect, lawyer, engineer, financier, merchant or industrialist—but to excommunicate women, unless they be perhaps a gifted actress or singer, was inevitably much easier, for their social life was everything. And because her social life was everything a woman had so much more leisure to be a custodian of purity: 'besides the guard which a man places round his harem, and the defences which a woman has in her heart,' Thackeray wryly remarked, 'hasn't she all her own friends of her own sex to keep watch that she does not go astray, and to tear her to pieces if she is found erring'. (*Pendennis*, pp. 518–19)

Feminine frailty was less forgivable too because women, it seemed, had far less opportunity or occasion to fall from grace. For the Victorian wife there were the snug walls of sheltered domesticity, her passionate absorption in her children, her insulation from evil by the barriers of propriety. For the Victorian husband there were the open streets where sex might be bought for a shilling. For the Victorian wife moreover there was the desexualizing nature of her upbringing, reinforcing what was considered her natural lack of appetite. There was also, perhaps almost as important, her conditioning in comparative physical debility. Clement Scott in a late-Victorian debate on the double standard expressed a common view of woman's relative constitutional sanctity from sin:

> If women were physically as strong as men, if they were never worn out or weary with child-bearing, if they were never sufferers from lassitude and fatigue, if they were endowed by nature with fierce power to battle, combat and endure, if, in fact, they were born animals as men are, instead of angels as women are, then indeed they might and ought to exact the same standard of sexual morality from the husband as from the wife. [99]

For the Victorian husband, born an animal instead of an angel, born into a sex in which appetite far from being lacking seemed almost incurably demanding, for the Victorian husband it was natural to believe like Thackeray in *Pendennis* that 'women are pure, but not men' (p. 164), it was natural to have different expectations of the sexes' moral behaviour. Even if he did not view his own shortcomings with indulgence, he would be likely to view the frailty of his womenfolk with a yet more severe disfavour. And he would be likely too to invest his wife with the responsibility of controlling his desires: the young Lord Shaftesbury prayed night and morning 'for a wife, lovely, beautiful and true; one with whom I may be safe from the snares of temptation'. [100]

The emphasis on woman's function as the saviour of a far more sexually vulnerable man is also central to the intellectual impoverishment of nineteenth century womanhood. That women were sometimes reduced to the level of simpering idiots is not to be credited simply to the crude, power-hungry egotism of their menfolk. In 1765 James Fordyce, the doyen of eighteenth century moralists on the fair sex, had claimed not entirely disingenuously, that feminine timidity and fragility served to disarm masculine egotism of its tendency to unchastity. For to men Nature seemed to say:

> 'Behold these smiling innocents, whom I have graced with my fairest gifts, and committed to your protection; behold them with love and respect; treat them with tenderness and honour. They are timid, and want to be defended. They are frail; O do not take advantage of their weakness. Let their fears and blushes endear them. Let their confidence in you never be abused—But is it possible, that any of you can be such barbarians, so supremely wicked, as to abuse it? Can ye find in your hearts to despoil the gentle trusting creatures of their treasure, or do anything to strip them of their native robe of virtue?' [101]

In a similar way woman's fragility and dependence were held the means of a general moral influence through the engagement of man's affections. 'In woman,' went a somewhat extreme view in 1835, 'weakness itself is the true charter of power, it is an absolute attraction, and by no means a defect; it is the mysterious tie between the sexes, a tie irresistible as it is captivating, and begetting an influence peculiar to itself—in short all independence is unfeminine: the more dependent that sex becomes, the more will it be cherished.' [102]

To a modern ear this last pronouncement, like Fordyce's, seems the worst form of patronizing masculine chauvinism. But we need to appreciate first that there was some excuse for masculine egotism at this time. The psychic pressures of the age, for example, that we considered in the previous chapters, weighed far more heavily on the man than on the woman. The middle-class woman was kept snug within the citadel of the home; the middle-class man faced the world abroad, the clash of new ideas, the nervous strains produced by technological change, the anxieties about the political and spiritual welfare of society, the harshness and the pressures of modern business life. It was surely understandable that men troubled by sensations of personal insecurity should seek to raise their self-esteem in domestic superiority, in a feeling that here at least they had power and control. For the wage-slave, enduring days of menial drudgery and indignity,[1] the worldly ignorance of his wife and daughters could provide a psychological buttress: not least by the escapist, vicarious enjoyment he might gain from their untroubled innocence, and by the boost to his self-esteem he might gain from pride in his role of selfless stoical protector. 'Matilda Rashleigh,' enthused a working-class paper in 1844, 'knew nothing of the world. Its cares, its blighting miseries, and its feverish short-lived joys were all unknown to her,—she lived in a world of her own—a world created by the purity and gentleness of her own heart—her ignorance was indeed bliss. . . . Dream on, we would say to such gentle, trusting hearts as Matilda Rashleigh; may it be long ere you awaken to reality, where there is so much more joy in the unreal.' [103]

We need to recognize too when considering the nature of Victorian masculine egotism that this view of feminine ignorance and weakness was steadily losing ground around the mid-century. It was still sufficiently strong in 1879, it is true, for Meredith to blast it comprehensively in *The Egoist*, and it indeed survived the century. But from the 1840s onwards society was increasingly sympathetic to a more feminist view of womanhood. The radical new women, like Ida in *The Princess* (1847), wanted complete equality with men: legal, social,

[1] For a vivid account of the dissolution of workday toil and humiliation in domestic peace and love see *Mark Rutherford's Deliverance* (2nd edn. 1888), pp. 247–53.

educational and professional. These were few in number. But the more liberal upholder of the doctrine of the sexes' separate but equal functions, such as Ida's creator Tennyson, was prepared to support a degree of liberation—in a woman's legal position, for example, or her educational opportunities. Full emancipation, claimed the new orthodoxy, was not to be considered. 'For woman is not undevelopt man,/But diverse.' And with woman diverse and created to play a quite separate but equally important role, crude talk of inequality was irrelevant:

> seeing either sex alone
> Is half itself, and in true marriage lies
> Nor equal, nor unequal, Each fulfils
> Defect in each. [104]

But if woman was not to be an imitation man, nor was she to be his slave and plaything. Limited emancipation, it was argued, was highly desirable as a means of producing more mature and enlightened mothers and wives.

By mid-century the qualities of ideal womanhood seemed more important than ever. In the eighteenth century to describe a beautiful woman as an angel was conventional hyperbole. But by the publication of Patmore's *The Angel in the House* (1854–6), which was to sell a quarter of a million copies in the following forty years, the image conveyed a much greater pressure of feeling. In an age of religious crisis the aura of quasi-religious homage with which the pure woman was invested formed at the least an unblocked emotional outlet for troubled minds, and at best it offered an existential basis on which to build a life—an alternative to, or confirmation of, God's perfect love for man. In an age of moral crisis, when traditional ethics seemed in danger of being swamped in material greed and animal enjoyments, the angel woman provided reassurance of the spirituality of man, and she offered too the prospect of moral protection and inspiration, an antidote to the Goddess-of-Getting-On and the perils of sensuality. In an age of emotional unbalance, when psychic strains were expressed in effusive sentimentality, the angel woman both encouraged the indulgence of fine feelings, the workings of the soul that seemed threatened by the demands of business, and later, the apparent claims of scientific material-ists,[1] and yet discharged these feelings safely without their turning into passions. James Thomson's poem 'The Deliverer' of 1859 illustrates how in the new orthodoxy, whereby each sex fulfilled defect in each, married love could deliver man from religious doubt, moral corruption and emotional sterility:

> Celestial flowers are set in earthly clay:
>> However small the circle of a life,
> If it be whole it shall expand for aye;
>> And all the Heavens are furled in Man and Wife.

> So thou, the man, the circle incomplete,
>> Shalt find thy other segment and be whole;
> Thy manhood with her womanhood shall meet
>> And form one perfect self-involving soul.

> Thy love shall grow by feeling day by day
>> Celestial love, thro' human, blessing thee;
> Thy faith wax firm by witnessing alway
>> Triumphant faith for ever glad and free.

> By her obedience thy soul shall learn
>> How far humility transcendeth pride;
> By her pure intuitions shall discern
>> The fatal flaws of reason unallied.

> Thou shalt see strength in weakness conquering,
>> The bravest action with the tenderest heart,
> Self-sacrifice unconscious hallowing
>> The lightest playing of the meanest part.

[1] Cf. Edward Burne-Jones' remark, 'The more materialistic Science becomes, the more angels shall I paint', quoted Jerome H. Buckley, *The Victorian Temper* (Cambridge, Mass., 1951), p. 164.

Chastity, purity, and holiness
     Shall shame thy virile grossness; the power
Of beauty in the spirit and its dress
     Reveal all virtue lovely as a flower.

Till love for her shall teach thee love for all;
     Till perfect reverence for her shall grow
To faith in God which nothing can appal,
     Tho' His green world be dark with sin and woe.

The model of womanhood given here by Thomson or by
Patmore in *The Angel in the House*, would seem incompatible
with the timid, fragile creature who saw everything in the wide
world through the coloured glasses of the proprieties. Havelock
Ellis in 1887 was to claim that 'woman was treated as a cross
between an angel and an idiot'. [105] There is a huge disparity
clearly between the simpering idiot of the etiquette books and
the inspiring, protective angel of the idealistic poet. But that
they co-existed was no accident of history. As we shall find
when we have examined the angel in more detail, the idiot was
in some measure her distorted mirror image: the more impressive aspects of Victorian sexual idealism were ironically a
source of the least attractive.

II THE ANGEL MOTHER

For early Victorians seeking in womanhood a symbol of
redemptive love and purity in antithesis to the immorality,
materialism and godlessness around them, seeking in womanhood comfort and counsel with which to meet the trials of life,
there was an obvious place to look, to the first woman they had
loved, their mother. And since Evangelical propaganda about
the duty of dedicated motherhood had been very effective from
the 1790s onwards, many had mothers it was not difficult to
reverence. Thackeray, for example, on revisiting his childhood
home in later years, was moved to write: 'All sorts of recollec-

tions of my youth came back to me: dark and sad and painful with my dear good mother as a gentle angel interposing between me and misery.' [106] Such nostalgia was the more intense for men suffering unhappiness in adulthood: the hero of William Smith's *Thorndale* (1857) considers, 'Well, I have been happy once! I have been a child!—I have been in heaven! I have stood in the smile, and lain in the arms of one of God's angels. I was the happy child of a gentle and loving mother.' (pp. 72–3) The poet Allingham in 'Half-Waking' dreams of sleeping in his childhood bed, his mother by the fire:

> If I should make the slightest sound
> > To show that I'm awake,
> She'd rise, and lap the blankets round,
> > My pillow softly shake;
>
> Kiss me, and turn my face to see
> > The shadows on the wall,
> And then sing *Rousseau's Dream* to me,
> > Till fast asleep I fall.
>
> But this is not my little bed;
> > That time is far away;
> 'Mong strangers cold I live instead,
> > From dreary day to day. [107]

Memories especially cherished were those of the mother's help in the troubled years of youth—the comfort she gave, for example in assuaging religious doubts. Sir Charles Tennyson has shown that the influence of Tennyson's mother was 'vitally important' in the poet's doubt-filled early manhood, and that this influence never ceased—after his mother's death Tennyson described her as 'the beautifullest thing God almighty ever did make'. [108] The portrait of her in *The Princess* indicates the nature of her influence:

> No angel, but a dearer being, all dipt
> In angel instincts, breathing Paradise,
> Interpreter between the gods and men.
> > (Pt. VII, lines 301–3)

The spiritual influence of Carlyle's devoutly religious mother was similarly enduring: 'Oh for faith!' he wrote, 'Truly the greatest "God announcing miracle" always is faith, and now more than ever. I often look on my mother (nearly the only genuine Believer I know of) with a kind of sacred admiration.' [109] Another and equally vital sphere of motherly influence was the moral, and especially the sexual. Witness Thackeray's opposition in *Pendennis* (1848–50) of the hero's Angel Mother and the corruption that almost claims her son. Witness particularly his description of her enduring talismanic power:

> All the lapse of years, all the career of fortune, all the events of life, however strongly they may move or eagerly excite him, never can remove that sainted image from his heart, or banish that blessed love from its sanctuary. If he yields to wrong, the dear eyes will look sadly upon him when he dares to meet them; if he does well, endures pain, or conquers temptation, the ever-present love will greet him, he knows, with approval and pity; if he falls, plead for him; if he suffers, cheer him;—be with him and accompany him always until death is past, and sorrow and sin are no more. (p. 607)

Thackeray in fact, unlike Tennyson, came to see faults in his mother: 'when I was a boy at Larkbeare,' he wrote in 1852, 'I thought her an Angel and worshipped her. I see but a woman now, O so tender so loving so cruel.' [110] But the enduring strength of his attachment is indicated by the fact that Mrs Pendennis was modelled upon her.

Blessed with such mothers, in fact or retrospective fantasy, it is not surprising that many Victorians chose their wives after such a model, looking to them for the same kind of comfort and inspiration. A. P. Stanley, for example, a bachelor in his late forties, became engaged in 1863 to remove the numbness and emptiness in his life caused by his mother's death some twenty months earlier. He wrote to his fiancée: 'You must be my wings. I shall often flag and be dispirited; but you, now, as my dear mother formerly, must urge me, and bid me not despair when the world seems too heavy a burden to be struggled against.' [111] In *Pendennis* Thackeray has Laura assume the role of mothering as well as later marrying his hero. Take, for instance, the scene when Pen is unhappy over his entanglement with Blanche Amory:

'Mamma left you to me,' she said, stooping down and brushing his forehead with her lips hastily. 'You know you were to come to me when you were in trouble, or to tell me when you were very unhappy.' (p. 658)

And note the way in which Helen Pendennis hangs over in spirit their final reconciliation: 'Pen's head sinks down in the girl's lap, as he sobs out, "come and bless us, dear mother!" and arms as tender as Helen's once more comfort him.' (p. 725) In *Liberty Hall* (1860) by Winwood Reade scenes in which the heroine looks after her sick lover demonstrate yet more clearly this assumption of the motherly role:

When she thought that he was awake, guileless as an angel, she would often come into the room. If his eyes were shut, she would kiss them till they opened; she would nurse him like an infant in her arms, and holding his head in her hands, would cradle it upon her bosom, and hide it all with her long and golden hair.

And he, like an infant, would lie still, caressing her, thanking her only with his eyes.

O, how they loved each other! (III, 265–6)

Situations in which a motherly heroine nurses and saves the soul of a sick, despairing hero are quite common in Victorian fiction. See the end of *Basil* (1852), for example, by Wilkie Collins, or Kingsley's *Alton Locke* ('Her voice was like an angel's when she spoke to me—friend, mother, sister, all in one'—II, 226). The conjunction of mother and sister here is particularly interesting (*Basil*'s saviour is his sister, just as in *Pendennis* and *David Copperfield* the heroines, Laura and Agnes, are at first quasi-sisters to their lovers). For the angel sister, in fact or nostalgic fantasy, was clearly sometimes not only a supplement but a substitute for the mother. In *Liberty Hall* the hero tells his mistress:

I cannot describe to you the holiness, the warmth of a sister's love, holy and pure without harshness, warm and tender without passion. It excels the love of the mother, it surpasses even the affection of the wife. A sister denies herself every thing, gives up every thing, her time, her amusements, to satisfy the whims of the too often ungrateful brother . . . when I was a boy, like other boys, I was ungrateful . . . But when I had become a man, when I had tasted the bitter cup of sorrow, when I had learned what it was to be wicked and to be unfortunate too, when my parents shrank from me, and I was removed from my companions, I found one who would always listen to me and sympathise with me when I wished to speak, and who would always cheer me, and console me when she found me silent and gloomy. (III, 170–1)

The plots of all these novels and also of many others show a remarkably similar pattern: the hero becomes entangled with a frivolous and often dangerous young woman, but he escapes from folly at last after much suffering to form a union with a mature and motherly angel.[1] Such a pattern may be explained in terms of rational idealism: that the Victorian confronted with the peculiar problems of his age sought their solution in a feminine ideal that had been tested and found effective. But there is an alternative explanation. There is a clear case to be made that the Victorian's ideal of a mature and maternal angel stemmed less from the problems of the age than from a widespread dependence on mothering induced in early childhood.

Many Victorian men, for example, continued to be extremely dependent upon their mother throughout their lives. Even in his thirty-fourth year, we are told, Browning still looked to his mother to buy his personal belongings for him, to pack his carpet bag when he went on a journey, to relieve him of all responsibility for his own material welfare:

As a grown man, he would not go to bed without receiving from her the goodnight kiss of his childhood: delayed in town, whatever

---

[1] In *Alton Locke*, as befits the novel's sombre tone, the union is not in marriage, but in death.

the hour of his return, he went at once to her bedroom in order to seek it. Even at night, the separation between mother and son was only partial. 'My room,' wrote Browning, 'is next to hers and the door is left ajar.' [112]

It was not until Ruskin was twenty-six that he was allowed to go abroad for the first time without his parents—even then they arranged that he be accompanied by a valet, a guide, and a travelling servant; and the letters that passed between parents and son, it has been remarked, 'resemble lovers' letters in their minute analysis of misunderstandings and grievances and unintended offences'. [113] Carlyle, who had once said of sick children that what they wanted was to get to sleep well on their mother's bosom, in his eighties spent his days dozing against the cushions of his carriage or lying quietly on a sofa at Cheyne Row. 'Ah, Mother, is it you?' he was heard to murmur when a hand touched his. [114]

Shortly after her death, when he was fifty-eight years old, Carlyle had written, 'It was the earliest terror of my childhood that I might lose my mother and it had gone with me all my days.' [115] The poet Francis Thompson late in life recalled the moment of childhood horror, the 'desolation and terror of, for the first time, realizing that the mother can lose you, or you her, and your own abysmal loneliness and helplessness without her'.[1] The death of the mother, though long expected, could be even to men of advanced years a crippling emotional blow. Browning, Henry Thomas Buckle and A. P. Stanley, all middle-aged men, were utterly prostrated for some months. [116] And the death of Queen Victoria, the 'Mother of England' as she was commonly known and loved, produced a national scale of grief: 'O Glorious, O Beloved! Mother, Queen', went a typically crude but deeply felt lament,

Our sea-salt tears are not for thee to-night,
Who dwellest in the everlasting light,

[1] Peter Butter, *Francis Thompson* (1961), p. 9. Thompson compared this feeling to that of first fearing oneself to be without God.

But for our orphaned selves. Our eyes have seen
A darker day than days of war's defeat:
Death in his cruellest fashion us doth meet,
Taking our Mother from us. Death has done
Today its direst deed, smiting not one
But every home in England! England weeps
While on her bier, England's Great Mother sleeps . . . [117]

One way of surviving the loss of a much loved mother was to take the happiness of the nursery into adulthood. Nonsense poetry, which enjoyed an extraordinarily widespread vogue amongst the Victorians, is an obvious illustration. For Lewis Carroll, Derek Hudson remarks, 'something vital went out of his life' when he lost his mother in early manhood, [118] and his writings would seem in some measure compensation for this loss. The works of Edward Lear, whose lifelong history of hypersensitivity, anxiety and psychosomatic illness stemmed from his rejection by his mother in early childhood, is a yet more clear-cut example. And an extraordinarily overheated attachment to his mother lay behind J. M. Barrie's obsession with the boy who never grew up. In his autobiographical novel *Margaret Ogilvy* (1896) he explains that his mother was the inspiration of all his writing:

> For when you looked into my mother's eyes you knew, as if He had told you, why God sent her into the world—it was to open the minds of all who looked to beautiful thoughts. And that is the beginning and end of literature. Those eyes . . . have guided me through life, and I pray God they may remain my only earthly judge to the last. They were never more my guide than when I helped to put her to earth, not whimpering because my mother had been taken away after seventy-six glorious years of life, but exulting in her even at the grave. (p. 5)

When we consider Beatrice Webb's father, who though a railway tycoon, knelt down every morning and night to repeat the prayer he had learned at his mother's lap, 'Gentle Jesus, meek and mild, look upon a little child', [119] we may reasonably conjecture that a wide range of Victorian men sought to return, in different ways, to the idealized world of childhood:

> Thrice happy state again to be
> The trustful infant on the knee!
> Who lets his rosy fingers play
> About his mother's neck, and knows
> Nothing beyond his mother's eyes.[1]

Where the mother was not yet lost to death, the intensity of her relationship with her son frequently suggests a degree of sexual enjoyment. The Angel Mother was not only a protective symbol of sexual purity; she was also the means, through her closeness to her son, of releasing inhibited sexual pleasures, her own as well as his. Browning, for example, once remarked that he so loved his mother 'even as a grown man he could not sit by her otherwise than with an arm round her waist'.[120] And hence the curious fact of women's necklines: Victorian ladies were terrified of exposing their legs or even ankles, but yet saw nothing indecorous in quite generous *décolletage*. The pleasure they gave and took was almost certainly partly sexual and partly an expression of their maternal function. The *Spectator*, for example, criticizing an American dress reformer, Dr Mary Walker, who lectured in London in 1851 in a long frock coat and trousers, conceded her the right to dress as she pleased but argued it was 'false to the ethical theory of a woman's dress, which should always be faintly enticing or fascinating. Woman's first function is to be mothers, and in any sound system of ethics, even the dress of the Second Empire which . . . passes the narrow line between enticement and allurement,

---

[1] Tennyson's 'Supposed Confessions of a Second-Rate Sensitive Mind', lines 40–44. Sado-masochism, *la vice anglaise*, represented another aspect of Victorian infantilist regression (Swinburne's portraits of his mother as Lady Wariston in *Lesbia Brandon* and Eleanor Ashburst in *A Year's Letters* are interesting in this context). But without adequate quantification of its extent, compared with that of the eighteenth century or our own, it is difficult to discuss as a distinctively Victorian phenomenon.

is a better dress than a mannish variety of the Bloomer Costume.' [121] How soaked in maternity Victorian sex-appeal was is demonstrated in Meredith's *The Egoist*, where Sir Willoughby is aroused by Clara Middleton's beauty, 'Her eyes, her lips, her fluttering dress that played happy mother across her bosom, giving peeps of the veiled twins.' (I, 233) Some Victorians were quite alive to the sexual element possible in the mother-son relationship. In *Pendennis* Thackeray explicitly describes Helen's anxiety over Pen's intimacy with Miss Amory as the 'anxiety with which brooding women watch over their son's affections—and in acknowledging which, I have no doubt there is a sexual jealousy on the mother's part, and a secret pang'. (p. 230)[1] And *Esmond* is very largely the study of the secret pangs of a woman torn between maternal and sexual love for her foster-son.

As such *Esmond* is also very largely a wishfulfilling fantasy for the son, a venting of his subdued longing for physical intimacy with his mother. Lady Castlewood plays the role of Esmond's mother: 'He flung himself down on his knees, and buried his head in her lap . . . "I am your mother, you are my son, and I love you always", she said, holding her hands over him.' (pp. 227–8) And she exchanges this role for that of his wife only when her own children desert her. Yet throughout she feels a deep romantic love for Esmond, a love which is crowned —despite her advancing years—with the child of their union. Sometimes an intense mother-son relationship could preclude the son from all romantic involvement. The autobiographical hero of J. M. Barrie's *The Little White Bird* (1902) explains his bachelor status with the admission it was old ladies, and not the young ones, who were ever his undoing: 'Just as I was about to fall in love I suddenly found that I preferred the mother.'

---

[1] Men too were subject to secret pangs. Monckton Milnes, who had himself been much upset at his sister's marriage, was warned by an aunt to expect some reaction from his prospective brother-in-law at his: 'brothers don't care for their sisters marrying and often don't fancy the man they choose'. Quoted James Pope Hennessy, *Monckton Milnes, The Flight of Youth 1851–1885* (1951), p. 1.

(p. 7)[1] Francis Thompson, who spoke little overtly of his dead mother but whose poetry abounds in maternal imagery, was content with his chaste love for the safely married Alice Meynell:

> For this was even that Lady and none other
> The man in me calls 'Love', the child calls 'Mother'. [122]

George Borrow, who was deeply devoted to his mother, ended thirty-six years of comfortable celibacy in a passionless marriage to a widow nine years his senior, a relationship reflected in the curious love between the hero of *Lavengro* and Isopel Berners. Sometimes, however, an intense mother-son relationship could involve the son in deep and perhaps passionate attachments to a substitute mother-figure. The common factor, for example, of the three women to whom Browning was strongly attached in early manhood was their age. Elizabeth Barrett was six years his senior, Eliza Flower nine years, and Fanny Haworth eleven. Robert Louis Stevenson, as he grew progressively more estranged from his own mother, looked consistently for alternative mother-figures, from his childhood nurse ('My second mother, my first wife,/The Angel of my infant life') [123] to the women he fell in love with as an adult, all of them once-married and a dozen years his elder— Mrs Sitwell, to whom he sent love-letters signed 'Your Son', Mme Garshine, and Fanny Osbourne, the mother of three children, whom he married. Disraeli too seems to have compensated for an estrangement from his mother in friend-ships and love-affairs with women older than himself: Sara Austen, Clara Bolton, Henrietta Sykes, Mrs Brydges Williams, and above all his eventual wife Mrs Wyndham Lewis, twelve years his senior.[2]

---

[1] Macaulay, it might be argued without facetiousness, never married because he found he preferred his sisters: see Eric Stokes, 'Macaulay: The Indian Years 1834–38', *REL* (Oct. 1960) I, iv, 41–50.

[2] One should note that Disraeli and Stevenson, unlike most of these other lovers of matronly angels, entertained a fairly liberal, even permissive view of sex: see Robert Blake, *Disraeli* (1966), pp. 101–7, 154; J. C. Furnas,

These extreme, but not uncommon, examples point to an ambiguity in the cult of the Angel Mother. On the one hand we can see that the womanly ideal of the early- and mid-Victorians was a response to the peculiar problems of the age facing the individual and society. We can, for example, readily understand Kingsley's love for a wife five years his senior, who offered the same guidance and solace in his religious and personal difficulties that his mother had offered before her; we can understand in *Yeast* that while Launcelot Smith in the masculine sphere of intellect was Argemone's superior, 'In questions of morality, of taste, of feeling, he listened not as a lover to his mistress, but rather as a baby to its mother.' (pp. 124–5) On the other hand, however, we can see that the cult of the motherly angel was also in some measure less a response to the problems of the age than evidence in men of a degree of emasculation, a reluctance to face the problems of adulthood, caused by an over-developed ideal of virtuous motherhood. Kingsley wanted man to respect woman's moral guidance with the trust of a little child, but he had no truck with effeminate molly-coddling: 'I am not a child, but a man,' he has Launcelot say, 'I want not a mother to pet, but a man to rule me.' (p. 208) Some Victorians, on the other hand, unquestionably did want petting from their mothers and mother-substitutes. This was the more likely with men suffering from poor health: Thomas Hood, for example, soon after the distressing death of his devoted mother fell in love with a woman seven years his senior; a friend wrote of their married life, 'she perfectly adored her husband, tending him like a child, whilst he, with unbounded affection, seemed to delight to yield himself to her guidance. [124] In sickness it was natural for the husband to expect to be cossetted like a child. But what are we to make of a man like Browning?—a leading figure in the cult of angel-worship, who when Elizabeth complained he played too much the woman's part in their

Voyage to Windward: The Life of Robert Louis Stevenson (New York, 1951), pp. 55, 362.

relationship, replied magisterially, 'You shall think for me, that is my command'. [125] There is a great deal of ambiguity in Browning's deferential posture; in the only poem, for example, he wrote in the first three years of his marriage, 'The Guardian Angel—A Picture at Fano', which begins,

> Dear and great Angel, wouldst thou only leave
> That child, when thou hast done with him, for me!

There is a great deal of ambiguity too about the quasi-religious side of Browning's ideal of woman. If the Angel Mother was a solution to the crippling anxieties Victorians might suffer through the problems of the age, it was also true that she could aggravate these problems. How far, for example, was Browning's painful struggle with disbelief, a vital element in his reverence for women, caused in fact by a tension between his naturally sceptical temperament and loyalty towards the faith and feeling of his Evangelical mother? How far was Rossetti's persistent instability, his dream-world of 'The Blessed Damozel', his agonies of conscience as he sullied his ideal, caused in fact by a tension between his naturally sensual temperament and loyalty towards the faith and feelings of his Evangelical mother? [126] With the crippling effects of an Evangelical mother in the case of Ruskin and the writer-diplomatist Laurence Oliphant there is little room for doubt: John D. Rosenberg and Philip Henderson respectively have demonstrated how the aggressive maternal solicitude of Mrs Ruskin and Mrs Oliphant towards their grown-up sons produced agonies of religious indecision and sexual eccentricity (with both men a virgin marriage combined with guilt-ridden auto-eroticism). [127] If these men suffered from excessive mother-love, others were crippled equally by the antithesis. We may perhaps question Phyllis Grosskurth's use of mother-deprivation as an explanation of John Addington Symonds' homosexuality; but just the same, it is remarkable how in Edward FitzGerald, Edward Lear and Samuel Butler homo-sexual behaviour seems to be connected with a distrust of

women which in turn seems associated with betrayal and
rejection by their mothers in early childhood.[1] If, in short, the
cult of the Mother Angel brought stability to fortunate sons
like Tennyson and Thackeray, it brought instability too to
other men less favoured.[2] And if there is some doubt as to its
connection with certain cases of homosexuality, there is no
question of its connection with another form of deviant
behaviour, the love of grown-up men for little girls.

III THE ADORABLE CHILD

At Oxford in the 1880s there was something of a craze for
little girls: undergraduates would take the dons' small
daughters out on the river, invite them to tea, and make them
mascots at some of their activities. This was no exceptional
student eccentricity; nor twenty years earlier had there been
anything unusual in Ruskin's enchanted involvement with the
schoolgirls of Winnington in Cheshire, his delight in joining
them in their games and dances, in reading them stories, and
writing them nonsense verses. Children, and especially girls,
were a natural form of escapism for an age given to sentiment
and whimsy, the more especially where, as with Ruskin,
escapist indulgence was essential to a man's psychological

---

[1] Phyllis Grosskurth, *John Addington Symonds* (1964), pp. 262-3; Alfred
McKinley Terhune, *The Life of Edward FitzGerald* (New Haven, 1947),
pp. 6-8; Vivien Noakes, *Edward Lear* (1968), pp. 58-9, 134; and Philip
Henderson, *Samuel Butler: the Incarnate Bachelor* (1953), pp. 4-5. Perhaps we
should put with this group the somewhat effeminate old bachelor Augustus
Hare, who had been both rejected by his real mother and betrayed frequently
by his adored step-mother: *The Years with Mother*, an abridgement of his
autobiography, ed. Malcolm Barnes (1952), offers in any case remarkable
evidence of the crippling effect on a child of over-conscientious Evangelical
mothering.

[2] One would like to know just what part Clough's childhood closeness to
and then sudden remoteness from his mother played in his strange personality
disorder: see Katharine Chorley, *Arthur Hugh Clough: The Uncommitted Mind*
Oxford, 1962), pp. 349-50.

equilibrium. The child offered ease and repose from the troubles of the day, a realm of trust, affection, playfulness and innocence in which the adult man was king: in the nursery world he faced no insuperable problems, no agonizing doubts; rather he could luxuriate in the absence of adult standards, in his freedom from misgiving or external criticism about his conduct and character, in his power to win admiration by a superior strength and cleverness. Tito, for example, the villain of George Eliot's *Romola* (1863), finds himself increasingly drawn to the solace of the child Tessa, her 'pretty trusting looks and prattle: this creature, who was without moral judgement that could condemn him, whose little loving ignorant soul made a world apart, where he might feel in freedom from suspicious and exacting demands'. (I, 223)

In another novel by George Eliot, *Silas Marner* (1861), we are presented with an alternative explanation of the cult of the little girl: 'In old days there were angels who came and took men by the hand and led them away from the city of destruction. We see no white-haired angels now. But yet men are led away from threatening destruction: a hand is put into theirs, which leads them forth gently towards a calm and bright land, so that they look no more backward; and the hand may be a little child's.' (p. 201) A child-angel, then, like Eppie, could exert the same redemptive powers as the Angel Mother. In Evangelical conversion fiction the phenomenon is quite plain: atheists, drunkards, gamblers, lechers and other sinners are mown down in swathes by the innocence of a child. In *Ministering Children* (1854) Maria Louisa Charlesworth describes the surviving power of a dead little girl to touch the hearts of those who knew her: 'The child spirit, who lives to minister to others' good, to ease the burden of the weary-hearted, to sweeten and bless life's bitter cup, to win the lost to the Saviour's feet, luring on, by words of truth, and bright examples of Heavenly love, from Earth to Heaven, from darkness to light, from death to life, has a record written on human hearts, hearts whose records are eternal.' [128] Seen in this context Dickens' Little Nell in *The Old Curiosity Shop* (1841) emerges as no mere exercise in pathos, but an affirmation, important to the Victorians, of the redemptive force of girlish innocence: 'If you have seen the picture-gallery of any one old family, you will remember how the same face and figure—often the fairest and slightest of them all—come upon you in different generations; and how you trace the same sweet girl through a long line of portraits—never growing old or changing—the Good Angel of the race—abiding by them in all reverses—redeeming all their sins.' (II, 141)

Some Victorians were unsympathetic to the Dickensian child angel, to Little Nell, Flo Dombey and their sisters: 'I'm never up to his young girls,' confessed the painter Daniel Maclise, 'he is so very fond of the age of "Nell", when they are most insipid.' [129] But these detractors were for a long time in a minority, and one is tempted to explain much of the adulation these figures received from Victorian men in terms of the latter's romantic involvement (Dickens' own involvement in these figures—their relationship to the dead Mary Hogarth—has become a critical commonplace). Certainly the appeal of the other little girl in *The Old Curiosity Shop* rests very heavily on romantic identification. The Marchioness is about eleven or twelve, with the stunted form of a child yet younger; and yet G. K. Chesterton read the passages about her and Dick Swiveller as 'perhaps the one true romance in the whole of Dickens'. [130] The text hardly supports him, but even without the epilogue, in which Dick has the child educated and several years later marries her, one can see that he was responding to something implicit in those passages. In some cases this romantic interest in the young girl has a mild, but definite erotic flavour.[1] Take, for example, Thackeray's description in *Pendennis* of his hero's infatuation with Fanny Bolton, the

[1] It will be obvious from my examples of this 'eroticism' that I am concerned only with the sexual aspects of child-worship; not, for example, with the more obviously 'erotic' aspects of child-pollution, -defloration, etc. To treat the latter would involve a considerable extension of the area of discussion.

porter's young daughter ('she was not a child, but she was scarcely a woman as yet'—p. 457). Pen's infatuation is both a flight from the fashionable world to an apparently ideal innocence and an outlet for his physical needs (witness the pleasure he gets from the night at Vauxhall, squeezing her hand, feeling her heart beating on his shoulder, and his later admission that he was tempted indeed to seduce her). Significantly Thackeray partakes of Pen's pleasures at Vauxhall: he asks genially if Pen kissed her when the lights were out, and implies that he did, asking what we would have done in his place. (p. 463) The novels of W. H. Hudson offer the reader a similar kind of vicarious pleasure: in *A Crystal Age* (1887) the hero describes his attraction to a beautiful girl of fourteen: 'I was absorbed in admiration of her graceful figure, and—shall I be forgiven for mentioning such a detail?—her exquisitely rounded legs under her brief and beautiful garments. To my mind the garment was quite long enough' (p. 24); fourteen to Hudson seems to have meant the maiden's prime—two of the three young girls who flutter the hero's heart in *A Purple Land* (1885) are of that age.

This romantic and sexual colouration around the young girl in fiction may seem no more than a harmless touch of fantasy. But sometimes men's whole lives were governed by this kind of romantic and sexual interest. In the fourth of his 'Sonnets of a Little Girl' Ernest Dowson writes:

> and in those pure grey eyes,
> That sweet child face, those tumbled curls of gold,
> And in thy smiles and loving, soft replies
> I find the whole of love—hear full and low
> Its mystic ocean's tremulous ebb and flow.

This for Dowson was no whimsical hyperbole but, as we shall see, a statement of literal fact. A few years after Dowson wrote this poem Lewis Carroll assured the illustrator of *Sylvie and Bruno* that 'naked children are so perfectly pure and lovely'.[1]

---

[1] Derek Hudson, *op. cit.*, p. 268. Hudson notes that his subject's enthusiasm for kissing little girls and seeing them naked was shared by another bachelor clergyman well known to us, Francis Kilvert (pp. 265, 267–8).

Now this for Lewis Carroll was less disinterested broadmindedness than a statement of psychological need. In 1879 and 1880
he had followed the fashion—in vogue from the 1870s to the
turn of the century—of representing nude little girls in photographs and pictures. Some mothers gave him permission to use
their daughters as camera-models, but others reacted so
forcefully that he not only gave up this particular line of
interest but photography itself, his hobby for the past quarter
of a century. Perhaps he was half-aware his motives were less
aesthetic than sexual: at any rate he instructed his executors to
destroy the negatives of these photographs, which he had kept
for the remaining eighteen years of his life, lest they got into
others' hands.

In this role of the child angel, her provision for a degree of
subdued sexual release, as in the other roles, her provision for
relaxation from the strains of adult life and her provision for
moral inspiration through her innocence, it is easy to see
analogies with the roles of the Angel Mother. Sometimes
indeed the child angel was described in explicit maternal terms.
In Dickens, for example, the good mother would seem conspicuous by her absence, with an occasional minor exception
like Mrs Maylie in *Oliver Twist*, whilst there are countless
weak and bad ones. The reason, it seems, lay in Dickens'
sufferings as a boy culminating in his struggle to escape the
blacking warehouse: 'I never afterwards forgot, I shall never
forget, I never can forget, that my mother was warm for my
being sent back.' [131] The good mother exists in Dickens'
novels, but mostly in the form of the motherly child. The
parent-child relationship, for instance, is frequently reversed:
suffering, motherless daughters, like Flo Dombey, Madeline
Bray, Agnes Wickfield or Little Dorrit, looking after delin-
quent parents.[1] Still more strikingly, one notices, the adoptive

---

[1] G. K. Chesterton in *Charles Dickens* (1906) points out that these young
girls are not children but 'little mothers': 'The beauty and divinity in a
child lie in his not being worried, not being conscientious, not being like
Little Nell.' (p. 122)

child-mothers of Dickens' boyhood, his nurse Mary Weller and his sister Fanny (both little older than himself) are celebrated in figures of an endearing childishness and yet a bustling maternal efficiency: in the descriptions, for example, of little Charley in *Bleak House* tending her orphaned family 'O! in such a motherly, womanly way!' (I, 252); or of the Marchioness looking after the sick Swiveller 'in as brisk and business-like a manner, as if he were a very little boy, and she his grown-up nurse'. (II, 97)

In the poetry of Thomson too the child-mother is quite prominent. Of the nature of his feelings for his own mother, who died when he was eight, we can guess from such lines as these from 'The Deliverer' about the angel who frees the poet from sin and despair:

> And when she spoke her voice was now so sweet
> In soft low music, tremulous with sighs,
> That one might dreaming hear his Mother greet
> With such a voice his soul to Paradise.

Of the nature of his feelings for Matilda Weller, with whom he fell in love when she was fourteen but who died very shortly after, we can guess from 'Mater Tenebrarum', where she is the mother-figure:

> Come down for a minute! oh, come! come serious and mild
> And pale, as thou wert on this earth, thou adorable child!

For Thomson, agonized by doubts about the existence of God, the essential goodness of humanity, the meaningfulness of life, Matilda alone through her purity and love could deflect his mind from suicide:

> What keeps me yet in this life, what spark in my frozen breast?
> A fire of dread, a light of hope, kindled, O Love, by thee;
> For thy pure and gentle and beautiful soul, it must immortal be.
>
> (*ibid.*)

The child angel in short was as vital to Thomson as the mothering angel to Tennyson. She was vital too to Ernest

Dowson, whose life followed a remarkably similar pattern: like Thomson, Dowson's childhood was deeply disturbed by his parents' instability (his mother later committed suicide); like Thomson, Dowson's end was premature and sordid—hastened by liquor and poverty. But like Thomson, Dowson found solace in a figure of girlish innocence, in 'Missie' Foltinowicz, eleven when he first met her, the daughter of a London tavern-keeper. From his teens he had sought in little girls the same talismanic powers of protective love and purity as other Victorians sought from angel mothers: in the third of his 'Sonnets of a Little Girl' he had declared his sweetheart's name to be his 'amulet',

> That whispered gently guardeth me from harm,
> It is my ritual, my mystic prayer. . . .

Now he had found his ideal. Like Matilda, Missie offered proof of the meaningfulness of life. However his love-affair ended, Dowson believed, was of minor importance: 'the important thing is that one should have just once experienced this mystery, an absolute absorption in one particular person. It reconciles all inconsistencies in the order of things, and above all it seems once for all to reduce to utter absurdity any material explanation of itself or of the world.' [132]

Thomson's persistent melancholia and dipsomania were clearly connected with the death of his angel child; one wonders, however, if he would have been much happier if she had lived. Certainly Dowson was tormented by a progressive alienation from his love as she grew older. 'What a terrible, lamentable thing growth is!' he wrote when she was sixteen, 'it "makes me mad" to think that in a year or two at most the most perfect exquisite relation I have ever succeeded in making must naturally end.'[1] Ruskin's infatuation with Rose La Touche was saddened by similar reflections: 'I shall not see her till November,' he wrote when she was thirteen, 'Nay I shall

---

1 Mark Longaker, *op. cit.*, p. 120. Dowson was not without ambivalence on this subject: see his poem 'Growth' of the previous year, where he celebrates the glory of his child-love's waking maidenhood.

never see *her* again. It's another Rosie every six months now. Do I want to keep her from growing up? Of course I do.' [133] This fear of incipient womanhood, it seems clear, was partly due to a fear of sex, a recognition that marriage, for example, would involve more than sentimental whimsy. Dowson, one imagines, had no thought of carnal congress with his Missie: in his love for her, as Arthur Symons noted, 'there was a sort of Virginal devotion, as to a Madonna'. [134] Ruskin was more ambivalent: with his child-wife Effie he abstained from intercourse, but with Rose he did intend to be husband in fact as well as name. [135] The incipient sexuality of W. H. Hudson's heroines is veiled in an interesting ambiguity. Yoletta, for example, in *A Crystal Age* provides sexual pleasure without feeling any herself: 'Yes,' she replies when the hero asked for a kiss, 'but you are keeping me too long. Kiss me as many times as you like, and then let us admire the prospect.' (p. 136) And she awakens to passion at the end only when Hudson has saved her from consummation by killing off his hero.[1]

Another factor in the love of little girls, apart from the problems of adult sexuality, was the fear of adult emotional complexities. A relationship with a child was safe and simple, but a relationship with a woman might be difficult and demanding. Lewis Carroll's problem may well have been not uncommon. 'He was a man,' remarks Derek Hudson, 'who carried his childhood with him; the love that he understood and longed for was a protective love. He had a deep instinctive admiration for women, yearning for their sympathy and often finding it. But it is probable that he could not reconcile in himself love and intimacy in his own life because he knew that he was pulled in two different ways (ambivalence is the modern term), and that in any close relationship something compelled him to seek distance and detachment.' [136] With some men an over-sensitive fear of involvement could lead to forthright

[1] The heroine of *Green Mansions* (1904), slightly older but only four-and-a-half feet tall, is the same kind of pliable living doll; and she too is frustrated by sudden death from enjoying her waking adult passions.

revulsion at adult femininity: one wonders what experience lay behind Dowson's cryptic reference to 'The perverse pleasure (to be observed in a hundred cases) with which a woman sets herself to degrade and obliterate the feminine ideal if she comes across a man with any faith in it'. [137] The solution to these difficulties was often sought in a supervision of the maturation of the child-love. Edward Benson, for example, a future Archbishop of Canterbury, in 1852 at the age of twenty-three confided to his diary a revealing picture of his future wife Mary Sidgwick, at that time aged eleven:

> As I have always been very fond of her and she of me with the love of a little sister, and as I have heard of her fondness for me commented on by many persons, and have been told that I was the only person at whose departure she ever cried, as a child, and how diligent she has always been in reading books which I have mentioned to her, and in learning pieces of poetry which I have admired, it is not strange that I, who from the circumstances of my family am not likely to marry for many years to come, and who find in myself a growing distaste for forming friendships (fit to be so called) among new acquaintances and who am fond indeed (if not too fond) of little endearments, and who also know my weakness for falling suddenly in love, in the common sense of the word, and have already gone too far more than once in these things and have therefore reason to fear that I might on some occasion be led [here the manuscript takes refuge in cipher] it is not strange that I should have thought first of the possibility that some day dear little Minnie might become my wife.[1]

In the following year little Minnie and Benson became virtually engaged, while she sat upon his knee. Other men were less fortunate in their efforts to protect themselves from hurt. Ruskin, for example, after the pain of his ruptured romance with Adèle Domecq sought to mould both Effie Gray and later Rose La Touche in his chosen image of womanhood; and the

[1] E. F. Benson, *As We Were* (1930), pp. 60–1. Lewis Carroll's brother Wilfred, like Edward Benson, married a girl twelve years his junior, to whom he had been attached since she was a child.

painter G. F. Watts, shyly essaying love for the first time in his mid-forties, hoped to guide the development of his child love Ellen Terry, who was thirty years his junior. But both men failed disastrously (Watts, it seems, like Ruskin suffering the humiliation of not only a failed but an unconsummated marriage). [138]

The love of little girls helps us to understand the more easily why the Victorian woman was 'a cross between an angel and an idiot'. Up to a point the mature angel-figure was expected to be child-like. She was expected, through the ennobling experience of love, to show her lover the radiance and innocence of a child:

> she grows
> More infantine, auroral, mild,
> And still the more she lives and knows
> The lovelier she's expressed a child.

She was expected, through the relaxed intimacy of love, to show her lover the liveliness and playfulness of a child:

> though discreet when he's away,
> If none but her dear despot hears,
> She prattles like a child at play. [139]

But she was expected too to possess an unchild-like moral grasp with which to inspire and guide her husband and her children. Too often unfortunately this last requirement was impossible to fulfil. For one thing, adult responsibilities were frequently cast upon her prematurely by early marriage: 'The day my frock was lengthened to a gown I stood at the altar,' complains Lady Blandish in *The Ordeal of Richard Feverel*. (p. 109, But, more important, the masculine 'dear despot' frequently wanted a doll-like immaturity in his wife. His own emotional maturity arrested by an over- or under-protected childhood, his natural egotism nourished by society's code of male supremacy, his feelings perhaps over-susceptible to the wounds of adult relationships, the Victorian man often cherished in his women-folk naïveté, subordination, and an undemanding tenderness.

The letters of Thackeray and Dickens to their prospective brides are revealing in this respect, for in each case the woman is frequently scolded as though she were some endearing but refractory child. [140] Mrs Thackeray (or 'Little Trot', 'Pussy', or 'Isabinda', as her husband loved to call her) was distinguished by not only the same charming artlessness and affection but also the same hopeless domestic incompetence as the first wife of David Copperfield, and perhaps it was not an unmixed disaster that their marriage, like the Copperfields', was soon cut short by tragedy. Certainly Dickens became thoroughly disillusioned with his child-wife. And yet it is remarkable testimony to the attractions of the doll-like feminine type that even after his detached and critical portrait of Dora Copperfield, Dickens fell prey once more to a schoolboy excitement over his immature first love, Maria Beadnell. It is remarkable too that even after his detached and critical portrait of this lady in the person of Flora Finching in *Little Dorrit*, and despite his interest in a new kind of strong-minded heroine like Estella Magwitch and Helena Landless, in his last novels Dickens' heart should still go out so uncritically to the familiar doll-like figures of Bella Wilfer and Rosa Bud. While such figures as these clearly represented a widespread masculine ideal, it is not surprising that many women were content to remain in happy idiocy rather than aspire to being angels.

5

The Welcome Social Outcast

I PERSECUTION AND INDULGENCE

'IF MEN COULD SEE US as we really are,' says the heroine of
Charlotte Brontë's *Shirley* (1849), 'they would be a little
amazed; but the cleverest, the acutest men are often under an
illusion about women: they do not read them in a true light:
they misapprehend them, both for good and evil: their good
woman is a queer thing, half doll, half angel; their bad woman
almost always a fiend.' (II, 37) The worst of all bad women for
the Victorians was the harlot and she was indeed seen as often
some kind of moral monster. In the year after *Shirley's* publication W. R. Greg, in the *Westminster Review*, complained about
the callous loathing with which prostitutes were treated: 'No
language is too savage for these wretched women. They are
outcasts, Pariahs, lepers. Their touch, even in the extremity of
suffering, is shaken off as if it were pollution and disease. It is
discreditable to a woman even to be supposed to know of their
existence. They are kicked, cuffed, trampled on with impunity
by everyone.' (LIII, 450) The prostitute's life, according to
Greg, was one of misery and despair, of poverty and squalor,
violence and disease: 'Their evidence, and the evidence of all
who have come in contact with them, is unanimous on this
point—that gin alone enabled them to live or act; that without
its constant stimulus and stupefaction, they would long since
have died from mere physical exhaustion, or gone mad from
mental horrors.' (p. 454) Even with gin, however, the prostitute's life, it seemed, was of very brief duration: within a few

years, according to most observers, disease, ill-treatment, malnutrition, exposure, and not infrequently suicide, took their inevitable toll. But despite this catalogue of sufferings, despite the impassioned eloquence of Greg and numerous other writers, respectable Victorians remained very often quite unmoved to charity: as late as 1898 the Bishop of Newcastle was complaining that 'too many professing Christians repudiate all responsibility for these outcasts of society. They will say no prayer for their conversion, give no alms towards agencies that are set on foot to win them back, and sometimes even suspect the motives of those who give themselves to this work with untiring sacrifice.' [141]

Suspicion of the motives of those working in reclamation suggests one obvious factor in all this callous antipathy to the whore: that society in fact did not believe in the catalogue of sufferings with which she was alleged to be afflicted. Certainly, even as Greg wrote, many Victorians were convinced that the typical prostitute, far from her image in sentimental novels as the poor, wretched wanderer of the night, was in reality positively revelling in a life of carefree sin, idleness and luxurious dissipation. This unsentimental view was largely endorsed a few years later by Dr Acton who published in 1857 not only his book on the reproductive organs but an influential study of prostitution. In Acton's opinion the wretched, gin-soaked slattern, ill-clad body at the mercy of wind and rain, careworn, emaciated face bedaubed with an inch of rouge, was very much an exception to the rule.[1] The average prostitute was pretty, elegant and fashionably dressed; enjoying greater wealth and affluence than her more virtuous sisters; and likely to leave her trade not by an early death but through re-entry to society by means of a respectable marriage. Acton in fact may have over-reacted from the sentimental stereotype. For the wretched wanderer of the night was not a novelist's fantasy but a

[1] Acton agreed that there were a few hundred miserable prostitutes doomed to an early grave, but saw these as mere 'drops in an ocean'—*Prostitution Considered in its Moral, Social and Sanitary Aspects* (1857), p. 53.

distressing reality for both interested laymen[1] and specialist missionaries, policemen and doctors throughout the century. In 1871, for example, William Logan, a fairly sensible and vastly experienced rescue worker, dismissed the Acton view as absurd, as 'nonsense, absolute and unmitigated'; [142] and in the 1890s the head of a Salvation Army home for fallen women and G. P. Merrick, who kept detailed case-notes of well over 100,000 women he had seen in Millbank Prison, were at one in repeating the old image of the prostitute's short, disease-ridden, gin-soaked life as though Acton had never written.[2] Mayhew's collaborator Bracebridge Hemyng, whilst agreeing in the main with Acton, was perhaps more judicious in generalization, conceding that there was 'a vast number whose lives afford matter for the most touching tragedies—whose melancholy existence is one continual struggle for the actual necessities of life'.[3] But whatever the facts of the prostitute's life and whether or not individual Victorians upheld the views of W. R. Greg or those of Acton, we are no nearer to understanding why the

[1] One recalls Hippolyte Taine's shocked reaction in the 1860s to the evening streetwalkers in the Strand and Haymarket. 'The impression is not one of debauchery but of abject, miserable poverty. One is sickened and wounded by this deplorable procession in those monumental streets. It seemed as if I were watching a march past of dead women. Here is a festering sore, the real sore on the body of English society.'—*Notes on England*, trans. Edward Hyams (1957), p. 31.

[2] See William Booth, *In Darkest England and the Way Out* (1890), pp. 53–5; and G. P. Merrick, *Work among the Fallen* (1891), passim. Merrick from his staggering collection of statistics calculated three years and six weeks as the average time prostitutes survived the hardships of their calling. Prostitutes of course were notorious liars, and the death rates from the census make this figure unlikely to say the least. Nonetheless Merrick would have to have been extraordinarily stupid to form his views of the prostitute's degradation after studying over 100,000 women of the kind described by Acton. Clearly there were huge differences between the wretches in the Millbank prison and their more successful and glamorous colleagues, and it was easy, one assumes, to over-generalize from both.

[3] Henry Mayhew, *London Labour and the London Poor* (1861–2) IV, 214. Curiously Mayhew allows the Rev. William Tuckniss in his preface to Hemyng's section on prostitution to talk in the conventional way of the prostitute's brief existence (IV, xxxviii).

Victorian whore was regarded with such remarkable venom. A sceptical Victorian, it is true, might well conclude that the thriving, contented prostitute was very far from needing charity. But it is not clear from this why she so often inspired active hatred and revulsion, why she was treated as some kind of moral monster, why even the poor unhappy woman who perhaps lapsed only once from virtue should be made the victim of brutal ostracism and persecution.

A more positive explanation of the abhorrence of the prostitute must begin with the nineteenth century fear of immorality. For the Evangelical mind, preoccupied with sin and the risk of eternal Hellfire, Biblical denunciations of the harlot were often alone sufficient to make her the object of terror and revulsion: her house was indeed the way to hell going down to the chambers of death. But with the variety of threats posed by sexual immorality to the stability of society there was a much more general basis for emotional execration. Pent-up fears of sex, of its insidious fascinations and its incalculable dangers, could be discharged upon a clear and convenient scapegoat. But, more especially, as a matter of conscious policy, harshly punitive treatment of the prostitute was vital to the sanctity of the home. If the home was to be the place of peace and the fount of civic virtues, it was essential both to banish fallen women from society lest they contaminate by example and temptation, and to make them bear the stigma of public obloquy. Ill-judged charity, wrote the Rev. John Thomas in 1809, was a positive social menace: 'If the youth of both sexes in this country saw—that Prostitutes became despicable; that infamy invariably attended them; that whatever professions of penitence they might make, they could not be restored to the bosom of society but by persevering and humiliating steps—would they not feel the *strongest* "incentive" to avoid, as a plague so pestilential a vice! But what wantonness of iniquity may not be expected to prevail, if virtuous society omit this duty, for which they are so highly responsible!' [143]

The prostitute's hard lot, however, was caused by more than

the nineteenth century fear of immorality. It was caused too by the complement to sexual fear, the apotheosis of sexual purity. In a negative way it was the result, as Bulwer Lytton noted in 1833, of society's preoccupation with chastity: 'Our extreme regard for the chaste induces a contemptuous apathy to the unchaste. We care not how many there are, what they suffer—or how far they descend into the lower abysses of crime.' [144] But, more positively, callous indifference and brutal persecution were both the reflex of the cult of female purity. On its lowest level men were sometimes moved by a kind of furtive pharisaic prurience. In Meredith's *Rhoda Fleming* (1865) the hero is first revolted by Rhoda's fallen sister, but when he looks on her 'affectionate pity washed the selfish man out of him. All these false sensations, peculiar to men, concerning the soiled purity of woman, the lost innocence, the brand of shame upon her, which are commonly the foul sentimentalism of such as can be too eager in the chase of corruption when occasion suits, and are another side of pruriency, not absolutely foreign to the best of us in our youth—all passed away from him in Dahlia's presence.' (p. 317) On a more defensible level men might be outraged by the affront of feminine unchastity to their faith in virtuous womanhood. For men anxious to worship women as angels, conscious of the importance of woman's role as wife and mother, conscious too of her natural proclivity to virtue, by constitution, education and social situation, feminine impurity was an immeasurably greater crime than masculine delinquency: 'men at most differ as Heaven and earth,/But women, worst and best, as Heaven and Hell.' [145] Their revulsion at fallen women was in proportion to their adoration of female purity.

This kind of feeling was clearly a crucial factor in what Trollope described as 'one of the marvels of our social system', [146] the vehemence shown to women offenders by even the most soft-hearted of their own sex. 'They shut their eyes,' wrote William Bell Scott, 'to every form of the Social Evil and take it as an impertinence in any man, poet especially, who draws their attention to these matters . . . "Serve them right" is

the verdict of the sweetest and gentlest of creatures.' [147]
Trollope himself in *Rachel Ray* (1863) explained the sweet
woman's harshness on the lines I have suggested: 'For a true
spirit of persecution one should always go to a woman; and the
milder, the sweeter, the more loving, the more womanly the
woman, the stronger will be that spirit within her. Strong love
for the thing loved necessitates strong hatred for the thing
hated, and thence comes the spirit of persecution.' (II, 200)
Such an explanation is however only partial. For a fuller
understanding of the virtuous woman's violent moral censure
we must return to the Victorian home, to see the operation of
another reflex of the cult of feminine purity. Many women, we
have seen, were brought up as virtual moral idiots, insulation
from a sullying knowledge of the world making them ignorant,
timid and conventional, especially in sexual matters: so it was
that ignorant distortions of the fallen woman's nature, timid
fears of the impulse she personified, apprehension of losing
caste by any laxity in censure, all combined to make her
predisposed to harshness. Above all, and these factors would
apply too to the more intelligent angel woman, there were her
jealous fears of the immoral woman's special and dangerous
attractions, and there were the paradoxical implications of her
own erotic ignorance—making her either unable to comprehend
why others should be less virtuous than she was, or, alternatively, perhaps unconsciously resentful of the pleasures they
were having.

In view of the strength of this spirit of persecution we might
expect Victorian prostitution to show the marks of vigorous
suppression. In fact, as is well known, it was rife: the outcasts
were omnipresent. Their exact numbers, even in London the
best documented city, are impossible to gauge. The lowest
tallies were those of the Metropolitan police which never went
above 10,000, but which, as the police were quick to emphasize, excluded many clandestine and part-time prostitutes. The
highest were those of the fourth estate, which occasionally
reached 120,000, and owed more perhaps to intuition than

arithmetic. Almost every round number between these poles received its advocates at some time or another, and some enjoyed a quite remarkable longevity: 80,000, the most popular guess after 1830, was still sufficiently common in 1907 for a rescue worker to think it worth demolishing. [148] The exact dimensions, then, of prostitution were unclear. But the essential facts were not. In May 1859 the *Edinburgh Medical Journal* discussed the difficulty of achieving any statistical precision, but then went on: 'Let any one walk certain streets of London, Glasgow, or Edinburgh, of a night, and, without troubling his head with statistics, his eyes and ears will tell him at once what a multitudinous amazonian army the devil keeps in constant field service, for advancing his own ends. The stones seem alive with lust, and the very atmosphere is tainted.' (XLVII, 1008) To any one who wished to look, *The Times* had remarked the previous year, it was plain that 'in no capital city of Europe' was there 'daily and nightly such a shameless display of Prostitution as in London'. [149] Nor was this a sudden new development. In December 1815, not long after the celebrations for Britain's victory over the French, a victory that was often ascribed to her superior morality, the *Anti-Jacobin Review* complained stiffly that 'notwithstanding our lofty pretensions to the character of a religious and moral people, there is no capital in Europe where prostitution is suffered to display itself in so shameless a manner as in London: Paris, though a sink of profligacy, is infinitely more decent in the above respect. There too the theatres are free from those disgraceful scenes which render those of London unfit to be entered by a modest woman.' (XLIX, 628)

Foreign visitors, one can appreciate, found the situation somewhat bewildering: they were astonished that a country so strait-laced in other respects could be so permissive in this. The German Pückler-Muskau, though certainly not a prude, was genuinely shocked by what he saw in the 1820s: 'It is most strange that in no country on earth is this afflicting and humiliating spectacle so openly exhibited as in the religious and decorous England. The evil goes to such an extent, that in the theatres it is often difficult to keep off these repulsive beings, especially when they are drunk, which is not seldom the case.' [150] How was it, wondered foreigners, that the respectable British with their cult of domesticity, with their determination to avoid anything in public discourse that might bring a blush to the cheek of modesty, could yet allow the streets and places of public amusement in their capital to be infested with open harlotry? Local observers too often found the situation rather puzzling. A writer in the *Lancet* (7 November 1857) remarked:

> The typical Pater-familias, living in a grand house near the park, sees his sons allured into debauchery, dares not walk with his daughters through the streets after nightfall, and is disturbed from his night-slumbers by the drunken screams and foul oaths of prostitutes reeling home with daylight. If he look from his window, he sees the pavement—his pavement—occupied by the flaunting daughters of sin, whose loud, ribald talk forces him to keep his casement closed. Yet he refuses to sanction any practical means for remedying the evil, or to lend his aid to its reform. (II, 479)

The typical paterfamilias in fact hardly lived 'in a grand house near the park', and if he found his pavement full of prostitutes, he would usually be in the van of any movement to displace them—in the interest of property values as well as morals. But the typical paterfamilias, as the *Lancet* suggests, did indeed show remarkable indulgence to the harlot, an indulgence of such latitude that the outcast in some ways was more privileged than those who banished her. For all the spirit of persecution, for all the brutal loathing directed by society at the prostitute, the prostitute was yet allowed in some respects virtually to persecute society.

In the first half of the century, for example, many respectable families were obliged to deny themselves the pleasures of the theatre. The saloons of theatres at this time were full of prostitutes openly plying their trade, frequently with the collusion of the managements, who far from discouraging them were often alleged to sell them cut-price season-tickets. Macready, it is true, succeeded in purifying both Covent Garden and Drury Lane, but the *Theatrical Journal* in congratulating him (27 July 1844) still felt forced to describe the other theatres as 'great public brothels . . . the very hot-beds of vice . . . houses of ill fame on a *large scale*'. (p. 236) For an innocent girl to enter the saloons was of course quite out of the question: apart from other considerations she might be mistaken for a prostitute herself by some undiscerning gallant. But nowhere in the theatres was she safe from the sight of vice: even in the auditorium she would be unlikely to miss the boisterous activity of harlots in the second tier of boxes. An American visitor of the thirties commented rather sardonically: 'How edifying to the young boarding-school misses who might be present. It was not necessary that they should go into the saloon, or look in as they passed, or observe what was going forward in the stairway and surrounding galleries; everything was visible, and necessarily visible too, from their seats.' [151] Around 1850 the prostitute took her trade to the casinos and pleasure-gardens that were now the rage following the introduction of the polka, like the Argyll Rooms and Cremorne, and left the more prosaic theatre to be enjoyed by sober respectability. But when these resorts entered an eclipse in the 1870s, she moved to the promenades of music-halls, like the Alhambra and later the Empire. Here again the respectable family suffered a restriction of its pleasures: even the Empire, which had the most decorous promenade of any music-hall, was not a suitable place for most fathers to take a modest wife or daughter.

The legitimate West-end theatres by this time had been purified within but many of the streets outside them, especially after the performance, were still thick with clamorous prostitutes. For by far the greater part of the century the route from St Paul's Churchyard to Regent's Park, through Fleet Street, the Strand, the Haymarket, Regent Street and Portland Place was a thoroughfare for harlots that imposed strict restraints upon all respectable heads of families. To conduct a wife or daughter through these streets at night was to run the gauntlet of dozens of unmistakable prostitutes accosting almost every man who passed and very likely jostling and insulting every lady. There were some areas indeed that a gentleman would skirt even when by himself: in the Haymarket, for example, at mid-century he would be lucky to escape physical molestation without abandoning the pavement for the middle of the street. [152] Even daylight presented certain difficulties: he would think twice before treating ladies to a stroll through the red-light district around Portland Place or the area around Charing Cross Station in the Strand. Fashionable shopping centres like the Strand or Regent Street furnished the biggest problem of all: to allow ladies to wander through them un-attended, window-gazing at their leisure, was to risk their being not only scandalized by streetwalkers, but, what was worse, accosted as such themselves. As late as the 1890s, when the streets in general were more decorous, it was inadvisable for a respectable woman to walk alone in Piccadilly, Regent Street, the Strand or Leicester Square. 'Although I was quietly dressed,' wrote Mrs Peel, a Fleet Street journalist at that time, 'and I hope looked what I was, a respectable young woman, there was scarcely a day when I, while waiting for an omnibus, was not accosted.' [153] A correspondence in *The Times* in January 1862 puts the picture nicely in perspective. A 'Pater-familias from the Provinces' had been outraged to find that two ladies of his family had been followed and accosted in Oxford Street, owing perhaps to their inadvertent intrusion upon the wrong side of Regent Street, the pavement that the prostitutes had seized as their own exclusive property. The *Saturday Review* (1 February 1862), in hazarding this suggestion, showed no surprise at the ladies' difficulty and very little sympathy: the best solution it could offer was for them to dress thoroughly unbecomingly, to procure poke-bonnets, to stint their skirts to a moderate circumference, and to cultivate sad-coloured underclothing—the best solution, that is, until the nation solved the problem through the statute book.

We are presented, then, with what seems a curious paradox: a society in which there was a violent hostility to the prostitute, and yet a society which preferred to suffer the greatest indignities from her rather than resort to legal intervention. To understand this ironical situation we need to recognize a quite different aspect of the question, to recognize that the violent hostility was very far from universal, that many Victorians' attitude to the prostitute was governed not by the spirit of persecution, but by the spirit of evasion.

II INTERVENTION AND EVASION

In 1862 the *Saturday Review* suggested a reform in either women's underclothing or the statute book as the solution to the problem of the streets. Twenty years earlier an attempt had in fact been made to affect the second of these alternatives. In 1842 the Committee of the London Society for the Protection of Young Females produced a Bill which, though it would not directly restrict the amount of street prostitution, would help to control the situation generally by giving the police more power over brothels. But the Government refused to introduce it in the Commons. After the Society had carefully reframed the Bill under the guidance of specialists in penitentiary work the Bishop of Exeter introduced it in the Lords in 1844. It passed its two readings without difficulty, but on its third, after a proposal that the question be deferred for more considered judgement and a hint from the Duke of Wellington that the Government might at some time take up the matter, the Bishop withdrew the Bill altogether. A few militants kept up the pressure for a year or so, but without much success; the issue was effectively dead. Forty years later the process was repeated. Between 1882 and 1885 the Criminal Law Amendment Bill, a roughly similar measure, was passed three times in the Lords only to hang fire in the Commons; and in May 1885, when it was talked out one night in the Commons, it appeared to have gone the way of its predecessor.

Parliament's inertia in this matter was often subjected to bitter criticism. Some critics accused politicians of a cowardly, wilful blindness, of hiding their heads at the mention of prostitution, of ignoring the problem in the hope that it would quietly go away; an accusation that does not seem very consistent with the alacrity with which the Contagious Diseases Acts were passed in the 1860s to control venereal disease in the prostitute population. Others were still more scathing in their charges: 'How can they be expected to legislate freely on the subject,—how can they fail to be shy of restrictive and punitive measures,—who are conscious, possibly, that any law, approaching in its principle and in its execution, to impartiality, must first affect themselves?' [154] These were the words of a clergyman of the forties. But the accusation he makes was even more common in the eighties, and not without cause—only weeks before the Criminal Law Amendment Bill was talked out in the Commons the Home Office appears to have been complicit in the extraordinary lenience shown Mrs Jeffries, a high-class bawd with many aristocratic clients. [155] But cynical self-interest as an explanation of Parliament's inaction seems hardly adequate. With both Bills it was not the allegedly libertine Lords but the Commons of the respectable Mr Peel and Mr Gladstone that was obstructive. Public opinion, not the machinations of evil men, was the real key to the problem. The Government, once W. T. Stead had roused the people in July 1885 with his 'Maiden Tribute' articles in the *Pall Mall Gazette*, took up the Bill with almost unseemly haste. But why did public opinion require Stead's sensational promptings before it demanded legislative action? The problem of prostitution had needed tackling throughout the century.

To an extent here, in the case of the general public rather than their statesmen, the charge of wilful evasion was well-founded. Many Victorians had a gift for not seeing the obvious when they chose. In the case of men evasion was often no doubt the product of a private sense of shame. The *Standard* (5 March 1858) explained society's toleration of prostitution as being largely due to

> . . . a very respectable, moral and middle-aged race. They may, it is true, have been guilty of certain short-comings in their youth, but they have now left all that sort of thing, and find it convenient to forget the existence, if they could, of those poor creatures with whom they have sinned; and never on any occasion to allude to, much less would they think of legislating upon, a subject so indelicate in its nature, and so fraught with disagreeable reminiscences. . . . (p. 4)

In the case of women evasion was no doubt often the product of an excessive feminine modesty. In *Blackwood's* May 1855 the novelist Mrs Oliphant expressed a fairly widespread view about prostitutes and purity: 'every pure feminine mind, we suppose, holds the faith of Desdemona—"I do not believe there is any such woman".' (LXXVII, 560) But Nelsonian blindness of this order can never have been an easy bloom to cultivate, and by the mid-fifties it was virtually impossible. Even if respectable citizens kept aloof from the indecent parts of London, they would still find it hard to evade the whore in literature and in the papers. The fictional prostitute had come a long way from the reticent ambiguities of the thirties, from Dickens' girl in 'The Pawnbroker's Shop' in *Sketches by Boz* or Nancy in *Oliver Twist*. By June 1859 indeed she had become so vividly familiar that *Tait's Edinburgh Magazine* protested that 'the subject of the "Social Evil" has been over-done'. (XXVI, 371) In these years too the occasional press complaints of earlier years about the state of the streets and theatres had given way to such an absorption in the problem of prostitution, that the *Saturday Review* was forced to remark 'the Social Evil question has become a very popular one—too popular by half'. [156] In the face of such exposure evasion, for whatever motive, was not a very practical proposition. Prostitution, wrote the novelist

Miss Mulock in 1858, 'in country cottages as in city streets, in books, newspapers, and daily talk, meets us so continually that no young girl can long be kept ignorant of it'. [157] Why then did public opinion not take action against the Social Evil? Why did it not support the ceaseless efforts of moral vigilants working to suppress it? The answer is that it did support them—twice. On two major occasions public opinion was mobilized in an attempt to solve the problem.

The first instance began in 1812. In that year the Guardian Society formed a Committee to discover the best means of both driving prostitutes from the streets and supplying a refuge for those who wished to reform—a twofold programme that was copied shortly by the Philanthropic Society's Fund of Mercy. By December 1813 a group of citizens had been stimulated by this activity to present a petition to the Lord Mayor and the Court of Common Council, signed by more than 2,000 house-holders, calling for energetic civic intervention. In October 1814 the Mayor, encouraged by the report of a special com-mittee he had appointed, had a proclamation published in the press and put up in every watch-house expressing his deter-mination to apply to prostitution the utmost rigour of the law. By the end of 1815 a new and very active Mayor was busily prosecuting brothels and committing streetwalkers to Bridewell in droves, and the press was full of enthusiastic letters and articles on the subject. On 11 February 1816 the *Sunday Monitor*, which had been running a series of lengthy progress reports, rejoiced that 'the nuisance of the prostituted streets is nearly removed'. (p. 3) A critic of the Guardian Society com-mented cynically the following year, 'a stranger, coming at that period to town, would have concluded that in a short time, London would be the purest city in the universe. What was the result of all this however! Why, that in a short time, within a little month the papers dropped the subject, and the business was forgotten; nay in spite of the continued exertions of the Lord Mayor, the streets soon became as much infested as before.' [158] The stone of Sisyphus was back where it had started, and there it remained for another forty years, until the vestry of St James's began to move it.

In the summer of 1856 a deputation went to the Home Office from St James's, Westminster, to plead for greater police control of prostitution; and the Home Secretary promised to investigate the matter. But two weeks later he simply reported that he was satisfied with the present arrangements. In the summer of 1857, however, the vestry and its colleagues in St Marylebone began to make some headway by engaging public interest in their efforts and thereby putting extra pressure on the authorities. By the end of October the *Lancet* was claiming that there was scarcely a journal of repute which had not begun to advocate the need for some practical reforms; and although this was a sizeable exaggeration at that moment, by January 1858 it had become much more like a fact. A series of meetings under the auspices of the Society for the Suppression of Vice and then a convention organized by St James's for the leaders of other metropolitan parishes to co-ordinate their programmes were enough to produce a minor flood of letters, articles and editorials in the press. With public opinion seemingly behind them the vestrymen looked to be making genuine progress. But soon the movement had lost the impetus it had gained. In March 1858 a deputation went to the Home Office to plead for stricter law enforcement, and the new Home Secretary, like his predecessor, promised to investigate the matter. But, as before, nothing materialized. Public interest fizzled out. And once more the vigilants were back almost exactly where they had started. In October 1857 the St James's vestry had succeeded in closing the Argyll Rooms, a favourite resort of London's harlots and their clients; in October 1858 the Argyll was re-opened and soon became as notorious as ever. The *Saturday Review* on 12 September 1863 gave the scene an ironic backward glance:

Five years ago, there was a great ripping-up of the skirts of society. . . . The 'Social Evil' was elaborately investigated from the sentimental, the classical, the philanthropic, the medical, the religious, and the statistical points of view; and sometimes the writer so warmed with his subject that the glowing descriptions which were intended to point a moral had themselves a mischievous pruriency. . . . And then amid much excited writing and highly-coloured purposeless description, all practical results were gradually lost sight of, until at length the subject, worn threadbare, gradually dropped out of notice. (XVI, 352)

It would be wrong to underestimate the truth of this observation. In 1857–8, as in 1815–16, the press interest in prostitution reform was doubtless partly spurious: some papers clearly took up this issue less from moral zeal than from an enthusiasm for a topic that was both novel and mildly prurient, or from a desire not to get out of step with their competitors. At the same time it would be wrong to underestimate the integrity of both press and public opinion. Some of the papers, through silence or explicit statement, had shown a coolness about the reformers from the beginning; and the dwindling of public interest in the movement seems to have been less the result of boredom than a growing recognition that these sceptics were being proved right, that mere law enforcement was not an effective solution: the whores chased out of the City in 1816 simply settled in the suburbs until the wave of repression ended; 'what is cut down in one parish,' noted the *Saturday Review* (16 October 1858), 'grows up in the next—the weeds are only transported from Norton Street to Brompton.' (VI, 374) Public opinion, if not sceptical about the reformers' strategy from the beginning, soon learned to become so. In 1857 Dr Acton chided the respectable paterfamilias for denouncing the casinos and night-houses for which the prostitute had abandoned the theatre: 'He rails and preaches against vice when he ought, as I view it, to thank her for doing what he could obtain of her neither by persuasion nor by force, I mean putting herself in a corner.' [159] A few weeks before Acton's book was published the Argyll Rooms had been closed down by the vestrymen of St James's. But a year later, when nearby inhabitants and tradesmen had testified that the locality had grown worse, not better, ever since, the lesson had been learnt: 'Last year, in a transport of moral and popular indignation, we closed the Argyll Rooms because they were the focus of all metropolitan vice. This year we open them, because, on the whole, it is better that the vicious population should be brought together than that it should be let loose on society.' [160] Many erstwhile enthusiasts for reform had made the chastening discovery that the problem was much bigger and more complex than they had thought, that legal sanctions could only work if society underwent profound economic and social changes, and that intervention for the moment might do more harm than good.

To begin with, a revolution was required in the condition of the poor. Large numbers of women were forced onto the streets by poverty—by atrociously low wages, by unemployment, or by improvidence. In the hopeless squalor at the base of the social pyramid prostitution was an accepted occupation that rarely attached any shame to its practitioners. For as the *Leader* instructed its middle-class readers (28 April 1860), morality meant very little to women in these conditions: 'Neglect, starvation, ignorance, vice, filth, and disease have surrounded them from infancy. They have been brought up with scarcely an idea of modesty or personal reserve; and the language to which they have habitually listened has been of the foulest and most blasphemous description. Intoxicating drink had formed the only, or almost the only pleasure of the class to which they belonged.' (p. 398) A perhaps more important factor than squalor and destitution was the drabness of existence for many respectable working women: for domestic servants and factory girls, for instance, working very long, hard hours for little pay and little recreation. In the provinces especially, with their comparative austerity, life was often, as the *Saturday Review* put it, 'one dreary routine of work, work, stitch, stitch, church-and-chapel-going', [161] a tedium that prostitution offered to replace with fancy clothes, gay living and financial independence. London was especially attractive for women of this type, for besides the appeal of its amusements there was the comfort of its size, offering greater safety from disturbance by police or reproachful past acquaintance.

Prostitutes in London were in very rich supply. They were also in exceptional demand. As the centre of the country's railway system, as the biggest commercial sea-port in the world, it had inevitably a large shifting population of likely clientele: of immigrants from Ireland and the Continent, of soldiers and sailors virtually debarred from marriage by the conditions of their service, of tourists and business travellers looking for diversion and with few respectable friends in town to help them find it. The size and anonymity of the capital was moreover an inducement to its respectable middle-class residents. Trollope in his *Autobiography* (1883) ruefully looked back on his loneliness as a youth: 'There was no house in which I could habitually see a lady's face and hear a lady's voice. No allurement to decent respectability came in my way. It seems to me in such circumstances the temptations of loose life will almost certainly prevail with a young man. . . . The temptation, at any rate, prevailed with me.' (p. 39) And the anonymity of London offered not only inducement to misconduct but protective cover from censorious remark.

It was this middle-class involvement in prostitution, as much as working-class conditions, that made the problem of legal intervention so intractable. For legal sanctions to be successful there would have to be not only a transformation of the economic and social conditions of the workers but a transformation too of the pattern of respectable middle-class life. There would have to be changes, for example, in the economic pattern of the middle-class marriage. In the lowest income groups of the bourgeoisie, amongst clerks and shopmen, marriage was often necessarily delayed. But amongst the more affluent sections, anxious to establish themselves securely in society, late marriage was very common also: a contemporary survey between 1840 and 1870 revealed that the average marrying age of men in the upper classes was 29.93 years. [162] For these men prolonged chastity involved not only the psychological pressures on male virginity and the denial of pleasure common to any period, but, as we have seen, in the light of nineteenth century medical opinion, a serious danger to their health. Doctors sometimes recommended prostitution to celibate patients, and one imagines other bachelors made out their own prescription. Marriage, then, was often delayed by prudential considerations. It was also often built on the same foundation. Grant Allen in the *Humanitarian* (November 1896) made a complaint that had been sounded throughout the century with insistent regularity: 'Men and women,' he wrote, 'are selected, or not selected, for considerations of wealth, rank, title, social position, creed, nationality, family convenience, fashion, and fifty other unessential accidents, rather than wholly and solely because they are here and now attractive to one another.' (IX, 343) In an age when divorce was a near impossibility, ill-sorted marriages, of convenience rather than love, were understandably a constant source of the middle-class demand for prostitution.

But a more deep-seated factor than prudential attitudes to marriage in the middle classes' commerce with the prostitute was the ironical workings of the idealistic view of sex. To appreciate more fully why intervention, to many Victorians, seemed a doubtful answer to the prostitution problem, we need to consider the ways in which the fear of sex, the cult of home, the pedestalized angel-woman all combined to foster the immorality they were intended to dispel.

III CONSCIENCE AND COMPASSION

The prostitute was the enemy of sexual purity. She was also in many ways its product. For Victorian sexual fears and sexual idealism were often counter-productive in effect, creating both a supply of potential customers for the prostitute and also a situation in which she was paradoxically not only the enemy, but the ally, of the purity ideal.

The counter-productive nature of the Victorian fear of sex is not difficult to appreciate. Parents, for example, watched anxiously the sexual development of their children, but they themselves, by reticence or interference, frequently nurtured the very tendencies they dreaded. Reticence on sex could produce an ethical unbalance in the young that might in time lead to involvement in prostitution. Kingsley in *Yeast* drawing on his own experience attributes the early lapses of Launcelot Smith to the prudery of his parents, who had always avoided all discussion of sexual love and kept even the relevant parts of the Bible carefully from his sight: 'Love had been to him, practically, ground tabooed and "carnal". What was to be expected? Just what happened—if woman's beauty had nothing holy in it, why should his fondness for it? Just what happens every day—that he had to sow his wild oats for himself, and eat the fruit thereof, and the dirt thereof also.' (p. 3) But parental interference could in some ways be even more disastrous. In the case of a young boy unable to respect or trust his elders, indoctrination and repression might serve only to provoke rebellion, stimulating rather than quenching his interest in masturbation, fornication and pornography. Steven Marcus' thesis about the connection of Victorian repression and pornography is here extremely relevant:

> For every warning against masturbation issued by the official voice of culture, another work of pornography was published; for every cautionary statement against the harmful effects of sexual excess uttered by medical men, pornography represented copulation *in excelsis*, endless orgies, infinite daisy chains of inexhaustibility; for every assertion about the delicacy and frigidity of respectable women made by the official culture, pornography represented legions of maenads, universes of palpitating females; for every effort made by the official culture to minimize the importance of sexuality, pornography cried out—or whispered—that it was the only thing in the world of any importance at all. (*op. cit.*, p. 283)

Repressive fears in short could lead to rebellious licence—not only for the individual young man but in society at large.

Puritan austerity inevitably caused a backlash; and the prostitute, like other symbols of immorality, gained new attractions from the vehemence of her detractors.

The cult of home too was a stimulus to the middle classes' traffic with prostitution. For it put in many cases an intolerable strain upon the married man's fidelity. For one thing, it led young men and women to form excessive expectations of the joys of family life. To an extent their eagerness for marriage often needed little encouragement: young men sought an outlet, perhaps a refuge, for their passions; young women were anxious to settle themselves, have babies, and avoid the privations and ignominy of spinsterhood. But with the developing consecration of woman as an angel in thousands of novels, poems, songs and sermons the imagined joys of wedlock became perilously idealistic: especially so when we consider how little, because of Victorian ideas of etiquette, an affianced pair often knew of each other's inner personalities. In *Anne Dysart*, her novel of 1850, Christiana Douglas delivered a salutary warning:

> most young men draw, in great measure, their opinion of women from works of fiction; for, except in company, where every body is doing the amiable and agreeable to the utmost, they are rarely or never intimate with any one of the sex till the fatal step is taken. Habituated, as I have said, to view all women, at least all who are to be considered praiseworthy, as formed exactly upon the model I have described, and with the false and absurd notion that it is *easier* for women than for men to practise all the virtues—quite natural to them as it were, they conceive that they have a right to feel aggrieved and injured because they find in their wives just such beings as themselves, possessed of rather more self-control perhaps, but with no more vocation to be angelic than they have. Instead, then, of practising that share of forbearance which they ought to have reckoned necessary from the first, they are unreasonably angry because creatures weaker than themselves have not attained to superhuman excellence. (II, 183)

Some husbands were wonderfully fortunate in their wives.

Others were chastened to learn that not all women could meet the claims of the ideal.

Others were severely disillusioned. For the home not only raised excessive expectations, it also seriously handicapped their fulfilment. Women in theory were educated with a view to the pleasure and moral edification of their husbands. Women in practice were often trained to irritate and bore them. 'Put yourself in the man's place,' says the cynic Barfoot in Gissing's *The Odd Women* (1893), 'Say that there are a million or so of us very intelligent and highly educated. Well, the women of corresponding mind number perhaps a few thousands. The vast majority of men must make a marriage that is doomed to be a dismal failure.' (I, 288–9) For the unidealistic Victorian not interested much in the angel-woman or in home as a place of peace, and more especially for the young man feeling his manhood and chafing against middle-aged notions of propriety, the domestic scene might be uncomfortable enough: a place of stultifying boredom, of vapid schoolgirl conversation, Sunday-school manners, and often oppressive nervous fuss. But for the disappointed idealist, who had married an angel only to find she was an idiot, the discomfort could be bitter in the extreme: his former ideals might now seem puerile extravagance, and his reaction against home and wife proportionate to his earlier adulation. For him as much as for the non-idealist the ease, raucous informality, and irresponsible pleasure of the brothel might be a necessary antidote to the stuffy tedium of the home. They might also be an antidote sometimes to the physical debility of his wife. Current notions of female delicacy, we have seen, were not always consistent with female health. The result for many husbands was weak, nervous wives continually suffering from lassitude and fatigue, all too easily worn out by the exertions of child-bearing and child-rearing. The result for many wives was unfaithful husbands. Rossetti is in this respect a classic example of disappointed idealism, a man who finding his ideal love turn into a sickly, irritable, and sometimes hysterical wife, looked for solace from a prostitute who was her opposite in everything. 'In this fact,' remarks his biographer, 'no doubt lay the secret of her hold upon Rossetti. Vulgar, vital, primitive, the antithesis of the overstrained ideal of "The Blessed Damozel", Fanny was the simplest, the most real of all the women Gabriel knew; she asked for no romantic sentiments, no heroics. Like the gypsy girl who had attracted Gabriel at Hastings five years before as he wandered about, somewhat disconsolately with the ailing Lizzie, Fanny was, for him "the image of savage, active health. . . ." ' After Lizzie's death came utter cynicism and far more recourse to prostitutes. 'In the life of the senses he sought to forget the unfulfilled promise, the vain idealism of the past, the long dreary embittered "courtship", the brief, unhappy marriage, the sordid, enigmatic end. In his new cynicism he took a bitter pleasure in destroying whatever of his former idealization of woman remained.' [163]

Perhaps the biggest strain of all, and the most conducive to infidelity, was sheer sexual frustration. Many husbands could never find sexual satisfaction in their wives. Apart from the question of women's health, and their incapacitation through pregnancy in an age when contraception was little used, there was the all-important factor of their attitude to sex. That the well-bred Victorian woman rarely experienced sexual pleasure was not myth, we have seen, but fairly common fact; and many a husband who began in worship at the shrine of angelic purity was forced to become in time a votary of sin. In Thomson's poem 'Virtue and Vice' of 1865 we see a husband driven increasingly to prostitutes by the sexless spirituality of his wife:

> She filled their home with freezing gloom;
> He felt it dismal as a tomb:
> Her stedfast mind disdained his toys
> Of worldly pleasures, carnal joys;
> Her heart firm-set on things above
> Was frigid to his earthly love.

The angel woman, it was hoped, would save men from prostitution; in fact for many unhappy, guilty husbands it was she who drove them to it. Ironically, and this is a final testimony to the interdependence of the angel and the outcast, in many marriages a loving husband, despite having a powerful sexual urge, might be as frigid as his wife. Freud explained this phenomenon in terms of the incest taboo, arguing that a youthful attachment to mother and sister prevented the adult man from fusing love and appetite: love for a wife chosen on the model of mother and sister meant feelings of tenderness which remained erotically ineffectual; appetite meant desire for an object, such as a prostitute, that evoked no reminder of the incestuous persons forbidden it. It is with this theoretical explanation in mind presumably that a recent biographer of Richard Burton has reconciled his enormous extra-marital sexual energy with his attachment to a notably frigid wife: 'She was the English virgin, pure and chaste; she was the scolding but nevertheless adoring mother, essentially untouchable and therefore endlessly exasperating and provocative, from whom he must flee and to whom he must return.'[1] Whether or not the theoretical explanation, or cases such as Burton, are too exotic for general application, it is certainly true, as Freud argued, that many a husband could not pleasure himself freely with a respectable middle-class woman: 'Full sexual satisfaction only comes when he can give himself up whole-heartedly to enjoyment, which with his well-brought-up wife, for instance, he does not venture to do. Hence comes his need for a less exalted sexual object, a woman ethically inferior, to whom he need ascribe no aesthetic misgivings, and who does not know the rest of his life and cannot criticize him.' [164]

Freud's approach to the interdependence of the angel woman and the outcast would have astonished most Victorians. But they would nonetheless have agreed that there was a connection.

1 Fawn M. Brodie, *The Devil Drives: A Life of Sir Richard Burton* (1967), p. 235. Cf. Philip Henderson's analysis of Oliphant: 'There was . . . in Laurence Oliphant a fundamental split between sensuality and affection due to his unconscious identification of the love of women with the love of his mother.' (*op. cit.*, p. 131)

If it were true that a sexual double standard was in human nature, that 'women are pure, but not men', then need followed for a safety valve for man's frailty, an outlet denied to him in respectable society. The whore was to this extent the ally of sexual purity, deflecting the danger of seduction from respectable wives and daughters and, equally importantly, deflecting from the marriage-bed any orgiastic practices husbands might desire. Thus it was many perfectly respectable Victorians were unenthusiastic as well as sceptical about the prospect of legal suppression. Their toleration of the prostitute in street and public place, their evasion of the problem except when it was forced upon their notice, was less the product of cowardly prudery than of a painful realization of society's need and guilt—the product in short of conscience. And it was the product also of compassion: until society transformed the situation of the poor and the working conditions of female labour it was ethically dubious to harass and victimize the girls they led to sin; and while the harlot was the guardian of society's marriage system, a system that was itself in some measure often little more than legalized prostitution, contempt, revulsion and persecution seemed savagely unjust. Sometimes indeed conscience and compassion led to a sentimental pedestalization of the prostitute as the martyr of society that approached the rapture normally given to the angel: 'On that one degraded and ignoble form are concentrated the passions that might have filled the world with shame. She remains, while creeds and civilisations rise and fall, the eternal priestess of humanity, blasted for the sins of the people.' [165]

Not infrequently conscience and compassion made for outright opposition to legal intervention, perfectly respectable citizens coming to the prostitute's defence. 'Many a gentleman of character,' it was remarked in 1858, 'had passed a night in a police cell for interference in the defence of prostitutes against the police', [166] a spirit of gallantry that was still in evidence in 1895, when an Oxford scientist, Professor Lankaster, and a distinguished actor-manager, George Alexander, were prosecu-

ted in successive months for protecting harlots from harassment
by the law. [167] The police understandably were often slow to
risk the odium that arresting prostitutes might bring them,
especially when they might not always be supported by the
courts.[1] *The Times* (21 February 1844) reported that a London
alderman named Farebrother had rejected a petition from some
citizens who had been disturbed by the activity of prostitutes
at night: 'These poor creatures must be somewhere . . . and why,
if acts of disorder were not proved against them, should they be
punished with imprisonment, or with the bad treatment which
they often suffered without being brought before magistrates
at all? He for one would not imprison a wretched woman merely
because she was brought before him by a policeman.' (p. 7)

On some occasions the policeman, and more especially his
instigators, the moral crusaders, received much worse than
mere obstruction in their efforts: they could be subjected to the
most bitter vilification, particularly from those who so accepted
the necessity of prostitutes as hardly to suffer any inconvenience
from encountering them. In 1848, for example, the tradesmen
of Regent Street, who had fought a long, costly, and unavailing
battle against the prostitutes in their midst, took the drastic
course of having John Nash's beautiful Quadrant demolished
by Act of Parliament. In the controversy that followed, a
writer to *The Times* (2 December 1848) exploded:

> It is the curse, Sir, of this nation to be beset with a myriad of
> canting hypocrites with great pretensions to religion and morality,
> but totally devoid of godliness and charity. That the condemned
> Quadrant afforded a temporary shelter from the pitiless storm to
> the houseless wanderer was sin enough in the eyes of these shop-
> keeping Philistines . . . but, Sir, I appeal to you, I appeal to every
> London pedestrian, whether they ever suffered any annoyance, in

---

[1] One should of course note that pity for the whore was only one source
of any lenience shown her by police and magistracy: the more organized
sections of London vice (like, for example, that ruled by Mrs Jeffries) clearly
enjoyed protection in some degree through bribery or influence.

any way, from the helpless creatures here attacked? . . . No. But this afforded your would-be saint an occasion to exercise his persecuting spirit too favourable to be lost. (p. 8)

The same accusations of hypocritical cant, of houseless wan-derers being cast on the mercies of pitiless storms, the same protestations of self-righteous prudery grossly exaggerating a trivial inconvenience, were heard forty-six years later, when in 1894 some moral vigilants led by Mrs Ormiston Chant sought to drive out the prostitutes from the Empire Theatre by abolishing its promenade. The newspapers were full of such letters as this, angrily attacking busy-body 'Prudes on the Prowl':

> How long is this great London of ours, so proud and yet so patient, to wait for that strong and irresistible voice of public disapprobation, that mighty roar of disgust, which is heard to-day in private in every assemblage of commonsense men and women, protesting against and execrating the tyranny of the self-satisfied minority? How long are we patiently to endure the shrill shriek of the emancipated female, to say nothing of the prurient grass widow? How much longer must we listen to the impudent piety of these provincial pedlars in social purity, who come red-hot from their Chicago platforms and tinpot tabernacles to tell this London of ours how she is to amuse herself and how she is to dispose of and harass and drive from pillar to post those unfortunate outcasts, whom we always have had, and always shall have, amongst us? [168]

The 'self-satisfied minority' was not in fact particularly self-satisfied. Mrs Chant, far from being a fanatical persecutor of defenceless outcasts, had been deeply involved for many years in welfare work to rescue them—like most of the vigilant pressure groups before her, from the Guardian Society to the Salvation Army. The bad woman in 1849, wrote Charlotte Brontë, was for most men a fiend; but by the 1890s neither those striving to control her with few exceptions, let alone those seeking to defend her, would have considered using any

such description. The greater charity to the outcast arose partly
because the fear of sex was now very definitely in decline, partly
because her existence was now both less extensive and in general
less obtrusive. Ironically the diminution in the prostitution
problem was in large measure due to the decline in sexual fears.
As middle-class thought became more liberal on such subjects
as contraception, marriage and divorce, and especially the social
role and sexual nature of women, the necessity of the outcast
proportionately decreased; and as the concern for sexual purity
and the idealization of the home began to fade, the purity of
the streets became at last a practical proposition.

6

Canting Hypocrites

I A TAX TO APPEARANCES

TOWARDS THE END of my first chapter I suggested it was all
too easy to make over-simple generalizations about Victorian
sexual hypocrisy. Some of the subsequent discussion (of the
double standard, for example, or the paradoxical indulgence
and yet persecution of the outcast) has, I hope, demonstrated
the need for historical empathy in this area. Now, as we
complete our exploration of the sources of Victorian sexual
attitudes and prepare to examine their chronological evolution,
it is essential to consider with this kind of historical empathy
the fundamental question of the exact correspondence between
professed ideals and actual belief. To what extent, for example,
was English morality in the nineteenth century merely a façade,
a pretension to virtue thoroughly belied by the existence of
widespread vice? To what extent was the blind eye turned,
wherever possible, to the prostitute, a blind eye turned also,
wherever possible, to a pervasive immorality beneath the
decorous surface of Victorian respectability? In 1822 Sir
Walter Scott drew attention to the discrepancy in English
morality between the apparent and the real: 'we are not now,
perhaps, more moral in our conduct than men were fifty or
sixty years since; but modern vice pays a tax to appearances, and
is contented to wear a mask of decorum.' [169] In his *Social
Topics* of 1850 John S. Smith amplified Scott's point, question-
ing whether any real progress had been made since eighteenth

century times when men were under little or no compulsion to
bother about appearances:

> it is one thing to have hooted immorality into concealment, and
> another to have actually lessened the sum of immorality . . . have
> we so driven immorality *in*, to fester even more foully in its hidden
> channels, or are we more moral in our lives, thoughts, and con-
> versations, individually and nationally, than we were in those days
> of blatant prodigality? Have we actually increased the amount of
> personal purity in this country, augmented the gross bulk of
> British morality, or have we merely, as is feared, succeeded in
> establishing a dominant show of morality which has small existence
> in reality? (pp. 63–4)

Smith's question about the 'sum of immorality' is un-
answerable with any certainty.[1] The statistics of prostitution,
we have seen, were highly problematic; and even if, as many
Victorians feared, they had in fact outstripped the growth in
population, this would not prove necessarily that there had
been no improvement in morality. Frederick von Raumer,
discussing prostitution in London in 1835, put his finger on a
very important point: 'Even if the number of prostitutes be
really greater than in Berlin, the fact is quite inconclusive as to
the greater unchastity. . . . Prostitutes are a distinct, an unfortunate, and, too often, a completely lost class. But the
"contrebande" which is carried on in private houses, is much
rarer here than elsewhere; indeed it is almost impossible.' [170]
Prostitution in England was a much more exclusive channel
than elsewhere for illicit sexual indulgence, and the amount of
non-prostitutional immorality was proportionately lower. Even
in the 1860s when 'contrebande' was more common, Hippolyte
Taine, though disgusted by the extent and flagrancy of British
prostitution, could yet conclude 'after diverse conversations and

---

[1] The *Saturday Review* (26 February 1870) sounds a note of healthy
scepticism: 'Of all useless inquiries, one of the most unprofitable is whether
the moral level of any particular stage or period of society is higher or lower
than that of the past. It is easy to make out a case either way' (XXIX, 274).

much observation' that the English were more chaste than his compatriots. [171]

It is difficult, then, to generalize about the extent of nineteenth century sexual licence. The figures for both prostitutional and non-prostitutional vice are much too uncertain for dogmatic interpretation. And even as we accept, for we clearly must, that immorality was indeed very widespread and that some of it doubtless involved the most despicable forms of humbug, we should still be wary of unqualified imputations of hypocrisy. For one thing, much of the vice we have been discussing was located in the unrespectable section of the working class which made no pretensions to morality and paid no tax to appearances. Again much of it which was located in the middle classes came, as we saw in the previous chapter, as a consequence of the constraints of respectability, its repressive indoctrination, its excessively idealized view of marriage and all that that involved: to stigmatize as hypocrites men who were more like casualties of prudery would be to adopt the logic of Butler's *Erewhon*, where illness is a crime. Above all, much Victorian vice exhibited a degree of shame and guilt that would surely abate the censure of all but the most self-righteous of moralists. Considering the easy accessibility of the whore, considering the peculiar Victorian pressures on masculine continence, considering the many rationalizations of misconduct that were available—the economic and social hardships of the harlot, the medical dangers of protracted and often involuntary celibacy, the frequent tedium, lovelessness and sexual sterility of the respectable marriage—considering all these factors, it is remarkable how vigorously many Victorians struggled against indulgence in immorality.

We might perhaps doubt this to be the case from Thackeray's famous remark in *Pendennis*: 'we are not about to go through Pen's academical career very minutely. Alas, the life of such boys does not bear telling altogether! I wish it did. I ask you, does yours? As long as what we call our honour is clear, I suppose your mind is pretty easy.' (p. 164) But we should note that this sweeping remark is very much at odds even with the characters of Thackeray's own heroes.[1] A few years later a writer to *The Times* (7 May 1857) expressed an alternative point of view: he believed that 'there are very many young men who are keeping themselves pure amid all the temptations of London life', and that of those who fell from grace 'many, perhaps most of them, are wretched under the convictions of their conscience'. (p. 12) This writer's belief was supported a little later by Taine, who noted the conscience-stricken faces of men entering brothels in the Strand and Haymarket: 'The mature man, the young man of the respectable classes, on that evening he is supposed to be travelling or at his club. He does not make himself conspicuous, does not offer his companion his arm: his expedition is secret and anonymous and represents no more than an escape of the beast which everyone of us carries within himself. . . . An Englishman in a state of adultery is miserable: even at the supreme moment his conscience torments him.' [172] For many Victorian men 'hypocritical immorality' was in fact involuntary capitulation to an irresistible compulsion.

Something of the same pattern is visible in the area of literary indecency. Like prostitution, pornography offered a hydra-headed problem for the would-be moral reformer, particularly in London: William Dugdale, for example, a notorious dealer in Holywell Street, the centre of the trade, was raided by the police in 1851 and deprived of 822 books, 3,870 prints and sixteen hundredweight of unsewn letterpress; in 1856 he was raided again for the umpteenth time and on this occasion some 3,000 books were taken—an indication of remarkable prosperity in view of his frequent spells in prison. Like prostitution

[1] Consider, for example, his description of Lord Kew in *The Newcomes*: 'He had passed a reckless youth, indeed he was sad and ashamed of that past life, longed like the poor prodigal to return to better courses, and had embraced eagerly the chance afforded him of a union with a woman young, virtuous, and beautiful, against whom and against Heaven he hoped to sin no more.' (p. 353)

pornography also offered problematic evidence as to the 'sum of immorality': the greater volume of traffic, for example, as compared with the eighteenth century may reflect increases in population, social affluence and publishing efficiency rather than any real change in sexual morality. And again like prostitution pornography exposed the Victorians to charges of hypocrisy that were often less than fair.

Many of its patrons, for example, were in large measure rebelling against the constraints of respectability. One thinks of Monckton Milnes with his extensive collection of sadistic materials at Aphrodisiopolis, as he called Fryston Hall, his home; of Swinburne and George Augustus Sala, two resolute iconoclasts dashing off their works of flagellatory pornography; or of Richard Burton, sedulously collecting salacious and gruesome stories on his travels in Arabia and Africa. In all of this there may be immaturity or emancipation, according to one's tastes, but there is surely little humbug. The same may be said for the Victorians' *sub-rosa* fondness for bawdy humour. In an age of such highminded literary purity it was surely quite natural for men, in smoking room or private letters, to relax with a little ribaldry. Sometimes smut found its way into the public domain as well. Cyril Pearl tells us that when a gentleman called Buggey announced his intention of changing his unfortunate name, the press commented good-humouredly on other people with similar problems: a list of embarrassing names published in *The Times* included Bub, Holdwater, Pricke, Poopy, Maydenhead, Piddle, Pisse, Honeybum, Leakey, Pricksmall, Quicklove, Rumpe, Shittel, and Teate. Pearl reminds us also how extraordinarily immune the writers of antiquity were from prudish expurgation: Bohn's famous Classical Library offered for five shillings not only full translations of Petronius, Martial, Catullus, Ovid and other classic writers, but also detailed annotations so that the more esoteric indecencies could be enjoyed by readers of limited scholarship. [173]

Occasionally the dabbler in bawdry or pornography was in

fact a crusader for sexual purity. Tennyson, for example, the idol of pure young maidens, was in private a practised teller of dirty jokes. Patmore, the high priest of angel-worship, kept hidden behind the bookshelves in his library a set of privately published books from the 'Eroticon Biblion Society', reprints of the world's forbidden erotic masterpieces. But again imputations of hypocrisy seem insensitive if we consider the enormous strain a very spiritualized view of woman could place upon men with powerful sexual urges.[1] One can only guess at the psychic disturbances such tension could produce. Tennyson, for example, who once flew into a fury at the very mention of de Sade, in private indulged the sadistic element that peeps out fitfully in his poetry: among the topics of conversation noted by his schoolboy son were such items as the following:

'A walled up room found with the skeleton of a man crawling from under the bed and the woman in bed.'
'A chieftain in Dahomey, I fancy, killed young girls to warm his feet in their bowels.'
'On the accession of a king in Dahomey enough women victims are killed to float a small canoe (with their blood).'[2]

Kingsley, another eminent idealist, whose novels we saw earlier exhibited a definite streak of sadism in their depiction of battered naked women, was led in private to give this impulse freer rein: the illustrations he drew for a *Life of St Elizabeth of Hungary* included the flagellation of a female figure in a chapel, angels supporting a naked woman on a cross with a group of repulsive howling animals at its base, and most elaborately of all a nude girl staggering, cross on shoulder, up a ragged

---

[1] One should note too the predicament of the highly sexed woman: Richard Burton claimed that the educated woman regularly lived 'in a rustle of (imaginary) copulation', relieving herself in French novels and in fantasy (*op. cit.*, VII, 404)—an over-generalization, but clearly based on some degree of fact.

[2] Charles Tennyson, 'Tennyson's Conversation', *Twentieth Century* (January 1959) CLXV, 37–8. Sir Charles remarks that he has not quoted the most disagreeable of these conversational specimens.

mountain track to the jeers and screams of ugly, evil monsters. This curious blend of sexual idealism, theological polemic and morbid eroticism Kingsley offered as a wedding present to his ascetic High Church bride. Here, as very often with the recourse to prostitution, sexual indulgence was less hypocrisy than the venting of an irresistible compulsion.

In 1828 William Hazlitt made a highly pertinent distinction: 'He is a hypocrite who professes what he does not believe; not he who does not practise all he wishes or approves.' [174] By this definition a great deal of Victorian moral behaviour escapes the indictment of hypocrisy: a large number of sincerely prudish Victorians were unable to practise all they preached. But by this definition too a great deal of Victorian moral profession is exposed in all its weakness. By this I do not mean the highly venial hypocrisy of those sincere dissenters from orthodox morality who felt obliged by fear of public opinion to profess what they did not believe. For even more than the penalties on the man himself who paid no tax to appearances there were also the intimidating penalties accruing to his family: 'Whoever has a wife and children,' remarked J. S. Mill, 'has given hostages to Mrs Grundy. The approbation of that potentate may be a matter of indifference to him, but it is of great importance to his wife.' [175] The kind of hypocrisy rather that I allude to is a variety of sexual attitudes we have barely discussed since the opening chapter. It is important to balance the weight we have given to various aspects of Victorian prudery with a reminder of the moral apathy and covert prurience that were also endemic in Victorian sexual morals. Many Victorians simply did not believe in the code they claimed to uphold. Their adherence was nominal, their concern only that they and others should pay the tax to appearances in the mandatory way. Even if their own personal conduct was as chaste in reality as in appearance, they were often guilty of conniving at others' sins. This was particularly the case, as moralists ruefully recognized, where the sinner had wealth and status on his side. 'We pride ourselves on the purity of our

morals compared with the continent,' complained Maria Smith
in her novel *Castle-Deloraine* in 1851, 'but in our dealings with
society we judge a man according to the place he holds in the
social scale, rather than by the conduct he has pursued in it,
and overlook the taint of vice itself if encircled by a coronet.'
(I, 176) Men of doubtful reputation indeed, far from being
banned from good society, were often especially welcome:
John S. Smith remarks that so far from a stand being made for
moral rectitude 'a certain amount of jaunty rakishness, a spice
of the Lothario, is rather desired than otherwise. It is almost
universal, that the roués of the town are precisely the men who
are never omitted in any invitation list, and to win attention
from whom is the chief ambition of the *belles*.' (*op. cit.*, p. 73)
The anonymous author of the novel *Broomhill* (1853) was
equally jaundiced about the moral apathy lurking beneath
maidenly decorum: 'If a man have a reputation for gallantry,
no matter even if it amount to a sin, you may depend on it,
half the women he meets will try to burn their fingers in the
same flame; the guilt that should banish him from female
society being but too often a passport to their good graces.'
(II, 225)

Women sinners too were sometimes afforded special treatment. In 1849 the dancer Lola Montez, or the Countess von
Landsfeld, the rumoured mistress of great men on the Continent, arrived in England and caused a general sensation.
Everyone talked about her, women copied her hair and clothes,
and tradesmen put her picture on snuff-boxes, fans and
souvenirs. In August, however, of that year the family of a
gentleman named Heald, to whom she had only just been
married, had her charged with bigamy before a packed and
excited court. Enough of her past life came into view to make
her abscond with the infatuated Heald. *The Times* (12 September
1849) gratified its readers' interest in her whereabouts by
publishing a letter from a gentleman in Naples: 'A youthful
bridegroom and a fair lady who, though still beautiful, once
was younger, answering in all respects the description given of

the enamoured couple who lately figured at the Marlborough Street police-office, appeared at, and disappeared yesterday from, Naples, with all the circumstances of eccentricity which have ever distinguished the movements of *la belle dame*, whether recognized as Mrs James, Lola Montez, the Countess of Landsfeld, or Mrs Heald.' (p. 3) The indulgent facetiousness of this letter—the writer goes on to say how the bright eyes of the lady had left a permanent impression on his heart—is typical of the press coverage Lola's travels were given in the next few years. Reports of arguments with managers, lovers and credulous tradesmen, lengthy reviews of her autobiography, descriptions of a Canadian lecture tour, all kept her a popular figure of interest. The *Saturday Review* (29 August 1857) commented cynically on the reports from Canada: 'It is only in Britain and her off-shoots that an audience can really relish the enjoyment of having a woman who has made herself notorious throughout the civilized world, and has gone through infinite adventures, come undauntedly before them, and heighten the poignancy of her looks and reputation by giving utterance to the language of an edifying morality.' (IV, 199) Perhaps taking the hint, in December 1858 Lola Montez arrived in England and started a highly successful lecture tour that lasted for several months. Notoriety served only for many Victorians to make her glamour more enticing.

The 'language of an edifying morality' was at this time not infrequently a cover for sexual titillation. The novelist's freedom, for example, was very restricted, but most of the respectable newspapers throughout the century carried accounts of salacious sex crimes and crim. con. or divorce actions.[1] Thomas Miller in *Godfrey Malvern* (1842) is conscious that his relative sexual candour as a novelist may, to some readers, make his book seem scarcely a moral work: ' "That may be, my dear lady!" we answer: "you have been reading *The Times* today: it reports a case of crim. con., an elopement, and a rape;—why

[1] Crim. con. was an enticement action brought by an injured husband against his wife's lover.

not burn it along with *Godfrey Malvern*? Both tell only the truth. It is not altogether a moral world!" ' (p. 287) Miller, however, is too charitable about the papers. Their excuse that they only told the truth about a not altogether moral world is thoroughly disingenuous in view of the amount of prurient detail that they offered. And after the Divorce Act of 1857 furnished them with new riches of materials their sense of civic duty ran with some suits to the length of several juicy columns for a week or more. The *Saturday Review* (8 January 1859), glancing at Campbell's Obscene Publications Act also of 1857, commented dryly: 'The great law which regulates supply and dammed seems to prevail in matters of public indecency as well as in other things of commerce. Block up one channel, and the stream will force another outlet; and so it is that the current demand up in Holywell Street flings itself out in the Divorce Court.' (VII, 36) Theoretically the pure young miss would be debarred from encountering this pollution but in fact, it was said, prohibition encouraged her often to read the papers on the sly. And indeed, such was the amount of nominal morality beneath the demand for purity in literature, sometimes there would be no parental prohibition: 'Mothers,' complained *Fraser's* in August 1860, 'who would not allow their daughters to open *Adam Bede* complacently permit them the unlimited study of the newspaper.' (LXII, 210)

It is doubtful whether the papers did the daughters much in the way of harm, any more than *tableaux vivants* or *equestrienne* actresses meant moral corruption for their brothers. And it is not here, in these examples of a relative moral laxity, that the Victorians are most open to accusations of hypocrisy. Traditionally in fact the most vehement attacks have been made in an opposite quarter, involving examples of their notorious moral censoriousness. 'It is the curse, sir, of this nation to be beset with a myriad of canting hypocrites with great pretensions to religion and morality, but totally devoid of godliness and charity.' The writer, the correspondent to *The Times* in 1848 I quoted in the previous chapter, makes a fairly common accusation. How just it is we can only determine when we have begun to examine the nature of Victorian moral cant.

II THE GRAND PRIMUM MOBILE

'We know no spectacle so ridiculous,' wrote Macaulay in 1830,

> as the British public in one of its periodical fits of morality. In general, elopements, divorces, and family quarrels, pass with little notice. We read the scandal, talk about it for a day, and forget it. But once in six or seven years our virtue becomes outrageous. We cannot suffer the laws of religion and decency to be violated. We must make a stand against vice. We must teach libertines that the English people appreciate the importance of domestic ties. Accordingly some unfortunate man, in no respect more depraved than hundreds whose offences have been treated with levity, is singled out as an expiatory sacrifice. If he has children, they are to be taken from him. If he has a profession, he is to be driven from it. He is cut by the higher orders, and hissed by the lower. He is, in truth, a sort of whipping-boy, by whose vicarious agonies all the other transgressors of the same class are, it is supposed, sufficiently chastised. We reflect very complacently on our own severity, and compare with great pride the high standard of morals established in England with the Parisian laxity. At length our anger is satiated. Our victim is ruined and heart-broken. And our virtue goes quietly to sleep for seven years more. [176]

It is the case of Byron that Macaulay has especially in mind. He might in fact have chosen better, for the widespread rumours of 1816 that led to Byron's exile, of gross adultery, incest and bestial cruelty, of sodomy and homosexuality, made him rather a special case.

Macaulay is on stronger ground, however, when he alludes to the fate of Edmund Kean, the actor, in 1825. After his exposure in the law courts as a liar and adulterer Kean was pelted and yelled down in the theatre and hounded to America. The abuse hurled at him was not merely vicious, but to some extent thoroughly hypocritical. His persecutors in *The Times*, for example, who led the pack against him, were themselves far from models of impeccable domesticity. [177] And it was *The Times*, one might add, that four years earlier on 8 August 1821 had greeted the death of a far more notorious sinner, Queen Caroline, with black columns and edges and pious, tear-jerking lamentations for 'the greatest, perhaps, the best woman of her day'. (p. 2) There is a similar contrast to be noted in the welcome given to Lola Montez in 1858 and the obloquy heaped earlier in that year upon the octogenarian poet, Walter Savage Landor. Landor was sued for libel by a scoundrel called Mrs Yescombe. From the trial it appeared, rightly, that he had written her obscenely abusive letters, and it seemed, wrongly, that she had aroused his particular venom by withdrawing a young girl from his society. He was crucified by the press and driven, like Byron and Kean before him, into exile. The press might be forgiven for misconstruing what had happened, and because of his political beliefs, they had little cause to like him.[1] But far from pitying an old man's senile errors of judgement, one or two papers indulged in an orgy of vilification. 'The most melancholy of moral abasements,' proclaimed the usually well-balanced *Saturday Review*, 28 August 1858,

is that of a hoary and lecherous old man. Filth and obscenity are never so unnaturally nauseous as from the chattering lips of age, and a tottering and toothless satyr generally keeps his foul life and conversation to himself and his associates. Mr Walter Savage Landor, we fear, has only lost the negative virtue of concealing his natural temper. Vice is not learned at eighty-five. Shamelessness is the result and consequence of moral causes—the rotten fruit of Gomorrah implies a long and steady growth in impudicity. (VI, 203)

The Victorian prude's denunciation of literary impudicity was open to the same kind of criticism as his alleged fits of periodical morality. In his *Autobiography* of 1850 Leigh Hunt

[1] A few months earlier, after Orsini's attempt to assassinate Napoleon III, Landor had been roundly criticized for his friendship with Orsini and his public and immoderate apology for tyrannicide.

notes the curious way in which, to suit English tastes, the title of his translation of a *fabliau* called *Les Trois Chevaliers et la Chemise* had been made *The Gentle Armour*: an earlier translator

> had no hesitation, some years ago, in rendering the French title of the poem by its (then) corresponding English words, 'The Three Knights and the Smock'; but so rapid are the changes that take place in people's notions of what is decorous, that not only has the word 'smock' (of which it was impossible to see the indelicacy, till people were determined to find it) been displaced since that time by the word 'shift'; but even that harmless expression for the act of changing one garment for another, has been set aside in favour of the French word 'chemise'; and at length not even this word, it seems, is to be mentioned, nor the garment itself alluded to, by any decent writer. (III, 217–18)

Charles Reade in a pamphlet defending his novel *Griffith Gaunt* (1866) coined the phrase 'The Prurient Prude' to describe the mentality that Hunt is condemning: the prurient prude is one who 'itches to attract attention by a parade of modesty (which is the mild form of the disease), or even by rashly accusing others of immodesty (and this is the noxious form)'. [178] It is ironic that Dickens, himself in his novels the scourge of prurient spinsters with both forms of the disease, should yet for all his purity have been the subject of their complaints. The *National Magazine* in December 1837 proclaimed him the purest writer of the day: 'and it is this circumstance which has not unfrequently raised our bile to hear affected mincing girls (who would come admirably under Swift's definition of a *nice* man, "one with *nasty* ideas",) who utter all their indelicate words in French, say they cannot read "Boz", he is *so low!*' (I, 448) Five years later the redoubtable Mrs Ellis in *The Daughters of England* lambasted the kind of maidenly prudery 'which is perpetually in quest of something to be ashamed of, which makes a merit of a blush, and simpers at the false construction its own ingenuity has put upon an innocent remark'. (p. 177)

Now there is much in these allegations of periodical fits of morality and of prurient prudery to justify the common view of Victorian moral hypocrisy. Public censure of an individual's private life exhibited sometimes a repellent degree of self-righteous self-display, priggishness and smugness, and worse a viciousness and malice that suggests the off-loading of the public's own moral guilt. In the same way moral censure of what was considered literary immodesty betrayed sometimes a prurient determination to discover immodesty where it did not exist, for the purpose of either self-display or alternatively surreptitious enjoyment, and a propensity to camouflage these intentions by bitter attacks upon the supposed violator of public decency. Nevertheless we should beware of being too censorious ourselves. Again, Hazlitt's comments on hypocrisy are very helpful. 'If any one really despised what he affected outwardly to admire,' Hazlitt remarks, 'this would be hypocrisy. If he affected to admire it a great deal more than he really did, this would be cant. . . . Cant is the voluntary overcharging of a real sentiment; hypocrisy is the setting-up a pretension to a feeling you never had and have no wish for.' (*op. cit.*, pp. 353, 366) Cant, in other words, is sincere at bottom, where hypocrisy is not.

Cant just the same has had over the years almost as bad a public image as hypocrisy. It was cant, for example, that aroused Byron's particular hatred. 'The truth is that in these days,' he wrote in 1821, 'the grand "*primum mobile*" of England is *cant*; cant political, cant poetical, cant religious, cant moral; but always *cant*, multiplied through all the varieties of life.' [179] On reflection, however, one might say that the grand primum mobile of *all* societies, of human nature itself, is likely to be cant. As Hazlitt put it, 'we almost all want to be thought better than we are, and affect a greater admiration and abhorrence of certain things than we really feel'. (*op. cit.*, p. 365) Perhaps today our emphasis is different: many of us who are young like to be thought cleverer than we are rather than 'better' and trim our opinions according to our company; many of us who are older would like to be thought more successful, more important, more fulfilled and happy than we are rather than 'better'. The social strategy is essentially the same, it simply operates in a different sphere.

And the fact that Victorian cant operated very largely in the ethical sphere accounts to some extent for its excesses. No department of human life is of greater complexity, requiring greater fineness of judgement, than the moral. The consistent chastisement of different moral offenders therefore inevitably presented the Victorians with enormous difficulties: 'all is arbitrary and capricious,' wrote Bulwer Lytton in this regard in *England and the English* (1833), 'often the result of vague and unmerited personal popularity—often a sudden and fortuitous reaction in the public mind that, feeling it has been too harsh to the last victim, is too lenient to its next.' (I, 371) And the difficulties were compounded by the none-too-rigorous ethical system that inevitably accompanied the cant of affecting to admire things more than was really the case. Again no department of human life is more unruly, more susceptible to volatile disturbance, than the sexual. Inevitably therefore the reproof of immodesty involved the Victorians in the conflicts to which prudery is ever likely to be vulnerable. A recent study of English prudery has suggested that when prudes 'inveigh or organize against sin they are consciously or unconsciously buttressing their own inner barriers against the pleasure they long for but fear to obtain'. [180] Such conflicts were especially common, one imagines, in an age so obsessed with purity on the one hand and sexuality on the other. And such conflicts, we should note, were a product not of hypocrisy but of conscious or unconscious cant. 'The virtue of prudes may be suspected,' Hazlitt noted, 'though not their sincerity. The strength of their passions may make them more conscious of their weakness, and more cautious of exposing themselves; but not more to blind others than as a guard upon themselves.' (*op. cit.*, p. 357)

Cant, I suggest, and much of it venial rather than outrageous humbug, is the characteristic weakness of Victorian moral censure. This is the light in which to read Macaulay's remarks about periodical stands against vice. 'We must teach libertines that the English people appreciate the importance of domestic ties.' Such was the sincere attitude of the bulk of the respectable population, even if many of them were not perhaps as sincere as they liked to think. And we should note finally how much of Victorian moral censure, even in what appears to be its least attractive manifestations, was in fact thoroughly sincere. I shall take two examples: first the vilification of *Don Juan* on its first appearance, and second the vilification of Oscar Wilde.

The reception of the opening cantos of *Don Juan* in 1819 needs to be placed in historical perspective. In the nervous years after the Napoleonic wars there was still enough conspiracy hysteria in existence, like that of 1797, to promote the fear that political sedition might be affected through moral subversion, and this subversion affected through immoral literature. In 1818 the *British Review* complained,

> It is a fact of very melancholy import, that the poetry,—we may say the literature of the present hour, is become the ally of immorality, infidelity and political disaffection. The man of feeling and reflection has need to tremble as he walks along our public streets, lest some new mischief in the windows of our booksellers' shops, some venal profligacy, some poison for the soul, some treason against God, should catch his eye, with its ominous label and fresh exterior, in the bloom of its first announcement. The town is gorged to satiety with profanation, obscenity, and scandal. (XII, 18)

The Satanic school of poetry, as Southey was later to call it, [181] which seemed devoted to spreading atheism and immorality, commanding as it did in Byron, Shelley and Leigh Hunt some of the most powerful pens in the kingdom, was a horrifying indication of the way the country might be going. Hence the torrid reception *Don Juan* encountered. It was not prurient prudery but anxiety that prompted the *British Critic* (August 1819) to describe the poem as 'a calm and deliberate design to palliate and recommend the crime of adultery, to work up the passions of the young to its commission, and to afford them the most practical hints for its consummation'. And it was anxiety not priggish smugness that prompted the same writer to claim that it was not by such works 'that the British nation is to be tricked out of that main bulwark of its national strength, its sturdy and unbending morality'. (XII, 202–3)

Fears for the future of the nation played a similar part in the violent hostility shown to Wilde in 1895. Modern commentators on this unhappy episode have almost without exception condemned the Victorians out of hand. Hesketh Pearson is not untypical: 'They damned Wilde with such vigour and thoroughness that, on this evidence alone, they must be considered the most vicious age in history.' [182] The affair did indeed exhibit the worst features of Victorian moral censure, its love of scandal and a scapegoat, its priggishness, its malice and its cruelty. But with historical perspective there is much to be said in the Victorians' defence. The reaction against Wilde had a number of sources. There was, for example, a good deal of understandable philistine resentment, resentment at his affectations to beauty and scorn for the bourgeoisie as illiterate and uncouth, even as he was being tried for a gross and ugly crime. There was the way he seemed to focus the threat of national decadence, to be a confirmation of Nordau's thesis in *Entartung* which appeared in translation simultaneously with his disgrace, that all modern art showed a disease and degeneration that menaced the human race. But the most important factor in Wilde's case was the most obvious: his sins were homosexual. At this point we need to widen the historical perspective. From the beginning of the century homosexual vice had been regarded with almost hysterical detestation: in its extreme form it had been punishable by death, the culprit being hanged on a special gallows so as not to contaminate murderers and robbers; and even minor offenders had been savagely treated in the pillory. [183] The vilification

Wilde received was an expression of this continuing detestation, directed at him not only for what he was but for what he appeared to have shown about English society. It was an expression of society's transferred guilt for the unnatural vice it had permitted within the shell of formal purity. Above all it was an expression of anguish and self-doubt. Victorian society was based in theory on an idealized love for woman; it was based in practice very largely on a system of male-bonding. [184] With women restricted socially by education, physique, convention and habit, male friendship was a keystone of society: sometimes passionate as with Tennyson and Hallam, sometimes raucous as with army officers and city swells, sometimes a product of all-male schools and all-male professions, sometimes a product of an economically conditioned protracted masculine celibacy. The Wilde case took the bloom off society's pre-Freudian innocence. It sowed suspicion and anxiety. It focussed a haunting fear as England approached the *fin de siècle* that her vast achievements in Empire and material progress, her place and standing in the world, had been built, not as she believed, on the secure foundations of national decency, but on the quicksands of a private moral hollowness. The vilification of Wilde was less an indication of vicious cant and hypocrisy than of a profound anxiety and insecurity.

III THE GLASS OF FASHION

The hostility to Byron and Wilde has a further significant aspect. Both men, besides being for their times figures of palpable immorality, were also men of Fashion. And our discussion of nineteenth century ethical postures, of prudery in its various manifestations, of hypocrisy and cant, of moral laxity and simple common sense, can go no further without an understanding of this phenomenon. The history of Victorian sexual attitudes, which we will soon begin to trace in some detail, is very largely the history of the relative strength at different times of prudery and of cant and hypocrisy, or, put in another way, of prudery and its philosophic antithesis, the ethic of the spirit of Fashion.

A very vivid picture of this ethic in its more extreme manifestations is given in an anonymous poem called *Fashion*, which was in its fifth edition in 1818:

> When at college the Fashion is—nothing to learn,
> A desperate fox-hunter thence to return,
> To drink, w—— and gamble, to brag and to swear,
> To speak and to look with an impudent air.
> Next—the title which Cyprian favour rewards
> The buck (to be finish'd) is put in the *Guards*—
> There the Fashion's extravagant, *crim. con.* and play,
> As the newspaper columns evince every day. . . .
> To squander a fortune; but, ere we retreat,
> To get deeply in debt, then in Bench or the Fleet,
> Throw your creditors over, and boast to a friend
> Of your *νοος* in thus carrying on to the end.[1]

Such a life-style, the extreme degree of fashionable licence, could hardly be further from the puritan cast of mind we examined earlier. Instead of the punctilious asceticism of Hellfire theology or mercantile prudence, the cultivation of temperance, frugality, industry, chastity and probity, it was characterized by hard drinking, heavy gambling, soft living, easy women and unpaid bills; instead of the pains of religious doubt or concern for the country's welfare, only irresponsible hedonism; instead of a compulsive need for purity in woman-hood, for home as a place of peace, only a shameless absorption in vanity and folly. A few years earlier a graphic account had been given of the manners of fashionable women. In November 1810 the *Universal Magazine* had complained that the latter had adopted 'a freedom of manners, a boldness of look and scantiness of apparel' which made them hard to distinguish from harlots; indeed when efforts were made to exclude the

---

[1] P. 47. 'Cyprian' was a slang name for prostitute.

Cyprian corps from the theatre law officers had been 'so far misled by appearances, that they were very near conveying a *nude* of high rank to the watch house'. (n.s. XIV, 377–8) Such a picture could hardly be further from the puritan style in womanhood we examined earlier. Instead of the naive innocence of the doll-like woman, her timorous, bashful modesty, her enslavement to the proprieties, in the mirror of Fashion we see a confident worldliness and assumption of independence; instead of the unstinting dedication of the angel-woman, her talismanic influence over children, hearth and husband, we find in contrast a devotion to selfish pleasure and an indifference to ethical obligation; above all instead of a strenuous purity, perhaps even a morbid fear of fleshliness, we are struck by the ostentatious, flaunted sexuality of the courtesan.

The chasm between the spirit of prudery and the spirit of Fashion in nineteenth century society was bridged by cant and hypocrisy. The excesses of the small world of Vanity Fair at any particular time were partly a defiant response to the stridency of the puritanism of the day. But they were also, more profoundly, a reflection of a prevailing lack of ethical rigour, of cant and hypocrisy, in society at large at that particular time. The periods when Vanity Fair was most profligate in its manners were times when the attitute towards it of the respectably behaved was notably coloured by moral apathy and conventionalism, even covert endorsement and admiration. In the second half of the eighteenth century, for example, moralists frequently complained that the bourgeoisie though in general very decorous in behaviour was more interested in establishing claims to Fashion than in purifying society's moral tone. And at the beginning of the nineteenth century moralists feared that the middle classes might become themselves positively debauched by the example of Fashion, seeking status through an adoption of the traditional aristocratic vices rather than the traditional bourgeois virtues.

This fear was understandable in view of the English middle classes' peculiar advantages in affluence, class mobility and literacy over their equivalents abroad. The upper middle classes might be influenced by their superiors through personal association, the lower classes through social osmosis or the circulating libraries' literature of Fashion. Francis Jeffrey in the *Edinburgh Review* (July 1806) noted with concern that 'in this reading and opulent country, there are no fashions which diffuse themselves so fast, as those of literature and immorality: there is no palpable boundary between the *noblesse* and the *bourgeoisie*, as in old France, by which the corruption and intelligence of the former can be prevented from spreading to the latter . . . if the head be once infected, the corruption will spread irresistibly through the whole body'. (VII, 460) In fact despite these fears the worst excesses of fashionable life were never repeated generally throughout society in terms of permissive conduct (only a small minority of the *nouveaux riches* succumbed to Fashion in this sense). But the excesses of fashionable life were reflected through society in terms of permissive attitudes.

On 11 December 1799, for example, *The Times* remarked of current styles in feminine couture: 'If the present fashion of nudity continues its career, the Milliners must give way to the carvers, and the most elegant *fig-leaves* will be all the mode.' (p. 2) In 1825 a similar joke was made:

> When dress'd for the evening the girls nowadays
> Scarce an atom of dress on them leave;
> Nor blame them—for what is an evening dress
> But a dress that is suited for Eve? [185]

The point here is not that the immodest fashions of Vanity Fair were being adopted in these years by general society: rather that there was a sufficient amount of free-and-easy tolerance in society, as typified by the facetious tone of these two writers, to encourage women of Fashion to persist in this immodesty. In the 1830s and 1840s fashionable dress inspired no comparisons with fig-leaves: indeed a novelist of 1844 had

to assure his readers that the previous generation had indeed
permitted such indecency; 'Monstrous as it may seem, I have
no doubt, were a woman to venture at noon-day into one of the
leading thoroughfares of London, dressed as every *élégante* was in
1817, she would be taken into custody.' [186] The principal
factor behind this improved decorum in fashionable life was the
greater universality enjoyed at this time by the puritan cast of
mind. Clearly the bourgeoisie's recent accession to political
power was also of some influence, but that this was of minor
importance is shown by the partial reversal in fashionable
manners in the latter decades of the century. In 1867 the
political power of the bourgeoise was extended further still;
and yet it was in 1867 that a writer complained: 'The low-
necked dress and bold look of the wearer are signs of the present
fast, frivolous and indecorous age'; [187] and by 1888 the
wheel in many ways had turned full circle: 'The excessive
nakedness of modern full dress is sometimes a pain and more
often an embarrassment to those who only observe. The
lowness of the bodice and the total absence of sleeves leaves an
impression of general nakedness.' [188] At the very time when
the supposedly puritan bourgeoisie was setting the social tone,
fashionable life, though free of most of its earlier grossness,
was once more indicating the amount of covert indulgence and
even approbation it was receiving throughout society.

In the Glass of Fashion, in the manners of Vanity Fair, in
the themes and tones of fashionable literature, we have an
index to the strength of prudery on the one hand and cant and
hypocrisy on the other at any particular time. We have also a
caution, a reminder, as we begin to trace the development of
nineteenth century sexual attitudes, that even at those times
when fashionable laxity was most on the retreat cant and
hypocrisy were still very much in evidence. In 1816 the
example of the Prince Regent encouraged a fashionable
licentiousness, but in 1816 too the success of the Evangelicals
encouraged a fashionable purity in which religion was little
more than the latest vogue:

Her outward signs at least will even raise
Your credit high in these convenient days.
Fashion, herself, the cause of virtue pleads,
Becomes chief patroness of pious deeds,
And lets us e'en pursue without restraint,
What once had stamped us *puritan* and *saint*. [189]

As we examine the evolution of the Victorian code of moral respectability, of the Victorian code of literary chastity and of Victorian concepts of ideal womanhood, we need always to remember how easily Fashion could put on her Sunday clothes, observing the form of puritan moral attitudes without any comprehension of their meaning, let alone commitment to the cause of their advance.

II

The Development of
Victorian Sexual Attitudes

7

The Rattle of the Bones

Up to this point my discussion of Victorian sexual attitudes has drawn together materials from a wide range of dates without very much stress on chronological distinctions. Enough has been said, I hope, to dispel any notion that the Victorians were some kind of monolithic entity, but what we require now is a comprehensive evolutionary scheme to place their attitudes in adequate perspective. Any assessment, for example, of standards of social decency, literary prudery or ideal womanhood in the 1850s must allow for historical relativity, must compare these standards with those prevailing a generation before and after. Such a scheme must also be very detailed, for previous historical surveys of sexual morals have usually been somewhat cursory and have therefore ignored or misunderstood rapid yet crucial fluctuations in attitudes. They have also in the main been somewhat uncritical of received conceptions of individual historical cases: an anxious Victorian moralist, for example, is not necessarily the best guide to contemporary standards of public morality any more than a censured Victorian writer is to contemporary standards of literary prudery. Much of my illustration, therefore, though I shall rarely suspend the argument to say so, will be designed to correct common misinterpretations of well-known individual cases.

Clearly what I am proposing is ambitious to the point of hubris. In making a detailed graph of English sexual attitudes from the middle of the eighteenth century to the beginning of

the twentieth (for these are my limits), even with the help of
the considerable secondary literature on this period, I am likely
to commit errors of my own through inadequate information
and subjective impressionism, not to mention shallow or
muddled thinking. Moreover, an attempt to synthesize such a
vast body of materials without over-simplification would seem
in danger, even without the interpretative tree-chopping I have
just mentioned, of becoming lost in a confused and cluttered
argument—the more so since I intend to emphasize always the
disparities, where they exist, between professed and actual
beliefs, the importance of Fashion as well as prudery.

Scale, detail and argumentative synthesis are inevitably
awkward bedfellows. And because of this I have decided to tell
the story more than once and from different angles; partly by
way of checking, corroborating and qualifying my interpretative
thesis and thus reducing error, and partly in order to help the
reader see immediately a pattern it took me years to see. The
next two chapters will analyse respectively the evolution of
public sexual manners and the evolution of literary prudery.
Essentially what I shall be suggesting in these two parallel
chapters is that the eighteenth century evolved generally
accepted codes in society and literature of nominal but not
actual sexual probity; that Evangelical moralists disturbed by
the implications of the French Revolution managed in the first
decade of the nineteenth century to arouse sufficient moral
urgency in the previously apathetic middle classes to affect the
evolution of tighter, more stringent codes by the 1830s, codes
which nevertheless still contained a large element of mere
conventionalism as well as genuine moral commitment and
which still showed, as in the eighteenth century, a huge
discrepancy in stringency as they operated respectively in
society and literature; that in the 1850s a reaction set in
against these codes which in literature involved a progressive
diminution of prudish restraints through pretty well to the end
of the century, but which in the area of public sexual manners
meant first a resurgence of the implicitly permissive attitudes

the Evangelical moralists had laboured to dispel, and then a fresh wave of moral urgency strong enough not only to curb the new excesses but gradually in the following decades to reform anomalies tolerated by the early-Victorian code. In diagrammatic terms one could say that from the 1790s onwards the force of prudery gradually represses the force of Fashion, that in the 1850s Fashion makes a comeback, that prudery then counter-attacks, apparently successfully in the sphere of manners where it enjoys majority support and unsuccessfully in literature where majority opinion is against it, but that in each area alike Fashion retains its power for the rest of the century. Given the parallel structure of the first two sections of these chapters the reader may, if he chooses, read them concurrently, rather than consecutively, by means of the subdivision numerals provided: the third section, dealing with the gradual imposition of new restraints in public manners and the gradual liberation from old restraints in literature, as the discrepancy in stringency between the early-Victorian social and literary codes was mitigated, inevitably do not show this kind of argumentative parallelism.

With the detailed analytical model of these two chapters as a background the argument of the next two, tracing the development of attitudes first to the ideal pure woman and then to the fallen woman, is rather simpler. Essentially what I shall be suggesting here is that the eighteenth century developed images of the pure and the fallen woman which were implicitly closer to empty moral gesture than rigorous moral commitment; that Evangelical propaganda of the 1790s and after fostered the acceptance of a new veneration for the good woman and a new abhorrence of the fallen; that by the 1850s these polarized images had undergone redefinition to the extent that they had now very much in common; and that these twin stereotypes then went into a gradual and parallel decline, partly because they were perverted by a resurgence of the empty moral gesture, by a return to the pre-Evangelical mentality, and partly because they became out-of-date, their idealism inappropriate to society's actual needs. Again, in diagrammatic terms, one could say that from the 1790s onwards the force of prudery progressively represses the image of woman encouraged by the force of Fashion, that in the 1850s Fashion makes a comeback, and that partly because of this, and partly because it gradually loses the support of majority opinion, the image of woman established by the force of prudery fades gradually away. Once more the reader may, if he chooses, follow the argumentative parallels in these two chapters concurrently, rather than consecutively, by use of the subdivision numerals.[1]

Skeletons are dry and lifeless objects at the best of times, and so, I fear, is the argumentative outline I have just offered. But it is also, I think, like the skeleton a necessary structural support. At any event I have rattled my bones now long enough: it is time to put some meat on them.

---

[1] The reader may also, if he wishes, cross-check references to significant dates: 1797, 1857, 1885 and 1895, for example, were years that produced noticeable changes in attitudes; and 1806, 1825 and 1869–70 were years that supplied interesting symptoms of underlying trends.

8

The Pattern of Sexual Manners

I 1750–1830

Eighteenth Century Decorum

1 IN 1822 SIR WALTER SCOTT, commenting on the social transformation of the previous sixty years or so, observed that the upper classes now no longer dared to 'insult decency in the public manner then tolerated; nor would our wildest debauchees venture to imitate the orgies of Medmenham Abbey.' [190] Scott's remark is both instructive and misleading. There had indeed been a big improvement in society's sexual manners, but not quite so big as Scott believed: for both the extent and the flagrancy of eighteenth century upper class immorality had been magnified by time. The legend of the Medmenham cult, for example, that Scott refers to, has been progressively whittled down by recent writers to the point where Medmenham would seem to have been less of a Hellfire Club than a country club, with pleasure gardens and facilities for sailing and fishing. [191] This last suggestion in a recent biography of Sir Francis Dashwood, the Abbey's owner, is slightly redolent of whitewash. But there is no question that Medmenham's infamy was largely the product of John Wilkes' political needs in the 1760s to blacken the character of his former friends and present enemies, Dashwood and the Earl of Sandwich; and that these two legendary satyrs were in fact both highly responsible statesmen and basically decent men. That Wilkes should choose this method to discredit them

indicates that society would not wink at the more exotic forms of vice. But indeed a large part of it, and not just Puritan enthusiasts, was unsympathetic to even quite mundane exhibitions of misconduct.

Society had in fact throughout the century become progressively more decorous in its manners. To some extent the change was due to the influence of middle-class sexual attitudes on the ruling aristocracy through such writers as the novelist Samuel Richardson. To some extent, after 1760, it was due to the influence of a pious and moral throne: the domestic example of George III and, within the confines of the court at least, the enforced ordinances of the devout Queen Charlotte. But the change came most of all perhaps from the aristocracy's independent redefinition of the nature of good breeding: its gradual acceptance of the idea that flagrant vice was a sign of inferior taste—an approach to ethics given philosophical foundation by writers like Lord Shaftesbury early in the century and its most developed practical demonstration in 1774 in *Lord Chesterfield's Letters to his Son*. The increase in propriety was admittedly very far from universal. As Chesterfield had himself remarked in 1755, a rake's progress in the fashionable world would often be helped, not hindered, by a flagrant display of sin:

> No vices nor immoralities whatever blast this fashionable character, but rather, on the contrary, dignify and adorn it: and what should banish a man from all society, recommends him in general to the best.
>
> He may, with great honour, starve the tradesmen, who by their industry supply not only his wants, but his luxury. He may debauch his friend's wife, daughter, or sister; he may, in short, undoubtedly gratify every appetite, passion, and interest, and scatter desolation around him if he be but ready for single combat, and a scrupulous observer of the moral obligations of a gamester. [192]

And when a few years later Vanity Fair took up French ideas of free love along with French fashions in dress, cuisine, literature and amusement, unchastity was for many a female rake an equally pressing social desideratum: 'there was hardly a young married lady of fashion', we are told, 'who did not think it almost a stain upon her reputation if she was not known as having cuckolded her husband.' [193] By the time of Scott's youth there were still numerous insults to public decency; but these excesses of Vanity Fair should not be taken as typifying general society. Even before Scott's birth a definite code of sexual respectability was in force, a code based, like the Chesterfieldian philosophy, not on morality so much as manners and decorum.

2 The first clause of the code was to the effect that flagrant unchastity in a woman disqualified her from appearing in good society. For a lady to stay respectable she must preserve the appearance of virtue. The world might guess; but it must never *know*, even if this involved adopting Nelson's strategy at Copenhagen. A woman with a past, to whose frailty a blind eye could not be turned, in the case, for example, of proven adultery or an extra-connubial pregnancy, though she might be acceptable within the limits of Vanity Fair, would in the best society be in danger of social ostracism. And a woman with a present, in the case, for example, of openly illicit cohabitation, would be lucky to escape oblivion even in Vanity Fair. She might live comfortably enough in town provided she accepted the confines of the demi-monde. But the expected and sensible course was exile on the Continent or in the obscurity of the countryside: in this way the children of the liaison, if not the mother, might be respectable. Mrs Polly Humphrey who enjoyed a discreet country life with Lord Chancellor Thurlow for thirty years was never socially acceptable, but of her three daughters one married a peer and another a baronet. Martha Ray, whose life with Sandwich was tragically cut short after nineteen years by a deranged, homicidal clergyman, was never respectable, but of her bastards who reached maturity one was an admiral, another a distinguished lawyer, and the other the

wife of an M.P. An anecdote about Martha Ray, who besides keeping house for Sandwich and bearing his children was the principal attraction at his musical evenings at Hinchingbrooke, illustrates vividly the system of decorum on which the respectable code was based. An observer commented:

> Miss Ray in her situation was a pattern of discretion; for when a lady of rank, between one of the acts of the Oratorio advanced to converse with her, she expressed her embarrassment; and Lord Sandwich, turning privately to a friend, said 'As you are well acquainted with that lady, I wish you would give her a hint that there is a boundary line in my family that I do not wish to see exceeded; such a trespass might occasion the overthrow of all our music meetings.' [194]

So much for the legendary satyr of Medmenham Abbey.

A respectable reputation then, even before the birth of Mrs Grundy, was essential for acceptance in good society. But only for women: Sandwich and Thurlow were not even embarrassed, let alone ruined, by acknowledging their illegitimate children. A gentleman would only be ruined by an exposed moral lapse if this were of a gross and perverted nature. In 1784, for example, Charles James Fox when charged with having had Pitt assaulted, could furnish the alibi that he had been in bed at the time with Mrs Armistead, who was ready to substantiate the fact on oath, [195] whereas William Beckford suffered eclipse and persecution for mere suspicion of homosexual practices. And yet in well-bred society it was preferred that gentlemen too should observe the proprieties, like Sandwich at his musical evenings, or like Dashwood in his amours (it is truly remarkable how little is known of them, and Dashwood was one of the most open and candid men of the age). [196] For a gentleman to be flagrantly immoral, to flaunt a mistress in town, to be the cause of a public scandal, of a divorce or crim. con. action, was at best bad form and at worst, where the woman involved was a lady, a damaging blow to his honour and prestige. How a gentleman

1. Sea-bathing at Scarborough, 1813 (Rowlandson)

2. 'Six of One and Half-a-Dozen of the Other.' From *Punch* 1856

3. Adah Menken as Mazeppa

BONUM EST HOMINI SVGVM
IN JVVENTVTE FERRE

4. One of Kingsley's illustrations for the 'Life of St Elizabeth of Hungary', his wedding present to his wife

6. A penile ring, to be used by sufferers from spermatorrhoea

5. The supposed effects of masturbation

7. Drawing by E. Gertrude Thomson for Lewis Carroll's 'Three Sunsets' 1898

8. Lola Montez

9. 'The Great Social Evil' by John Leech.
TIME:— Midnight. A Sketch not a Hundred
Miles from the Haymarket.
Bella. "AH! FANNY! HOW LONG HAVE
YOU BEEN *GAY*?"

10. Skittles, the queen of the
'horsebreakers'

11. 'The Champion Wife' and her erring husband

12. 'A Merry Night at Cremorne'

13. The Sistine Madonna by Raphael

of the best society was expected to behave is nicely shown in a letter written to a friend in 1790 by the first wife of Richard Brinsley Sheridan, explaining that her marriage had almost come to breaking point through Sheridan's misconduct and indiscretion. [197] From this letter it is clear firstly that society would have penalized Sheridan if his affair with Lady Duncannon had not been hushed up (he would have been 'an object of Ridicule and Abuse to all the World'), and secondly that what hurt his wife most was not his infidelities so much as his atrocious lack of propriety, his imprudence in simultaneously just missing a public scandal and actually precipitating a semi-public scene (being caught *in flagrante* with a governess)— she had been upset most by his bad manners, not his morals, and now that the potential and actual embarrassments were over, she was happy to dismiss his infidelities as 'vagaries'.

3 It was this amoral basis to the code of polite respectability that the moralists of the 1780s and early 1790s most attacked. Amoral sexual decorum, it was argued, like nominal Christianity, was in fact more dangerous to virtue than open profligacy and godlessness: it concealed moral deformities with elegance and attraction. Wesley's *Arminian Magazine* (September 1789) talked of 'the deluge of depravity which has been pouring in upon us' (XII, 496), and in the same year the Duke of Grafton, a reformed rake, of the very great increase within the last twenty years of every description of vice; [198] but by depravity and vice they meant principally the dereliction of civic duties like honesty and reverence—the consequence of servants being set bad examples by the religious and moral apathy of their employers. As the lessons of the French Revolution began to be absorbed, as the upper classes started to see the importance of commanding the masses' respect and of sedating subversive tendencies with piety and moral zeal, the warnings of these moralists found a very receptive audience: Hannah More's *Thoughts on the Importance of the Manners of the Great to General Society* (1788) reached its eighth edition in 1792 and her *Estimate*

of the Religion of the Fashionable World (1791) reached its fifth by 1793. 'Reformation', it was claimed, 'must begin with the GREAT, or it will never be effectual. Their example is the fountain from whence the vulgar draw their habits, actions, and characters. To expect to reform the poor while the opulent are corrupt, is to throw odours into a stream while the springs are poisoned.' [199]

~ The effect of this agitation on the manners of the great does not seem immediately very appreciable. The tone of aristocratic morals in the 1790s would seem to be set by the notorious roistering of the royal princes or the extraordinary situation in Devonshire House, where the three legitimate children of the Duke and Duchess shared the nursery and schoolroom with the Duke's illegitimate children by the Duchess' dearest friend and house-guest, Lady Elizabeth Foster. But in fact society had, if anything, tightened its code of decorum. What is interesting about the anomaly of Devonshire House is that propriety was stringently observed: the illegitimate children of Lady Elizabeth, and a bastard son of the Duchess by Lord Grey, were all born in absolute secrecy abroad, [200] and though the paternity of Lady Elizabeth's children was probably plain to the Devonshires' friends, great pains were taken to conceal it from the children themselves and to avoid gossip in the world at large. [201] In a similar way Nelson's bastard daughter by Lady Hamilton was born in a state of elaborate secrecy and remained ignorant until after her mother's death that she was anything more than their adopted child. [202] A lady's reputation was perhaps of greater delicacy than before. Certainly Nelson was most concerned by his cohabitation with Lady Hamilton despite the covering presence of her husband: he went to the length, we are told, of having her avow with him the innocence of their relationship before the altar of their church. And though a gentleman's reputation, as in the case of the royal princes, still enjoyed its privilege, discretion was perhaps more essential than before. The Prince of Wales, for example, never set up house with Mrs Fitzherbert, and Beau

Brummell learnt to his cost the error of openly referring to the nature of their liaison. [203] When the Duke of Clarence first began living with the actress Mrs Jordan they were frequently seen together in the theatre and other places, but soon hostile remark in the press and personal insult to the lady obliged the prince to retire with her to the countryside, where he remained almost in exile for the following twenty years. [204]

The manners of the great then, while not flagrantly permissive, still retained the amoral basis to which the moralists were objecting. And it was clear that they would continue to do so while nominal religion and moral apathy prevailed throughout society. For it was not just the great who were lacking in moral zeal: their code of decorum rather than ethics was underpinned now as before by a great deal of indulgence in middle-class society. Indeed, moralists claimed, the middle classes were becoming progressively more lax in moral standards: 'Everywhere we may actually trace the effects of increasing wealth and luxury, in banishing one by one the habits, and new-modelling the phraseology of stricter times; and in diffusing throughout the middle ranks those relaxed morals and dissipated manners, which were formerly confined to the highest classes of society.' The writer is William Wilberforce, the book his very influential *Practical View of the Prevailing Religious System of Professed Christians in the Higher and Middle Classes in this Country, Contrasted with Real Christianity* (1797), pp. 376–7. In the same year another Evangelical, the Rev. Thomas Gisborne, in another much-read book argued that the middle classes in London were particularly susceptible to contamination by the moral laxity of upper-class manners: susceptible

> . . . by means of the softening appellations which fashion, enlisted in the service of profligacy, has devised for the most flagrant breaches of the laws of God and man. Hence not only among the unprincipled, but in virtuous families, among women of modesty, and by women of modesty, conversation is not unfrequently turned to topics and incidents, of which, to use the language of

an Apostle, 'it is a shame even to speak'. . . . The evil now in question contaminates the country also; but, though not restricted to the metropolis, it is there most prevalent. [205]

4 This year, 1797, was crucial year in British moral history. It was a year, we have seen, of peculiar nervous stress: of fears of a French invasion, of rebellion in Ireland, mutinies in the Fleet, and to cap everything a panic about an insidious foreign conspiracy to undermine religion and morality. It was a year, in short, when sexual subversion seemed for many the greatest peril facing the nation. From this time the propaganda of the moralists took on a new emphasis: a conviction that though nominal religion and amoral manners were terrible enough, there was now the added danger of open vice in fashionable circles, that alongside the traditional decorum of the aristocratic code there was now in Vanity Fair a resurgence of flagrant depravity. The pressures and dangers of war meant for the moral conservative anxiety and alarm; for the fashionably irreverent they meant glamour and excitement, a kind of holiday time of heedless gaiety and reckless self-indulgence, a mood in which it was especially dashing to espouse the fashions of dangerous France. 'The levity and licentiousness of French manners', noted the *Annual Register* in 1798, explaining the increasing propriety of the bulk of the upper classes, 'had certainly made an alarming progress in the higher, and, what were called, the fashionable circles; from whence they must pass on to the lower orders.' (p. 229) Must pass on, indeed, the moralists feared, when affluence and class mobility guaranteed a flow of arrivistes eager to embrace the latest fads. In 1801 an energetic pamphleteer John Bowles, in his *Reflections at the Conclusion of the War*, expressed a common anxiety that peace with France meant only more contamination, and in the following year he developed his argument in some *Remarks on Modern Female Manners, as Distinguished by Indifference to Character, and Indecency of Dress*. His claim was that fashionable manners had woefully deteriorated (an interesting contrast to

Scott's view twenty years later on England's steady improvement since the debauchery of the 1760s): in no way was this
more obvious than in the social acceptance in higher circles of
women of known profligacy and in the adoption of French
indecencies in feminine couture.

As England entered the nineteenth century the sexual manners
of Vanity Fair were often ostentatiously permissive, in marked
contrast to the traditional decorum of well-bred aristocracy.
'To see our young gentlemen cutting a swell, as the fashionable phrase is,' complained the *Oracle* in 1800, 'and adopting
the manners and language of brothel bullies, for that's the go;
to behold our amiable young ladies striving to rival in appearance and knowingness the nocturnal trampers of the Strand, is
undoubtedly a very edifying prospect.' [206] These were the
years of the great courtesan, of Mary Anne Clarke, the ex-
mistress of a stonemason, now living in splendour in Gloucester
Place on £1,000 a year from the Duke of York; of Harriette
Wilson and her sisters holding court in Hyde Park or the opera
to a cluster of adoring young noblemen from the army and
universities. But this affront to respectability was less pervasive
than it might seem. The demi-monde lived within definite
limitations: Harriette Wilson might be the kept woman,
mistress or friend of important noblemen associating with
the highest in the land, but she herself would not be invited to
mix freely in their circles. Vanity Fair too was more decorous
than the minority of extremists would suggest. It is true that
disreputable women were often given acceptance: Harriette's
younger sister Sophia, for example, after her marriage to Lord
Berwick. But society as a whole retained its embargo on fallen
women. Lady Holland, who had eloped with Lord Holland
when already married, borne their first son out of wedlock, and
yet gradually won acceptance through the strength of her connections, was admittedly something of an exception. But one
should note that the Hollands had made some gesture to
decorum (they had taken care that the bastard was not born in
Holland House [207]). And for all their continuing discretion

both were subjected to wounding slights: Lord Holland was much embarrassed when the Lords in 1800 against his counsel decided to make it illegal for divorcees to marry their co-respondents (the Bill was later defeated in the Commons); and Lady Holland had to be circumspect when making up her guest lists to avoid the humiliation of a snub. Mrs Armistead similarly, who had been a prominent woman of the town before living with and finally wedding Fox, threw a successful ball in 1806 through her husband's popularity and connections, but again one should note the nervous apprehensions of her friends beforehand. The significance of ostentatious licence in a section of Vanity Fair lies less in its extent and influence among the great than in what it represented: the fact that a large section of the middle as well as upper classes had still not yet been jolted from moral apathy by the moralists, that the activities of notorious men and women were a constant source of indulgent, prurient gossip in the press, that there was even a certain amount of imitation throughout the bourgeoisie of their raffish styles of deportment and of dress.

Middle Class Pressure for Reform

5 'The levity and dissipation of the middle ranks,' wrote the Evangelical Mrs West in 1806, 'are the singular and alarming characteristics of the present times. The middle classes, where temperance, diligence, and propriety used to reside, the favourite abode of rectitude, good sense, and sound piety, have undergone a change within the last fifty years which must startle every considerate mind.' [208] But if much of the middle class was still enjoying too many of the comforts of affluence to be alarmed by the moralists' propaganda, a very large element was now firmly committed to the cause of virtue. The Evangelical Mary Sherwood wrote of the picture of England she received in 1809 when she had been in India four years: 'From what we heard then we supposed that since we had left England, the cool green island had become a land of saints.' [209] And in 1811 the *Christian Observer*, celebrating its tenth

anniversary, remarked on the renaissance of militant moral commitment through the land: 'The circumstances with which we are most forcibly struck is the different aspect which the Christian world exhibits at the present moment from that which it bore at the commencement of our course. Nor is its aspect altered only; it is improved beyond the fondest dreams of a visionary. If one could suppose some calm, calculating Christian Observer to open his eyes, after a ten years sleep, on the passing scene, would he not find himself in a new creation?' [210] Part of the reason for this rapid growth in moral earnestness was the growing impact of Evangelicalism on the beliefs of the upper classes, the impact that had begun in the 1790s with their sudden concern for moral piety in the masses. But another vital factor, especially in the lower middle classes, was the very affluence and class mobility that was stimulating the moral apathy of Fashion: the middle classes had received large numbers of prospering Christians from the proletariat beneath them. The development of Sunday schools in the eighteenth century had exempted many workers from the constraints of manual labour: with their improved education they became clerks and shopmen, factory superintendents and overseers, often schoolmasters, merchants, and industrialists; and they carried their sobriety and religion into their superior social station. The phenomenon was particularly marked among Methodists with their emphasis on industry and frugality, their system in commerce of favouring each other with capital and custom but discriminating against the ungodly and immoral. By 1815 one person in thirty-four in the nation was a Methodist, and their influence was enormous.

In the changing social climate some members of aristocratic society were becoming understandably sensitive to an increasing hostility to the state of their morality. Their concern was aroused especially by the Mrs Clarke scandal of 1809, when the mistress of the Duke of York, the second heir to the throne and the nation's commander-in-chief, was accused of using his influence in the sale of military appointments, and the Duke himself was charged with complicity. For seven weeks, while Mrs Clarke and her associates were examined before the Commons, the country could talk of little else, and amongst other vituperative expressions of disgust at royal licence effigies of the prince were burnt in Suffolk and Yorkshire. George III, for all his mental vagaries, had wit enough to see the dangers of such a scandal in an age of revolution: 'This is the severest blow to our family since they left Germany. The people will bear with me because I am old, but they [my family] will suffer for it.' [211] On top of the pressure from the Evangelicals against aristocratic moral laxity there was now the threat of radical demagogues exploiting the public's moral improvement as a political tool. It was this accession of virtuous indignation by the left wing, who had never themselves been noted for any remarkable degree of chastity, that seriously inhibited the moralists' propaganda. Undue exposure of aristocratic licence might do more harm than good, weakening the authority of the governing class as well as setting the masses a bad example. Thus it was only one Evangelical journal (and this a provincial one) made an attack on the prince by name. In fact the political dangers of this scandal were shown very shortly to be more apparent than real. In 1809 the prince was acquitted of corruption but felt obliged by public outcry to resign as Commander-in-Chief. In 1811 he was reappointed and, such had been the reaction in his favour in the interim when the machinations of his exposers came to light, his reinstatement was accompanied with a good deal of public approbation.

6 Nevertheless the lesson had been learned, and it was only a question of time before aristocratic manners took on a new degree of strictness. That they were not to do so immediately was partly because of the advent of the Regency. The Prince Regent, for all his intelligence in some respects, thought the best answer to public censure of his morals was to imprison Leigh Hunt and his brother. It is true he was unable to reverse the progress of decency in any dramatic way: he was not

allowed, for example, by Queen Charlotte to discontinue his father's practice of banning divorcees from court (Lady Holland was excluded from his inaugural fête at Carlton House), and the Queen in 1815 went to the lengths of ostracizing her new daughter-in-law, the German wife of the Duke of Cumberland, because of widespread rumours of her immorality. But if the Regent did not produce a dramatic deterioration in aristocratic manners, he certainly both impeded their general improvement and encouraged the minority element in Vanity Fair to new excesses of ostentatious laxity. The excitements of war, we have seen, brought for some fashionables a heedless irreverence and rage for pleasure. The coming of peace, like the end of another war almost exactly a century later, produced yet fresh and greater extravagances, a reckless carnival made the more pleasurable, as in the 1920s, by the existence of serious post-war problems—the mass unemployment of a peacetime economy aggravating already smouldering political unrest. This mood of wilful hedonism, of a reckless readiness to shock, is well illustrated in the characters of Byron and Caroline Lamb. With the Regent as head of state and a degree of sexual permissiveness open in Vanity Fair but touching the middle classes too, the flamboyant nature of their intrigue was only to be expected. In fact the lady went too far: after Lady Heathcote's ball, where she caused a great scene and apparently tried to kill herself, and still more the publication of her novel *Glenarvon* (1816), in which she exposed the whole affair to the general public, not even the forgiveness of her husband, the future Prime Minister Melbourne, nor the distinction of her family could save her from social ruin.

But though one element of society seemed more licentious than ever, the social tone in general was improving, the temper of the age was becoming more austere. 'It appears to me', wrote Hannah More in 1818, 'that the two classes of character are more decided than they were; the wicked seem more wicked, and the good, better.' [212] Whilst Fashion was having its fling, a new moral seriousness was sweeping through society.

The cabinets of Lord Liverpool, for example, as David Spring points out, [213] had few, if any 'Regency' characters in them. Some of his ministers, like Vansittart and Harrowby, had Evangelical connections, and Liverpool himself, if not an enthusiast, was very much on the side of sobriety and respectability. The universities too had undergone an extraordinary change in manners. In 1792 Francis Jeffrey had claimed it was possible to acquire nothing in Oxford except praying and drinking. [214] But in 1812 the Earl of Dudley wrote of his astonishment at the improvement that had taken place, one, he considered, of the most important of his time. [215] And in 1816 Coleridge was struck by 'the late and present condition of manners and intellect among the young men of Oxford and Cambridge, the manly sobriety of demeanour, the submission to the routine of study in almost all, and the zeal in the pursuit of knowledge and academic distinction in a large and increasing number'. [216]

By 1820 and the coronation of George IV the temper of the country was less inclined than ever to tolerate flagrant immorality in its rulers. And when Queen Caroline, who in 1815 had gone abroad to escape the persecution of the Regent, returned to demand her rightful position by his side, the lesson of the Mrs Clarke scandal was presented with redoubled clarity. The Queen's arrival was the signal for widespread demonstrations in her favour, an increasingly sober people eager to believe the best of her and the worst of her dissolute husband, to make her a symbol of purity in antithesis to the permissive corruption of the previous decade. The radicals inevitably took up her cause, and in the ensuing atmosphere of mob violence and anti-monarchist propaganda the aristocracy not surprisingly took alarm: Lady Jerningham, four days after Caroline's arrival, wrote that the country was nearer to disaster than it had been since the days of Charles I—a fear that gathered momentum as for a whole summer the country was in a state of virtual emergency. The King, hoping for a divorce, had the Queen arraigned before the Lords to answer for her adulterous misconduct while abroad, but the whole affair rebounded on his head. Notwithstanding the weight of evidence against her the people's mood was such that the Government at length declined to prosecute further. Their withdrawal was greeted joyously as a triumph for public morality: 'All here is ecstasy,' Macaulay reported from Cambridge. ' "Thank God, the country is saved," is written on every face and echoed by every voice.' [217] George IV, in short, was a sad anachronism, doomed to the scorn and hisses of an increasingly moral people.

7 The old order, however, of aristocratic sexual manners was not yet dead. Known immorality in a public man did not yet herald his social ruin. It is true that, when in 1824 and 1825 Harriette Wilson sought to blackmail a lot of the gentlemen who were to figure in her *Memoirs*, a great many were desperate to avoid the scandal of public exposure. But though many paid her off and others held panic-meetings in London clubs to organize legal protection, we should recall also the Duke of Wellington's legendary response of 'Publish and be damned'. In 1825 public scandal might be embarrassing. But it was not yet socially fatal. As Macaulay later remarked of this year, 'men, whose gallantries were universally known, and had been legally proved, filled some of the highest offices in the state, and in the army, presided at the meetings of religious and benevolent institutions—were the delight of every society, and the favourites of the multitude.' [218]

Nevertheless there was clearly now an ethical vigour in society, pressing increasingly the cause of moral reform. 1825 was also the year when Hannah More remarked: 'It is a singular satisfaction to me that I have lived to see such an increase in genuine religion among the higher classes of society. Mr Wilberforce and I agree that where we knew one instance of it thirty years ago, there are now a dozen or more.' [219] The Evangelical moralists, who thirty years before had complained of middle-class moral apathy, could now rejoice in a great deal of middle class moral dynamism. They could rejoice too, if their observation was sufficiently objective, in the vast improvement in the working classes' morality and manners. The middle class as a whole retained its nervous image of proletarian licentiousness, but close observers saw a very different picture. Francis Place, himself of humble birth, and with voluminous records in hundreds of scrapbooks of England's social changes, wrote in 1829: 'I am certain I risk nothing when I assert that more good has been done to the people in the last thirty years than in the three preceding centuries; that during this period they have become wiser, better, more frugal, more honest, more respectable, more virtuous than they ever were before.' [220] A large section of the proletariat was still quite free from the bourgeois pattern of manners. But an even larger section was ready to support the middle classes' cause of social purity, and ready to rejoice when a new king and a reformed Parliament would mean the replacement of the old aristocratic sexual code with a new and more stringent model.

II 1830–1870

Early-Victorian Decorum
8 A writer in 1870 looking back on the period before the Great Exhibition of 1851 commented: 'Never had a nation been so respectable as was England during the twenty years which preceded that event. Our Court, especially during the latter but larger portion of the time, had been a very pattern of royal propriety; and the members of our aristocracy, most of whom in their quest of happiness, are by no means independent of princes' favour, encouraged the cause of virtue by paying it at least an external homage. '[221] David Spring has argued interestingly that the improvement in the aristocracy's manners by 1830 was due in some measure to the restoration of its own traditional self-disciplined code of conduct; to a reaffirmation

of the traditional structure of authority in the aristocratic family. [222] But it is clear that there was a good deal of 'external homage' to the cause of virtue in direct response to middle-class opinion: 'Our men of rank', said the *Morning Chronicle* (1 October 1827), 'may occasionally *assume* a virtue which they have not, they may sometimes be greater hypocrites than their forefathers were; but hypocrisy is, at all events, an homage offered to public opinion, and supposes the existence of a fear of the people.' (p. 3) And it is clear too that 'the very pattern of royal propriety' that came in 1830 with William IV's accession also reflected the existence of a fear of the people. For William out of deference to public opinion from the very first dissociated himself quite deliberately from the morals of his notorious predecessor. His German wife Queen Adelaide, who from her experience in Europe had been made acutely sensitive to the monarchy's vulnerability if its sins were left unchecked, [223] was even more demonstrative. 'Queen Adelaide,' wrote Greville, 'is a prude, and will not let the ladies come *décolletées* to her parties. George IV, who liked ample expanses of that sort, would not let them be covered.' [224] King William, in consequence, despite the known immorality of his former years and the clutch of Fitzclarences cluttering up the court, came to be much loved by his people as a model of domestic propriety.

In 1832 the Reform Act strengthened the people's hand still further in their call for a purification of the manners of the great. 'We may perceive everywhere, indeed,' noted Bulwer Lytton the following year, 'that Fashion has received a material shock. . . . A graver aspect settles on the face of society.' [225] The cause of virtue was strengthened yet again in 1837 when a pure young queen succeeded to the throne. Her insistence on spotless character in all applicants for court office, together with the virginal modesty of her demeanour, helped accelerate the improvement in sexual manners of the nation's public men. This at first sight may not seem consonant with the facts: both Lord Conyngham, as Lord Chamberlain, and

Lord Uxbridge, as the Lord Steward, immediately installed
their mistresses as housekeepers in Buckingham Palace; in 1837
a future Prime Minister, Disraeli, and a past Lord Chancellor,
Lyndhurst, both narrowly escaped involvement in a divorce
suit against Mrs Sykes; and two or three years later the
Secretary of State for Home Affairs, Lord Palmerston, was
caught red-handed in Windsor Castle bursting into the
bedroom of one of Her Majesty's ladies-in-waiting. But in fact
even those not yet abreast with the changing situation were
shortly to become so: it is Disraeli's Mr Tadpole who points
out, 'We must go with the times, my Lord. A virtuous middle
class shrinks with horror from French actresses; and the
Wesleyans—the Wesleyans must be considered;, [226] and
Palmerston learnt to his cost the error of outraging royal
propriety—his escapade at Windsor was the foundation of the
court's long hostility towards him. [227] Even before the
Queen's accession in fact a new code of manners had emerged,
reflecting the impact of middle-class opinion and the influence
of the court, a new, more stringent code that required only the
enthronement of Victoria to complete its power and scope.

   The first feature of this code was that exposed immorality in
a public man was no longer a forgivable lapse in taste, but a
fatal moral crime. Melbourne, it is true, escaped unscathed
from his appearance in the Norton divorce case in 1836, but
only because the evidence against him was ludicrously inadequate. If he had been found guilty of adultery with Mrs
Norton, it is very unlikely that his career could have weathered
the storm (he had in fact, prior to the trial, been willing to
resign the premiership). *The Times*, 24 June 1836, acting as
spokesman for middle-class morality, accepted the verdict but
added that any man who could waste his time on such 'con-
temptible and unmeaning frivolities' had sufficiently demonstrated (quoting the *Standard*) 'his utter unfitness for the station
that he held'. (p. 3) The second feature of the new code was
that the definition of decorum in the case of women was much
stricter than before. In 1790 Mrs Sheridan was not too

discomforted by the thought of an amicable separation from her husband; but by the Victorian era desertion of a husband, even a bad one, was as scandalous as earlier being divorced had been: not only was Lady Holland, forty years after her original offence, still not allowed to be received by Queen Victoria, even the innocent party to a suit was debarred from court until 1887. Melbourne in 1836 was quite justified in warning Mrs Norton that even if she were cleared of adultery her name would be tarnished and her social life blighted. Conjugal purity was not enough: it was improper now even to be the occasion of an open marital breakdown, it was improper now even to occasion unfounded rumours of adultery. The new definition of decorum is well illustrated in the case of Lady Blessington. Twenty years before Victoria's accession Lady Blessington, who prior to her marriage had lived in adultery for some years with a certain Captain Jenkins, had begun to win acceptance in aristocratic society by the charm of her attractions as a hostess. But rumours of her relationship with Count D'Orsay, which seemed to be confirmed when he was married to her step-daughter, wrecked her progress towards rehabilitation. The visitors to her salon were almost entirely male, and the middle-class publisher, Samuel Carter Hall, who himself believed in the purity of her conduct, described the rationale of this virtual ostracism: 'It is not enough for a woman to *be* pure; she must *seem* pure to be so; her conscience may be as white as snow, but if she give scope to slander and weight to calumny her offence is great. She taints those who are influenced by example, and renders vice excusable in the estimate of those whose dispositions incline to evil.'[1]

---

[1] Samuel Carter Hall, *Retrospect of a Long Life* (1883) I, 113. Of course much of the hostility to Lady Blessington came more from jealousy and malice than from high moral principle. There is poignant irony in the many sermons she delivers to the heroine of her *Victims of Society* (1837), the imprudent subject of much ill-natured gossip—sermons about the need to seem as well as be pure that are identical in import to the remarks I quote from Hall.

9 With a new social code of this degree of stringency the tone of upper class life was becoming increasingly more sober. The rips and rakes, the bucks and bloods of Vanity Fair, who had formerly crowded the social scene, were a small minority by the thirties, their haunts out of fashion and replaced by the more sedate pleasures of London club life. In 1831 the prospectus of Surtees' *New Sporting Magazine* announced that its pages would be closed to such 'low and demoralizing pursuits' as prize-fighting, bull-baiting and cock-fighting; and four years later bull-baiting and bear-baiting were made illegal. The great race meetings, such as Doncaster and Ascot, declined in patronage; the gambling craze of the twenties subsided, the Government closing Crockford's and similar institutions in 1845; and heavy drinking went out of fashion—according to Palmerston in 1844, 'the greatest topers are those who take half-a-dozen glasses'. [228] In 1855 Thackeray in *The Newcomes* looked back nostalgically at a more robust generation, when the young Earl of Kew drank hard, kept racehorses, gambled furiously and did who knows what besides: 'He began life time enough to enjoy certain pleasures from which our young aristocracy of the present day seem, alas! to be cut off. So much more peaceable and polished do we grow; so much does the spirit of the age appear to equalize the ranks; so strongly has the good sense of society, to which, in the end, gentlemen of the very highest fashion must bow, put its veto upon practices and amusements with which our fathers were familiar.' (p. 108) The most indecorous practices and amusements to which young gentlemen now aspired were usually little more than bonneting policemen, fighting cabmen or running off with door-knockers. Much has been written of the boisterous, table-thumping bawdry of their supper-rooms. But in fact these clubs were mostly in obscure alleys and cellars far from the public gaze, sometimes requiring almost a pass-word for admittance, and men who patronized them would not boast of the fact in polite society. Much has been written of Renton Nicholson's Judge and Jury Club, founded in 1841, where the entertainment was

enlivened with both *poses plastiques* and Nicholson's speciality, bawdy mock-trials of salacious crimes and crim. con. actions. But one of the reasons for Nicholson's long immunity from prosecution was his discretion: the majority of Londoners were either unaware of the club's existence or deceived about its nature—from Nicholson's autobiography of 1860 and from the club's publicity he quotes, its activities would all seem as innocent as charades around the fireplace. Much has been written of the flourishing night life of the fifties, of gay times with gay ladies in the Argyll Rooms, Kate Hamilton's and Cremorne. But in fact these haunts, though more public than the supper-rooms before them, were also, as Dr Acton strongly emphasized, in general far more decorous: music and dancing in displacing largely all-male sedentary drinking had brought with them in most cases order, restraint, sobriety and refinement. [229]

The Beginnings of a Counter-trend

10 By the end of the 1850s, however, a counter-trend to this developing decorum became visible. It arose largely, one suspects, from society's enforced recognition of the amount of vice flourishing still beneath these decorous improvements. In 1857, we have seen, there was a great deal of press agitation about the extent and flagrancy of the Social Evil. In 1857 too the new Divorce Act was passed, and there was in consequence much discussion about the health of the marriage-system, a discussion and scepticism that grew proportionately with the steady flow of unsavoury divorce suits reported in the papers. Previously prostitution had been a public shame and divorce a private shame that had not been frequent matters of general discourse. Now suddenly immorality was recognized as a pervasive social fact: the detailed modes in which prostitution was conducted, the varying grades of brothels and harlots, their relative costs, pleasures and disadvantages, the detailed modes in which marital intrigues might be conducted, the tactics and subterfuges shown in the diaries and letters of adulterers and adulteresses, these were becoming an open feature of social life.

In this new climate of overtly recognized vice it was perhaps inevitable that the high-class courtesan should begin to make her comeback. Since the heyday of Harriette Wilson in the opening years of the century the demi-monde had kept itself pretty well under cover. But now glamorous ladies of pleasure were coming once more into the eye of Fashion. Escorted by their noblemen protectors they began to figure prominently at the opera and the races, and more especially in Hyde Park and the hunting field, where their skill in driving and riding earned them the title of 'pretty horsebreakers'. *The Times* (17 July 1860) quoted the *Morning Post*'s complaints of the shameless way in which young men openly associated with these harlots: 'We see them descend from their mother's box at the Opera to exchange persiflage with notorious individuals—we detect them rising from their chair in Rotten-row, by the side of Lais and Aspasia, to chat with Lady Alice or Miss Fanny over the rail— . . . Such things were not done even under the dissolute sway of the Regency; they certainly should not be done in the respectable reign of Victoria.' (p. 9) This resurgence of permissiveness in the world of Vanity Fair caused inevitable concern to the morally conservative already distressed by the publicity about prostitution and divorce.

'Vice,' commented *Tait's Edinburgh Magazine* in February 1858, 'unhappily, has only in the eyes of some people, to become fashionable, and it becomes venial.' (n.s. XXV, 110) This alarm at the erosion of sexual standards, the fear indeed of England's moral decline and fall, is the more readily comprehensible when we consider the strain being imposed on traditional sanctions against immorality by the growth of religious scepticism. With Darwin seeming to invite man to rule his life on the basis of animal amorality, with books like *Essays and Reviews* seeming to shake the citadel of religion from within, one can appreciate, as England entered the 1860s, the effect of 'pretty horsebreakers' on worried moral conservatives.

On 18 January 1861 the *Record*, prompted by readers' complaints about the growing laxity of society's sexual manners, took up an unequivocal position: 'It is high time that a faithful and uncompromising opposition be offered to this awful plague which is assuming such proportions. . . . There must be no hesitation or squeamishness in the matter. Men who are known to live in open sin should be first remonstrated with, and then proscribed from society, if they disregard the solemn admonition. Young men whose habits are degrading must not be welcomed to our houses, because their manners are fashionable and their conversation sparkling.' (p. 2) Solemn admonitions notwithstanding, in only a few months London fashionable life took on a yet more alarming character with the public début of Catherine Walters, better known as Skittles or Anonyma, the most famous of the horsebreakers. Skittles quickly set new styles for the demi-monde. Respectable women of Fashion too were not slow to copy the *élan* of her slang, dress, deportment and equipage, nor to pester male acquaintances for details of her origin, residence and activities. She was in short the cynosure of the hour. Her portrait figured widely in the windows of photographers and fashionable modistes and milliners. It figured too, more sensationally, in the Royal Academy exhibition of 1861 in a painting by Sir Edwin Landseer, a painting that was one of the two most popular of the year. A letter to *The Times* on 27 June left no doubt about the identity of the sitter, and it left no doubt also about the power and influence now exerted by the courtesans. It was written supposedly by 'Seven Belgravian Mothers' complaining that they were unable to marry off their daughters because fashionable men found the horsebreakers more attractive. A writer signing himself 'Beau Jolais' joined the discussion on a rather more serious note: the horsebreakers, he claimed, were not only more glamorous, sophisticated and amusing than the average fashionable miss, they also, in his experience, made for their protectors perfectly decorous, and much more comfortable and economical homes. The domestic virtues of the courtesan quickly became something of a cliché. In the *National Review*

(April 1862) the highly respectable W. R. Greg argued that, for some years past, society had grown both duller and more expensive in its habits whilst the demi-monde had gone quite the other way: 'as the one has grown stupider and costlier, the other has grown more attractive, more decorous, and more easy. The ladies *there* are now often as clever and amusing, usually more beautiful, and not unfrequently (in external demeanour at least) as modest, as their rivals in more recognized society.' (XIV, 453)

As the demi-monde flourished, the morally staid became increasingly alarmed. The day after *The Times* published its letter from the 'Seven Belgravian Mothers', the *Daily Telegraph* had scoffed at the idea of the nation's moral decline. But a few months later, on 13 December, its tone was very different:

> So surely as the physician, listening at the stethoscope, can catch the muffled sound which means death, so certainly the philosopher and the publicist may foretell the ruin of the country if the fatal tone at its heart cannot be arrested. It means that marriage is being set aside, that lust is being written for love, that fashion is compiling on sand a new version of the laws which God wrote on stone. . . . Our journals are full of causes which shame the courts, our streets are full of a sad sisterhood whose misery will weigh us down like a millstone. Elegant writers do not blush to talk the slang of the 'demi-monde'; leading journals doubtfully balance the 'wife' with the 'horsebreaker': and a famous opera employs the Divine strains of music and the genius of great artists to make a consumptive harlot a fit spectacle for honest women. In circles to which the people look up it is voted slow to deserve a wife by chastity, and to keep a wife by manly work, which God's law and Nature's enjoin. . . . The correct thing, now, is a boudoir at Brompton or St. John's Wood. (p. 4)

This last concern, the time-honoured one about the circles the people looked up to, the fear that the tastes of Vanity Fair would become diffused throughout society, was a commonplace of the sixties. On 19 August 1865 the *Saturday Review*, discussing the freedom with which gentlemen paraded their im-

morality at the Opera or in the Park and the indifference of the
fair sex at their doing so, remarked, 'It is possible that at present
this evil may, for the most part, be confined to the "higher
classes", or a section of them, but social manners soon spread.
Tyburnia treads on the heels of Belgravia, and Bloomsbury
presses close on Marylebone, and Islington and Hackney must
follow the course of fashion.' (XX, 232)

11 In fact, as far as any general deterioration in social manners
was concerned, the alarm of anxious moralists was unfounded.
A large section of the middle classes was resistant to the
pernicious example of Fashion, for the fear of sex remained a
powerful influence in the land. The spirit of asceticism, the
class-conscious concern for genteel respectability, the alarmist
fears for the safety of Church and social order that Grant Allen
was still complaining about in the 1890s, were very much in
force. The worship of home and family, the need for peace and
harmony within the domestic sphere, the crippling effects of
sexual miseducation, all proved mighty disincentives to a
dissolution of moral standards. Indeed, for all the growing
laxity in the upper reaches of society, the middle class in
general was becoming yet more decorous in its manners. This
trend was especially noticeable in the lower-middle classes. In
1857, the year when the great concern arose about the state of
the nation's morals, Dr Acton in his book on prostitution
stressed the improvement in lower-middle class manners he had
witnessed since his first encounter with London nightlife
in 1840:

> Among the London youths I found the systematic streetwalkers,
> frequenters of night houses, disorderly brawlers, assailers of female
> modesty, habitual companions of positive prostitutes, to be much
> more unblushing, and, considering the comparative population at
> the two periods, more numerous than they now are. The 'gent' of
> 1840, much such a creature as I have described, had over-run the
> town. He was not to the same extent as our genteel fathers,
> inclined to disorder, and mistake drunkenness for jollification. So

far he was improved, and he welcomed with enthusiasm the invention of casinos and the naturalization of the then recent polka. But although by no means an extinct animal he is no longer *the* feature of the town. He has in great measure left the unprofitable arena to the gently born and bred. The latter now rule at Cremorne and in the Haymarket, while your snob *pur sang* is girding up his loins for the race of life in which he presses hard upon his betters, 'coaching himself' in his Crosby Halls and in the public libraries, chess clubs, debating classes, and other multifarious educational institutions. (*op. cit.*, pp. 165–6)

In January 1862, just one month after the *Daily Telegraph*'s gloomy Jeremiad about society's moral depravity, *Temple Bar* endorsed this view of the lower-middle classes' self-improvement. But it claimed too that this moral advance was observable in the upper classes also, that the gently born and bred had also in large measure left the unprofitable arena of London nightlife. The callow young gentleman of the 1840s, with no thought in his head but the coarse amusements of Cider Cellars and Coal Holes, was now a thing of the past: indeed, speaking of the Judge and Jury Club, it remarked, 'The saddest reflection with this exhibition—which is now happily relegated to the scum and outscourings of society—is, that it was originally fostered and promoted by "gentlemen".' (IV, 289–90)

But if social manners in general, despite the example of Vanity Fair, had grown more decorous and sober, there was still a lot of substance to the moralists' complaints. For beneath the decorous surface of middle-class life there was a widespread sympathy and admiration for the excesses of the fashionable world. The 1860s were a time of peculiar stress for the morally committed, but for a large section of the public they meant a resurgence of uncommitted, nominal morality. Amongst the upper-middle classes increasing affluence from the mid-nineteenth century boom, increasing contact with the Continent, and especially the French, increasing freedom from political anxieties and religious inhibitions, were producing a widespread reaction against early Victorian moral stiffness. A long letter to *The Times* (3 July 1862) is symptomatic of the change. The letter purports transparently to be a complaint that the thoroughfare from Apsley House to Kensington was choked with carriages each evening between five and seven o'clock. Actually it is a panegyric about Skittles' queen-like presence in Hyde Park, her regal progress attended by aristocratic lady imitators:

> Where she drove, they followed; and I must confess that, as yet, Anonyma has fairly distanced her fair competitors. They can none of them, sit, dress, drive, or look as well as she does; nor can any of them procure for money such ponies as Anonyma contrives to get—for love.
>
> But the result of all this pretty play causes a great public nuisance, and it is on that account, and not at all on account of my admiration for Anonyma and her stepping ponies, that I now address you. . . .[1]

This admiration for Skittles was sometimes found in rather surprising places. The respectable Mr Gladstone, for example, was her close friend for some time in the sixties. 'He unfailingly remembered my birthday', Skittles later recalled, 'and often sent me little presents. He was a much gayer man than people gave him credit for and he waltzed beautifully. In his grave manner he had an irresistible charm, and he was flattered by the company of beautiful women.' Perhaps indeed the Grand Old Man was somewhat more than 'flattered' by Skittles' company: in 1918, remembering a game of skittles and a tour of St Paul's they had once enjoyed together, she remarked, 'I'm an old woman now, and perhaps it is an old woman's vanity, but I do believe that secretly Gladstone had a mild passion for me. Never once did he give any hint of this except to say occasionally that our talks were something he would always cherish.'
[230]

---

[1] P. 12. This article caused *The Times* appreciable discomfort in August 1871 when it criticized Charles Reade for portraying a horsebreaker in *A Terrible Temptation* and was met with the rejoinder that Reade had taken his model from *The Times*' own columns.

If an austere moralist like Gladstone could enjoy the company
of the demi-monde, it is not surprising to find in the popular
fiction of the sixties evidence of a widespread indulgence and
sympathy towards fashionable immorality. Simultaneously
with the emergence of the horsebreakers there had been a
significant development in literature, the emergence of a 'fast
school' of novelists.[1] In theory the latter, notably Ouida and
Miss Braddon, painted moralistic pictures of fashionable vice.
In practice their morality was blatantly nominal, a mere excuse
to dabble in a titillating subject. Their popularity, Mrs
Oliphant claimed in *Blackwoods* (September 1867), was an
indictment of the nation, for unlike, for example, French
novels they had little to recommend them but their prurience:
'We do not gulp down the evil in them for the sake of the
admirable skill that depicts it, or the splendour of the scenery
amid which it occurs. On the contrary, we swallow the poorest
of literary drivel . . . for the sake of the objectionable subjects
they treat.' (CII, 261) But what is significant about fast novels
is not simply the prurience underlying their nominal morality
but the evidence they offer of the fantasies of much of the
respectable bourgeoisie, evidence that the attitudes, if not the
conduct, of the fashionable world were echoed in all sections of
society. For as Lord Strangford remarked shortly after Mrs
Oliphant's broadside, protesting against Ouida's distortions of
aristocratic life, 'If this be not a true picture of the English
upper classes in the middle of the nineteenth century, it gives
at least the ideal excellence to which the lower classes aspired'.
He went on very severely, 'the taste for Ouida's novels confirms
what we know from other sources of the curious ignorance and
vacuity of mind of the English middle classes of the period!'
[231]

12 The horsebreakers then focussed a quite pervasive loosening
of moral attitudes throughout the bourgeoisie. But not all of it

[1] I will discuss these novelists more fully in the following chapters.

was attributable to the influence of Fashion. Some of it was a
clear-headed, rational response to a new image of society. In
the *Westminster Review* (July 1864) Justin McCarthy, discussing
the popularity of Anonyma, noted that the institution of
marriage now seemed virtually on trial: 'What English people
used to think Madame George Sand very wicked years ago for
saying, newspapers, and books, and even sermons, not un-
commonly say now. It is discovered that throughout English
social life immorality is a much more general institution than
successful and satisfactory marriage.' (n.s. XXVI, 40) The early
Victorian code, it was now seen, was based on the partnership
of marriage and prostitution. Many early Victorians of course
had always known this, and from their realistic awareness of
society's moral problem, its dimensions and its seeming
intractability, they had derived a degree of worldly tolerance of
sexual misdemeanours. With the social revelations of the late
fifties and the sixties this kind of attitude to morals became
inevitably more common. Indeed with a certain minority
sexual liberalism went a good deal further: perhaps, they
thought, the answer to society's moral problem lay in reforming
the marriage system, in the liberation of women, the adoption
of contraception, the countenancing of easier divorce, even the
acceptance of free love. But to another, and far more widespread, body of opinion the solution lay not in loosening sexual
standards, but in tightening them, in making a militant effort
to purify society. And in the last three decades of the century
England was to see a moral crusade on numerous different
fronts that was to make society, in externals at any rate, more
decorous than it had ever been before.

III 1870–1900

The Struggle for New Restraints
In the last year of the 1860s the omens for a social purity
crusade did not seem very favourable. To anxious puritans

society in 1869 appeared from top to bottom riddled with moral laxity. In the fashionable world the horsebreakers, their male protectors and female imitators, seemed an index of this malaise. 'Although morality', commented *Vanity Fair* on 28 August, 'for the last twelve years has flowed at the same low ebb, it has sunk many fathoms nearer the mud since the days of our fathers. . . . Society, rotten at the core as it has long been, is now so at the surface, and until the ban of ostracism is set on those men who so flagrantly outrage decency, it will remain so.' (II, 122) And the raffish London nightlife, especially around the Haymarket, seemed an equally intractable problem for the puritan. A new effort was being made to clean it up, but sceptics felt that this attempt would be no more durably successful than the last: 'Vice is suffering at present from a rather violent spasm of morality, and is naturally anxious about its future, but we do not think it has much cause for uneasiness. On the contrary, to all seeming, its prospects generally were never fairer or more promising than at this moment . . . the whole tone of feeling in society is in favour of vice, and this must prevail in the long run.' [232] Parliament, too, to many seemed on the side of vice, for in this year it extended the scope of the Contagious Diseases Acts which forced prostitutes suspected of having V.D. to submit to medical examination and, if the latter proved positive, to three months quarantine in hospital. The Contagious Diseases Acts seemed superficially a cynical enshrinement of the Victorian double standard, a condonation and protection of masculine immorality. But they received no criticism in the press, and an agitation against them in October was almost totally ignored. The omens for the social purity movement did not seem propitious, and in the beginning of 1870 they seemed less so, when the heir to the throne and leader of fashionable society had his name dragged through the divorce court as a result of his friendship with Mrs Mordaunt.

In June 1866 Queen Victoria had written the Prince of Wales that, society being now so lax and bad, he had a duty to deny himself amusement in order to keep up the previous moral tone. She explained that she and her husband had always been 'civil to, but kept at a distance from, the fast racing set', although during her youth, 'its manners at least were good and none knew its faults'. Latterly the manners of its members had worsened to such an extent, and their faults become so widely known, that the Prince of Wales was bound to mark his disapproval by 'not asking them to dinner, nor down to Sandringham—and, above all, not going to their houses'. [233] But the Prince went his own way, and far from keeping a distance from the fast racing set became closely associated with it, and with the demi-monde as well. *The Times* (24 February 1870), commenting sympathetically on his imprudence with Mrs Mordaunt (from the divorce suit it appeared he had committed no real misconduct), warned him 'how watchfully he must walk whose life is the property and study of the world'. It cited the wonderful example of his father, and went on: 'We do not doubt that the future years of the HEIR APPAR-ENT will show, by their fidelity to this example, the influence of the lesson he has had to learn, and that Englishmen will see exemplified in their King that is to be a life purified from the semblance even of levity.' (p. 8) The Prince, however, was not to be a pattern of royal propriety. His idea of decorum was not the middle-class model exhibited by his father, but the pre-Victorian aristocratic model. Society might be permitted to guess, for example, that Mrs Langtry was his mistress, he simply took care that it did not know for certain through open scandal. Their liaison was by no means shrouded in secrecy, but it was not ostentatiously flaunted; and there was no chance of public exposure, for the situation was accepted by both the Princess and by Langtry (who had faded into the background and disappeared).

Not all the upper classes were prepared to condone the Prince's laxity. In the 1880s a deputation of noblewomen led by Lady Tavistock asked the Archbishop of Canterbury to stop the moral rot that was ruining London society. Some young married women, they claimed, had no standard of morality at all, and the centre of this mischief was the Marlborough House set. They wanted the Archbishop to start a moral mission for women of that class to restore the old idealism that was waning, and to warn the Prince of Wales about the harm that he was causing. The Archbishop did indeed institute at Lambeth a series of well-attended devotional meetings, but he did not approach the Prince, feeling that derogatory gossip was an inadequate warrant for such an intrusion on his privacy. The Archbishop's highminded scruples, however, were not the Prince's greatest ally. Running through even the more moral upper classes there was a widespread toleration of his laxity. In the early 1880s, for example, when Mrs Langtry was being snubbed by certain aristocratic ladies, the Prince asked Gladstone to lend her his support. Gladstone dutifully made formal calls, went to dinner whenever possible, and allowed her to make social capital from his friendship. The G.O.M. was clearly moved by more than kindness to the Prince: he was obviously enthralled by the lady's company and even gave her the code sign which enabled the letters of the few to pass unopened by his secretaries—a privilege she exploited so often as to cause the latter some concern. Gladstone's behaviour is an illustration of the fact that the Samuel Carter Hall definition of decorum, that a woman must not only be pure but give no excuse for rumours of impurity, was now a much less common feature of middle-class morality. In February 1870 *The Times* had said the Prince of Wales must give no scope for gossip and lead a life purified from the semblance even of levity. On 10 March 1888, commenting on his twenty-fifth wedding anniversary, it paid tribute to his contribution 'to what may be called the religion of the family throughout England':

What the country has gained by this example of a happy strenuous family life in the highest place, it is difficult to state too strongly. At a time when, so to speak, all our institutions are being cast into the furnace, it is of enormous value to see, in the family next

the Throne, a type of life which, aiming at no impossible or
ascetic standard, is yet such as may be regarded without blame and
imitated without harm. (p. 13)

With this degree of Nelsonian morality quite general we can
appreciate that any crusade for society's moral improvement
had a number of serious obstacles to surmount.

The campaign instituted in 1869 against the Contagious
Diseases Acts was a case in point. In the early seventies its
propaganda, meetings and activities were almost totally boy-
cotted by the press, or alternatively subjected to vituperative
attacks. The intransigence, however, of press and Parliament
was by no means solely the product of cynicism and hypocrisy,
of their deliberately turning a blind eye to masculine immorality. With statistics seeming to indicate that the Acts were
both curbing the incidence of V.D. and also in fact, through
rescue work in hospitals, being of moral as well as physical
benefit to the prostitute, it was quite easy for sincere and
intelligent people to be resolute regulationists. Nor can one
wholly blame them for avoiding discussion of the Acts, for
they recognized that these measures, though necessary, were
obnoxious to the instincts of a great section of the people. Nor
indeed can one wholly blame even their hostility to the
agitators; for some of the latter were injudicious propagandists,
suggesting, for example, that venereal diseases were intended
by God to punish promiscuity. It was not a cynical, amoral
male supremacist but a sensible and dedicated rescue worker
who argued that 'be those Acts right or wrong in principle,
wide and fearful harm has been done to the cause of purity in
more ways than one, by the fanatical and ignorant agitation
that has been fomented and carried on amongst ladies married
and single, the vast majority not having the slightest practical
or accurate knowledge of what is being raved about'. [234] But
despite these self-inflicted handicaps and despite the other
obstacles in its path the cause of purity made steady progress
through the seventies. A sizeable measure of public opinion was

quickly aroused to militancy: in 1870 the abolitionists defeated an advocate of the Acts in a by-election at Colchester, in 1871 they presented Parliament with a petition for repeal containing a quarter of a million signatures, and by 1873 they had converted the Protestant churches solidly to their position. Parliament remained obdurate; but after 1874, when the distinguished statesman James Stansfeld brought his political expertise into alliance with Josephine Butler's personal charisma, it became at least more temperate and open to reason. Eventually in 1882, though a Select Committee of the Commons reported enthusiastically on the Acts, a minority report given by Stansfeld tipped the balance for the abolitionists. In 1883 the Acts were suspended, and, despite a rearguard action by regulationists, in 1886 they were abolished.

While the militants were making progress in this matter, steady advances were also being made in purifying the tone of London's nightlife, in shutting down the haunts of prostitution, the disreputable night-houses, casinos and pleasure-gardens. In 1870 one of the best known pleasure-gardens, the Highbury Barn, lost its dancing licence and went out of business the following year. In that year, in 1871, its principal rival, the Cremorne Gardens, lost its licences for music and dancing, and though it regained them in 1874 and survived the attacks of moral vigilants for three years more, it was demolished in 1878. In most of these cases the militant's cause was assisted by economic factors. For one thing, with the decline of the 'gent' these haunts enjoyed progressively less quantity and quality in their patrons. For another, the urban development of London made their sites often too valuable to waste (Cremorne, for example, was turned into building lots and the Haymarket into offices and shops); whilst their growing, uncouth rowdiness became intolerable to landlords and tenants of increasingly expensive residential property. Clearing the prostitutes from the promenades of music-halls did not allow the militant these advantages. In 1894 Mrs Chant persuaded the London County Council to refuse the Empire Theatre its licence unless its promenade was abolished. But her action, as we saw earlier, produced a good deal of violent hostility in the papers. The vigilants were alleged to be an unrepresentative minority of 'Prudes on the Prowl'. When the Empire re-opened, with flimsy canvas barriers cutting down the promenade to a gangway, a group of young men fulminating against Puritan killjoys, tore them down; and their leader, the nineteen-year-old Winston Churchill, orated, 'You have seen us tear down these barricades tonight. See that you pull down those who are responsible for them at the coming election.' [235] Despite, however, the rhetoric of Churchill, despite the formation of a 'Sporting League' by the cricketer W. G. Grace to keep those who voted against the Empire off the Council, despite all the vituperative letters in the press, the 'unrepresentative minority' of puritans was solidly vindicated at the coming election, and the L.C.C. under Sir John McDougall proceeded to attack the promenades of other music-halls.

Four years earlier Grant Allen had complained, 'Just now, a certain number of well-meaning dissenting ministers and sleek provincial journalists assume to speak with authority in Demos's name, and believe themselves to be expressing his inarticulate views when they preach the doctrines of some curious mixture they describe as social purity'. [236] Now it is true that a large proportion of the working class was anything but puritanical in its morals. Of this the puritans were but too well aware. And yet the latter could fairly claim that their movement embraced all sections of the people. Their leaders were often drawn from the aristocracy, the established church, the universities and the professions, but their appeal extended well into the working class. When Parliament, for example, was debating the repeal of the Contagious Diseases Acts in 1883, a crowd of women spent the night not far away kneeling in prayer in the street, and these women included the ragged and miserable inhabitants of the slums as well as ladies of rank and station. When in the same year Miss Ellice Hopkins, who had been touring the country preaching moral purity, addressed a

miners' meeting in Bishop Auckland, some one hundred and
fifty men were moved to come forward and sign the five rules
of conduct she expounded; in so doing they became the founder
members of her White Cross Society which was soon to
become nationwide. In a similar way other agencies for moral
reform, like the other purity leagues, or the Church Army or
the Salvation Army, drew some of their strength from Allen's
supposedly unpuritan Demos.

But the main grass roots of the purity movement were in the
lower-middle class. For it was here that one found now,
commentators agreed, the nation's greatest moral sobriety. 'If
English morality could be judged by the standard of morals
which exists among the lowest section of the middle class,' the
Fortnightly remarked in December 1885, 'the small shopkeepers
and other employés on the same level, there would be no reason
not to congratulate ourselves most heartily upon it. Between
the lowest class and the professional class there is a happy
interspace of virtue.' (n.s. XXXVIII, 775–6) Much of this
sobriety owed more to the British Goddess Sleek Respectability
than to any great moral earnestness, but the shopkeeper class
was nonetheless a vital ally of the purity movement. With its
growth in numbers and in wealth, its new power in national
and local politics, and with the self-confidence in expressing
its opinion that these developments afforded, the lower-middle
class was now an active influence on the conduct of the
country's affairs. The same pattern was observable in the
upper-working class, in the aristocracy of labour, whose life-
style was so close to that of the lower-middle class as to be
virtually indistinguishable. A writer in 1873 noted that skilled
artisans were 'as conscious of the superiority of their lot over
that of their poorest brethren as is the highest nobleman in the
land. And they are right: for their lot does just offer them the
opportunity of being gentlemen in spirit and in truth; and to
the great honour of the age be it said, many of them are
steadily becoming gentlemen.' [237] Again the morality of this
class owed a lot to genteel affectation, but much of it was

militantly earnest, the morality of men active in chapel and trade unions, for example. With the confidence gained from numbers—it amounted to about a tenth of the working class— and more especially from an enhanced prosperity and prestige as it outstripped in material progress the rest of the proletariat, the aristocracy of labour as much as the lower-middle class was playing a forceful part in society's affairs.

Even before the extension of middle-class power through the Reform Act of 1867 aristocratic levity had kept itself within certain limits. 'The aristocracy,' Bagehot remarked in 1865, 'live in the fear of the middle classes—of the grocer and the merchant. They dare not frame a society of enjoyment as the French aristocracy once formed it.' [238] But after 1867 public opinion was a yet more pressing consideration. In February 1870 Queen Victoria wrote that, though her son was cleared of committing adultery with Mrs Mordaunt,

> . . . Still, the fact of the Prince of Wales's intimate acquaintance with a young married woman being publicly proclaimed will show an amount of imprudence which cannot but damage him in the eyes of the middle and lower class, which is most deeply to be lamented in these days when the higher classes, in their frivolous, selfish, and pleasure-seeking lives, do more to increase the spirit of democracy than anything else. [239]

In the event the Prince was booed in the streets, catcalled in the theatre, and hissed at Ascot as late as June. With the rise of the spirit of democracy and the rapid expansion of the popular press, criticism of the Prince became a regular feature of the age. And in 1875 *Reynold's News* in particular, which had kept up a consistent barrage of attacks on the Marlborough House set, made great capital from the case of Colonel Valentine Baker. The Colonel, a friend of the Prince of Wales, was convicted of sexually assaulting a young lady in a railway carriage, but what outraged the left-wing papers more was the extraordinarily light sentence he was given. The judge, claimed *Reynold's News* (8 August 1875), seemed

. . . to have forgotten that he was looking on one of the most cowardly ruffians that ever stood in a place where a vast number of ruffians had already appeared before him, and only saw in the atrocious criminal in the dock the highly-favoured colonel of hussars, the intimate friend and associate of the Prince of Wales, the Duke of Cambridge, &c.—and he regulated his sentence accordingly . . . so flagrant, so shameful a miscarriage of justice as that witnessed on Monday at Croydon, is sufficient to arouse the indignation of every honest-hearted Englishman who has ever been brought up to believe that English justice really knows no distinction of person. (p. 5)

Outraged public opinion was somewhat mollified when the unfortunate Baker was cashiered from his regiment. But it became inflamed again in 1882 when Lord Wolseley, with the Prince of Wales' support, appointed Baker (who had distinguished himself in the Turkish army) as commander-in-chief of the new Egyptian army. The Cabinet was obliged to revoke the decision; and two years later Wolseley's appointment of Baker as his principal intelligence officer, when organizing an expedition to relieve Gordon at Khartoum, was similarly vetoed by the War Office.

The attacks on Baker show to some extent the way in which public morality might be exploited for political ends. But by this time the militant puritans were increasingly prepared to exploit political tensions in the interest of public morality. Sixty or seventy years earlier the Evangelicals had been so worried by the danger of revolution they had tried to play down the embroglios of the Duke of York and Mrs Clarke and Queen Caroline and George IV. But the puritans of the eighties had no such inhibitions. In April 1885 they instigated the prosecution of Mrs Jeffries, a notorious bawd with many aristocratic patrons, with the clear intention of creating a major scandal, of having the sins of the great exposed in open court. Their hopes, however, were to be frustrated. At the police-court hearing the police, the magistrate, and the Home Office all seemed to be complicit in a cover-up. In the following month the Middlesex sessions proved even more disappointing: before the proceedings got under way the counsel for the prosecution and defence apparently reached an understanding with the judge that if Mrs Jeffries pleaded guilty she would get off with a fine; as a result no evidence was heard. The purity movement made little secret of its suspicions: indeed at a public meeting in Luton, James B. Wookey, the secretary of the Gospel Purity Association, claimed to know the names of the men responsible for this conspiracy of silence; they included, he said, Lord Fyfe, Lord Douglas Gordon, Lord Lennox, Lord Aylesford and the Prince of Wales. The purity movement too did not scruple to draw a political lesson from this 'conspiracy'. 'The inferences,' said the *Sentinel*, one of its journals, 'point to a state of moral corruption, heartless cruelty, and prostitution of authority, almost sufficient, even in this country, to goad the industrial classes into revolution.' [240]

Stung by their failure with Mrs Jeffries the puritans quickly tried another tack. In July in the *Pall Mall Gazette* W. T. Stead at their instigation astounded the nation with his 'Maiden Tribute of Modern Babylon' articles. In these reports lurid evidence was given of the sexual exploitation of the daughters of the poor by the depravity of the upper classes. The objective primarily was to pressure the Government to pass the Criminal Law Amendment Act, which would give these girls much greater legal protection. But the political point was also heavily emphasized: 'If ever there is a social revolution in this country it will be over this very question. . . . It is the one explosive which is strong enough to wreck the Throne.'[1] Again the suspicion arose of Government complicity in aristocratic vice. The Government acceded to Stead's pressure and passed the Criminal Law Amendment Act, but then almost immediately took its revenge by having Stead himself charged with abducting a young girl. Stead's offence was purely technical: he had used quite innocently a girl called Eliza Armstrong to demon-

[1] *Pall Mall Gazette* (28 July), p. 1; (6 July), p. 2. Not surprisingly the Prince of Wales was one of the first to cancel his subscription to the paper.

strate the workings of the trade in female virgins. But he was sentenced nonetheless to six months imprisonment. The actions of the Government and the appreciative response of much of the London press were, however, much less disgraceful than they might seem. Laying aside any prudish aversion to Stead's sensational articles, and laying aside any resentment at the inflammatory political prejudice they exhibited, there were substantial grounds for the hostility to him. For one thing, with the *Pall Mall*'s circulation jumping from fewer than 13,000 to hundreds of thousands and with newsboys hawking copies at half a crown a time, many regarded his combination of moral pretension and salaciousness as the worst possible kind of hypocrisy.[1] For another, his revelations were widely regarded not only as hypocritically prurient but as gross distortions of the truth[2]: they were, it is true, supported by the superficial investigation of a somewhat prejudiced puritan committee, but even purity workers were amongst those who rejected them as spurious. [241] Finally, the evidence of the trial, where a rich old debauchee who had deflowered a thirteen-year-old girl turned out to be Stead himself, destroyed for many what was left of his credibility.[3] Stead's credit, however, remained good with most of the religious and radical journals, and in the provinces especially he was regarded as a hero and a martyr.

[1] George Bernard Shaw, who initially had offered himself to Stead as a newsboy, showed a not uncommon reaction: 'Nobody ever trusted him after the discovery that the case of Eliza Armstrong in the Maiden Tribute was a put-up job, and that he himself had put it up. We all felt that if ever a man deserved six months' imprisonment Stead deserved it for such a betrayal of our confidence in him.' Quoted Frederick Whyte, *The Life of W. T. Stead* (1925) I, 304.

[2] See, for example, the *Standard* (11 November): 'the wonder grows that it should ever have been possible for a moment to conceal such atrocious proceedings under the mask of a holy purpose'. (p. 5)

[3] *The Evening News* (9 November) explained the matter with an engaging cynicism: 'the hideous narratives of obscene practices which Stead professed to have revealed were based merely on gossip he had picked up from prostitutes when wandering about brothels "in a state of intense mental excitement" and obfuscation, due to unwonted indulgence in champagne and cigars'. (p. 2)

London cynics could say what they liked; Stead's politico-moral strategy, his expert blend of sentiment and sensation, his moral flourishes in the courtroom and in prison, had won new masses to the militants' cause. The purity movement was now stronger in numbers and more aggressive in posture than it had ever been before.

On 10 September 1885, commenting on the implications of Stead's trial, the *Methodist Times* promised little quarter for eminent moral delinquents: 'When this side issue has been settled, the cause will pass to a more august tribunal, the Supreme Court of the Public Conscience of the Nation. All impure men must be hounded from public life.' (I, 601)[1] In the ensuing election puritan propaganda did indeed play a prominent part, but a greater coup was enjoyed by the militants shortly afterwards when a possible future Prine Minister, Sir Charles Dilke, offered himself for arraignment and chastisement. In February 1886 Dilke was named in the Crawford divorce case. Mrs Crawford admitted adultery with him, but when he declined to give evidence he was dismissed from the suit on a technicality (a wife's confession was accepted as evidence of her own guilt but not of the man's she cited). In the face of an anomalous verdict, where effectively Mrs Crawford was found to have slept with Dilke but not Dilke with Mrs Crawford, it was somewhat injudicious of the *Daily News*, with a couple of other papers, to rejoice that Dilke's character had now been vindicated after full and open trial and that he would now be welcomed back to public life with fervour. The *Pall Mall Gazette* and a number of religious and

---

[1] One M.P. whose earlier life would not have stood too much scrutiny was the radical Labouchere, a firm supporter of Stead and the author of a subsequently notorious amendment on homosexuality to the Criminal Law Amendment Act. Labouchere had lived in sin for some time with his eventual wife, Henrietta Hodson, a famous actress. During the 1868 election he was assailed by hecklers so often with the cry "Ow's 'Enrietta?' that he is alleged to have opened one meeting by announcing 'I wish to convey to you all the gratifying intelligence that Henrietta is quite well'. See Hesketh Pearson, *Labby* (1936), p. 67.

provincial journals quickly expressed their outrage at this enthusiasm, their outrage that Dilke should be presented as a paragon of virtue while the woman was held up to obloquy, their outrage too that an important statesman should make no attempt to defend himself from the slur of moral corruption. Within a few days many of the nationals had come round to insisting he clear his name by a further recourse to the courts. And the result, as is well known, was calamitous for Dilke. Four years later the puritans' strength was seen again, in the case of Parnell and Mrs O'Shea, when Gladstone was forced to destroy the hope of Ireland by pressure from the Nonconformists of the National Liberal Federation. Finally a year later, in 1891, the radical element in the social purity movement was delighted, after the loss of Dilke and Parnell, to have at last the Prince of Wales at bay. The Tranby Croft scandal, which exposed in court the nature not of the Prince's sexual habits but of his gambling, precipitated a torrent of well-nigh universal vituperation. The Prince's stock with the general public had never been so low.

With these penalties on exposed immorality it is not surprising that aristocratic society showed a marked degree of schizophrenic hypocrisy, that it tended to turn a blind eye to the laxity in its midst but, in the event of any scandal which affected its prestige with the world outside and in particular cast a shadow on the Prince, that it punished the offender with some violence:

> What it resents, anathematises, and punishes is not the commission but the detection of the fault. It connives at the sin; it shrieks at the scandal. So long as the sin does not amount to more than a well circumstantiated but discreetly whispered suspicion, though a suspicion it may be that involves something very like certainty, all is well. But directly it is bruited abroad outside the limits of society, so soon as, to use the common phrase, it gets into the papers, society lifts its hands in horror.[1]

[1] *Fortnightly Review* (December 1885) n.s. XXXVIII, 778. E. F. Benson, *As We Were*, pp. 91–2, gives a good example of the savagery with which, especially

This kind of hypocrisy, however, was by no means an aristocratic monopoly. The country had become infinitely more
decorous through the work of moral militants, but the support
they enjoyed contained a large amount of purely conventional
moral posturing. For the spirit of Fashion though chastened in
terms of open breaches of decorum was nonetheless a very
potent factor in the nation. In 1870 the fear had been expressed
that the laxity of Vanity Fair represented in fast novels fitted
the mood of even the respectable middle classes:

> The world liked the new way of seeing itself. It had been well-
> behaved long enough, or had made believe to be, and it welcomed
> any generous attempt to represent it as courageous enough to be
> wicked. Even those persons who on the whole preferred to stand
> more or less upon the old way were pleased to hear of the new ones.
> Thus all parties were satisfied—both those who, rising in insur-
> rection against a dull generation, imagined that loose morals and
> ill manners were a proof of spirit; and those who, subscribing
> liberally to the circulating libraries, thanked heaven that they
> were not as one of these. [242]

And this fear, that the respectable classes paid often little more
than lip-service to the idea of social purity, was clearly
vindicated in the years to come.

We see it, for example, in society's ambivalence on the
question of wild oats. Even as the purity militants were
strengthening the official insistence on a single standard of
chastity in the sexes, a large body of opinion was becoming
ever more permissive towards the indiscretions of young men.
This development is mirrored strikingly in the literature of the
period. In *Pelham* (1828), Bulwer Lytton could still joke
publicly about his hero's youthful errors; in the next three
decades such levity was for private pleasure only[1]; but in the

---

in the case of women, this hypocrisy could operate: the unfortunate woman
he cites was Lady Henry Somerset, who caused a scandal by making public
the reasons for her separation from her husband and was ruthlessly punished
for her error.

[1] One recalls Dickens' fun in 1848 on the subject of English chastity with
the over-solemn Emerson: see Edgar Johnson, *op. cit.* II, 645.

succeeding years gentlemanly debauchery could once again be treated with amusement by a novelist like Reade in *A Terrible Temptation* (1871) or with implicit admiration by fast novelists like Ouida. We see too a moral levity, beneath the increasing decorum, in society's ambivalence towards marriage. Dilke, on being reminded before his court case of Wellington's alleged reply to Harriette Wilson, is reported to have responded, 'An aristocratic society then rather enjoyed a scandal. To-day the middle classes rule and adultery to them is as bad as murder.' [243] His remark over-simplified the climate of the 1820s, but it over-simplified too the middle classes' attitude to adultery in the eighties. Only a few months earlier a writer had lamented that, among the austere middle classes, scandal was often as much the subject of flippant conversation as in permissive Vanity Fair:

> even the eminently serious and respectable, the husbands and wives who have never given a handle to calumny, severest of matrons and the chastest of maids, gossip about infidelities and the rumours of infidelities imminent or accomplished, which may wreck homes, with as much zest as, if they understood French sufficiently well, they would chuckle over the scarcely veiled indecencies, the innuendoes, and *équivoques* of a play by Halévy or Albert Milhaud, [244]

One should not overstress the polarity, in these examples of ambivalence, between militant puritanism on the one hand and nominal morality on the other. For sexual liberalism was stronger now than at any time in the century. An indulgent attitude to immorality was more than ever a sign of decreasing moral seriousness. But it was also more than ever a sign of healthy tolerance, generosity and respect for others' privacy: advocates of free love, for example, were no longer beyond the social pale. Nonetheless the striking fact of late-Victorian morality is the ambivalence of progressive sexual decorum in the public sphere and a large degree of insincere conventional-ism in the private. Officially, for example, contraception was taboo. Unofficially its use in the respectable classes was becoming very widespread. The turning point had been the trial of Annie Besant and Bradlaugh in 1877 for publishing a tract on contraception called *The Fruits of Philosophy*. But though the middle class in general was finding birth control a blessing, it was prepared to support, here as elsewhere, the puritan militants who were harassing and prosecuting birth-control propagandists. One of the most galling obstacles that the Neo-Malthusians met with, in their efforts to bring the blessing of contraception to the masses, was the smug conventionalism and silence of the classes who already enjoyed it. The late-Victorians' hard-won code of social purity concealed in many ways a rather repellent inner hollowness.

9

The Pattern of Literary
Prudery

I 1750–1830

Eighteenth Century Decorum

1 IN 1826 SIR WALTER SCOTT told a famous story about his great-aunt. The old lady had asked him, it seems in the early 1790s, to obtain for her the works of Aphra Behn, which she remembered enjoying in her youth. With some misgiving about the propriety of the author Scott had sent them but marked the package 'private and confidential'. The next time he saw his aunt she thrust the books into his hands and recommended him to burn them. 'I found it impossible to get through the very first of the novels,' she said; and she added, 'but is it not odd that I, an old woman of eighty and upwards, sitting alone, feel myself ashamed to read a book which sixty years ago I have heard read aloud for large circles consisting of the first and most creditable society in London?' [245] Some years before this incident took place the old lady's hostility to Restoration coarseness was already very prevalent. In 1777 Sheridan, the major playwright of the age, had written *A Trip to Scarborough*, a bowdlerized version of a play by one of Mrs Behn's contemporaries, Vanbrugh's *The Relapse*, and for it David Garrick had written an explanatory prologue:

> As change thus circulates throughout the nation,
> Some plays may justly call for alteration;

204

At least to draw some slender covering o'er,
That graceless wit which was too bare before:
Those writers well and wisely use their pens,
Who turn our wantons into Magdalens . . .[1]

Nor was this a sudden new development: a change had been
circulating throughout the nation from the beginning of the
century; and shortly after the time when Mrs Behn was read
aloud to the delight of good society a remarkable tightening of
the standards of literary chastity had been affected. This may
seem surprising when we recall the carefree bawdy of such
popular writers as Fielding, Smollett and Sterne. It may seem
less so if we recall also that even the level-headed Dr Johnson
said of *Tom Jones* that he 'scarcely knew a more corrupt work';
that the 1758 edition of *Peregrine Pickle* was bowdlerized of
some eighty pages by Smollett himself after protests from his
readers; and that *Tristram Shandy* was from the beginning
harshly censured and later strictly censored.[2]

It is natural to ascribe this advance in literary prudery to the
growing influence on literature of the emergent middle class:
to their concern for domestic purity, their aspirations to
gentility, and their church-going, sermon-reading piety. Certainly two of the most important literary puritans of the 1740s
were the London printer Samuel Richardson, who introduced
the word 'indelicacy' to the language and made the prudish
Pamela a figure of perfect bourgeois purity, and the Methodist

[1] Dramatic bowdlerization had of course been perpetrated by Restoration
writers too, but their expurgations of Shakespeare, for example, were
prompted by notions of taste not decency (the first bowdlerization of
Shakespeare on moral grounds appears to be Thomas Hanmer's edition of
1744—Quinlan, *op. cit.*, p. 240).

[2] See *Johnsonian Miscellanies* ed. George Birkbeck Hill (1899) II, 190;
Perrin, *op. cit.*, pp. 253-4; Alan B. Howes, *Yorick and the Critics* (New Haven,
1958), chs. 1 and 3. One is inclined similarly to recall the existence of
Cleland's *Fanny Hill* and Wilkes' *Essay on Woman* (if he indeed wrote it), to
forget that Cleland was summoned before the Privy Council and obliged
to renounce all further writing in this line, and that Wilkes was punished
by losing his seat in the Commons, being forced into exile, and being
imprisoned upon his return.

John Wesley, whose *Collection of Moral and Sacred Poems, From
the Most Celebrated English Authors* (1744), was the first English
bowdlerized verse-anthology to be published.[1] But it would be
a mistake to see the advance of prudery only in middle-class
terms. For a significant proportion of the upper classes too,
with their developing conception of good breeding, gave firm
support to the movement for literary purity. Indeed a writer in
The World (10 May 1753), an upper-class magazine, complaining about modern novels adopts a distinctly bourgeois tone:
'The thing I chiefly find fault with is their extreme indecency.
There are certain vices which the vulgar call fun, and the
people of fashion gallantry; but the middle ranks, and those of
the gentry who continue to go to church, still stigmatize them
by the opprobious names of fornication and adultery.' (p. 114)
But if aristocratic breeding helped in the advance of literary
chastity, after 1760, when the development of circulating
libraries turned the novel into an industry, the role of the
middle classes became increasingly predominant. For the
explosion in novel production required both writers and readers
from the purity-conscious bourgeoisie, and especially, given the
amount and nature of female leisure, from the purity-conscious
middle-class woman. The tone of literature became inevitably
more modest and genteel.

2 Amidst the prevailing decorum the spirit of Fashion, the
desire for spicy tales of gallantry, appeared to have little chance.
In October 1770 the *Critical Review* warned its readers against
the novels of Treyssac de Vergy, a young Frenchman enjoying
the favour of England's Vanity Fair, who had the effrontery to
profess 'that the favourable reception which he meets with from
his fair readers is in proportion to the immorality of his
writing'.[2] De Vergy's speciality lay in luscious, but one must say

---

[1] For detailed discussion of Richardson's impact on the growth of prudery
see R. P. Utter and G. B. Needham, *Pamela's Daughters* (1937); for Wesley
see Perrin, *op. cit.*, pp. 35–8.

[2] Here, as elsewhere, I am indebted to J. M. S. Tompkins' pioneer work,

discreetly unerotic, fictionalized accounts of contemporary scandals or lives of famous rakes, actresses and courtesans. But this style of fiction does not seem to have been widely popular; de Vergy's vogue was short; and disreputable publishers were sometimes forced to re-issue their wares with different titles— in September 1771 the *Critical* was complaining that *Cupid turned Spy upon Hymen, or Matrimonial Intrigues in Polite Life* was the very *Cuckoldom Triumphant, or Matrimonial Incontinence Vindicated* that it had reviewed and censured the month before. Yet though the bulk of literature was becoming very chaste, we cannot rule the spirit of Fashion out. Literary chastity, like the decorum of aristocratic sexual manners, often had little connection with strict morality. The upper classes' code of sexual manners was supported firstly, we have seen, by their political and social pre-eminence. But it was also supported, I suggested, by the moral apathy, the nominal religion of a large section of the apparently virtuous middle class. This nominal morality is very obvious in the middle classes' literature, an area where they were practically pre-eminent, where *they* enjoyed the sanctions and the power. By nominal morality I mean not so much the cheerful laxity of writers like Robert Bage in *Barham Downs* (1784); nor the vacuous edification, the squeamish sentimentality of lady novelists by the score. I mean the combination of prurience and purely conventional morality apparent in lots of later eighteenth century novels, blatant titillation not so far removed from that of de Vergy being smothered in decorous didacticism. In February 1775 the *Monthly Review* gave a synopsis of a novel called *The Morning Ramble; or History of Miss Evelyn*, which furnishes a vivid illustration:

A young lady in love with her supposed uncle.—An old dotard in love with this same young lady, his supposed grand-daughter.—

The Popular Novel in England 1770–1800 (1932). Also helpful on the eighteenth century taste for tales of gallantry is Robert Mayo, *The English Novel in the Magazines, 1740–1815* (Evanston, 1962), pp. 184–90).

These amours made honest by the help of a gypsey, whose child the loved and loving fair one is said to be.—Her virgin chastity attempted by the ancient lover, and rescued by the younger.—Her virgin chastity again attempted by the friend of her beloved *Adonis*, and again rescued by a mad adventurer.—The rescued fair conducted by her new inamorato to the mouth of a dismal cave, (in which he threatens to end his life before her eyes, unless she consents to repay his services with those charms which he had preserved) and there terrified into a promise of marriage.—A *third ravishment*, and a murder, introduced for the sake of *variety* and *entertainment*, into the husband's story of himself.—The wife, unmindful of her holy vow, on a sudden suffering her first passion to rekindle.—Her husband in a fit of jealousy, encountering his innocent rival.—The hapless fair rushing between their swords.—Wounded.—Expiring.—Lamented. (LII, 186)

3 It is not surprising in view of this nominal morality, false sentiment and latent prurience that the moralists of the 1780s and early 1790s were mostly hostile to the novel. Some of them indeed regarded novel reading as fraught with spiritual peril: 'Novels, generally speaking,' warned the *Evangelical Magazine* in August 1793, 'are instruments of abomination and ruin. A fond attachment to them is an irrefragable evidence of a mind contaminated, and totally unfitted for the serious pursuits of study, or the delightful exercises and enjoyments of religion.' (I, 79) Even the best fiction, thought extremists of this type, was a dangerous indulgence, an invitation to levity, a distraction from moral duty. The more moderate Evangelicals, like Hannah More and Mrs West, did not go this far, and in fact sometimes wrote novels themselves as a means of proselytization. But Evangelicals of all persuasions were agreed in proscribing the greater part of popular fiction on the grounds of its deficient moral content: its treatment of good, they argued, was sentimental, conventional, platitudinous, and unrelated to the specific requirements of vital religion; its treatment of evil, they cautioned, was too often a titillating dabbling in impurity.

The effect of Evangelical propaganda against the suspect morality of popular fiction does not seem immediately very appreciable. The Minerva Press, which was founded in 1790, was famous for its improving works by large numbers of pious ladies, like Mrs Bennett, Mrs Roche and Mrs Meeke. But one of its biggest successes of the 1790s was Elizabeth Helme's *The Farmer of Inglewood Forest* (1796) which purports to offer a sober moral lesson but is in fact amply endowed with prurient thrills. It shows simple rustic virtue being attacked by the insidious force of Fashion: of five young people placed in its snare two remain safe in happy rural wedlock, but the other three, a young man and two girls, are each corrupted by a fashionable rake. The young man's decline into drinking, wenching, gambling, rape and murder is painted in lurid detail: we see him, for example, raping one girl and saved at the last from raping another, who turns out to be his own daughter; there is also an affecting scene in a brothel where he nearly sleeps with his own sister, and her history as mistress, courtesan and common prostitute rivals his in prurient detail and pseudo-moral authorial comment. The popularity of this novel shows that, for all the moralists' efforts, a large section of the bourgeoisie was still far from Evangelical strictness. The purely nominal morality to be found in middle-class literature was still complementary to the combination of surface decorum and inner moral laxity of aristocratic sexual manners.

4 Indeed there was a good deal of evidence for anxious moral conservatives that the standards of literary purity were not only not improving but in fact becoming worse; that the loosening standards of Vanity Fair in terms of sexual manners were being mirrored in a new licentiousness in literature. Most blatantly there were the journals of Vanity Fair, freely advertised and sold, consisting largely of gossip about fashionable whores and reports of crim. con. actions and the juicier sexual crimes. Their titles are indicative of their contents: *The Rambler, or The Annals of Gallantry, Glee, Pleasure, and the Bon Ton* (1783–90), for

example, or *The Bon Ton Magazine, or Microscope of Fashion and Folly* (1791–6). More serious for the moralist, since it argued a more general degeneracy of standards, there was the popularity of a new school of fairly salacious fiction, often adapted from French and German sources. In 1796, for instance, moralists were scandalized by the translation from the German of *Horrid Mysteries* by Peter Wills, of *Maurice, a German Tale*, of *The German Miscellany, Consisting of Drama, Dialogues, Tales and Novels*, and of *Laura, or The Influence of a Kiss*. But they were scandalized most by an English original of that year, written in the very same vein, Matthew Lewis' *The Monk*. The latter, to their chagrin, for all its heady concoction of seduction, rape, incest and sadism, for all its crude, adolescent prurience,[1] met in 1796 a most favourable reception: the *Monthly Mirror*, the *Morning Chronicle* and the *Analytical Review* all praised it highly and indeed only the *Dublin Flapper* raised its tiny voice in protest. [246] The following year, however, was a very different matter. 1797 was a crucial year for English literary prudery. In a year of peculiar nervous stress, in particular of a widespread fear of a conspiracy to subvert the nation's morals, and in a year when the purity of the home and therefore the purity of family literature had never seemed of more importance, it was inevitable that a new degree of prudery should emerge and with it a violent backlash against the current permissive trend. In 1797 a few hostile notices of *The Monk* led to a well-nigh universal storm of censure in the press. Foremost among the attackers was Coleridge in February in the *Critical Review*: 'The Monk is a romance, which if a parent saw in the hands of a son or daughter, he might reasonably turn pale.' (XIX, 197) Lewis, it seems, was under threat of prosecution until he agreed to recast the book in a new edition. His later

[1] A typical incident is the scene where the Monk views the half-exposed bosom of the fatal Matilda: 'and, oh! that was such a breast! The moonbeams darting full upon it enabled the monk to observe its dazzling whiteness: his eye dwelt with insatiable avidity upon the beauteous orb' (1959 edn, ed. Louis F. Peck, p. 187). This passage was one of the many Lewis cut for the expurgated edition in 1798.

writings were dutifully chastened, but he was nonetheless persecuted for the rest of his life by critics seeing immorality, blasphemy and subversion in everything he wrote.

The Evangelicals then had made their point, or had had it made for them by the emotional climate of 1797: a large section of the bourgeoisie was now converted to the need for a purification of popular literature. As England entered the nineteenth century, however, the battle was far from won, and moralists were still concerned by a resistant permissiveness in the literature of Vanity Fair. Fashion journals, for example, continued to delight in prurient scandal and reports of titillating crimes: in March 1804 the *Lady's Magazine, or Entertaining Companion for the Fair Sex* gave an account of the trial of two brothers, one a clergyman, for abducting and raping a certain Rachael Lee; the main feature of the evidence, and the end of the indictment, was the latter's fatal admission that on finding further resistance useless she had torn from her breast a gold locket, crying 'The charm that has preserved my virtue hitherto, is dissolved!' and adding, as she threw it away, 'Now welcome pleasure!' (XXXV, 164–5) But the mild prurience of this story, compared with the more blatant indecencies of the fashion journals of the previous decade, illustrates that even Vanity Fair accepted certain limits. Moreover though Vanity Fair might still appreciate the frank eroticism of *The Monk*, the book in general was in eclipse and the literature of Fashion much more chaste. John Thorpe, Jane Austen's incarnation of the spirit of Vanity Fair, complained 'Novels are all so full of nonsense and stuff, there has not been a tolerably decent one come out since *Tom Jones*, except *The Monk*'; [247] but the majority of fashion conscious readers were content with the new decorum. This did not mean, however, that the moralists were content. For them the decorum of much fashionable literature, where it seemed to cover an inner moral laxity, was as dangerous as open licentiousness. Moore's *Poems of Thomas Little* (1801), for example, which went through eight editions in five years, contained love poems of what seemed an unspeakable cynicism and voluptuousness. A sizeable proportion, in short, of the respectable middle class had yet to be converted to the cause of militant purity.

Middle-Class Pressure for Reform

5 In 1806, however, a stand was made. Moore's *Epistles, Odes and Other Poems* was subjected to an attack led by Jeffrey in the *Edinburgh* as violent as that on Matthew Lewis. Like Lewis, Moore was particularly susceptible to censure by virtue of his place as the darling of fashionable society, but the fact that Moore's work was so much less erotic in its content indicates how aggressively puritanical many spokesmen for middle-class opinion were becoming. Of the nine reviews I have seen none was prepared to defend the book's morality, and most of them were vehemently hostile. A new conception of the writer's moral duty, a new intensified fear of the dangers of impure literature, were becoming characteristic of responsible opinion. 'The publication of a licentious book,' alleged the *Annual Review and History of Literature* in 1806,

> . . . is of all high crimes which can be committed against the well being of society, that for which there is the least temptation and the least excuse. It is a sin to the consequences of which no limits can be assigned, and those consequences no after repentance can counteract. Whatever remorse of conscience the writer may feel, will be of no avail; the agonies of a death-bed repentance cannot cancel one single copy of the thousands which he has sent abroad, and as long is he heaping up guilt upon himself in perpetual accumulation. (V, 499)

In this new literary climate it was inevitable that fastidious expurgators should seek to soften the writer's agonies of repentance. Bowdlerization of plays and of domestic literature had been common for over half a century, but with the increasing stress on the family unit as the salvation of society it was becoming both markedly more common and considerably more prim. In 1806 the Rev. James Plumptre began his expurgated and amended *Collection of Songs*, a monument of fastidious absurdity. [248] And in 1807 the first *Family Shakespeare* appeared, edited it seems by Thomas Bowdler's sister. It is indicative of the extreme prudery of an Evangelical minority that even the Bowdler *Shakespeare* was often attacked for being too permissive. The *Christian Observer*, for example (May 1808), thought it unsafe for young people (VIII, 326–34), and the Rev. James Plumptre that the editor 'should have gone further, and omitted, or altered, many words and expressions, which still hold a place in the work'; [249] if Plumptre, however, represented a much greater degree of squeamishness than the Bowdlers, he in turn was liberal compared with the *Eclectic Review*, which in November 1809 severely censured one of his books for daring to defend the potential moral utility of the theatre.[1] On the other hand, if these enthusiasts found the *Family Shakespeare* insufficiently purified, many others found it distinctly over-prudish. The *British Critic* (October 1807) tersely remarked: 'There are doubtless squeamish people to whom these mutilations will be acceptable. In printing from Beaumont and Fletcher, such a process would have been necessary; Shakespeare, we should think, might have escaped.' (XXX, 442) Responsible middle-class opinion had rejected the open licentiousness of Lewis; it had rejected the suggestive levity of Moore; but much of it was not yet ready to accept the castration of England's greatest poet. And yet in a few years even the prudery of Bowdler was very widespread.

6 As England entered the years of the Regency the Evangelicals, though pressing hard, had not converted the whole of the middle classes to support their brand of purity. For a start, there was still a good deal of nominal literary chastity. The old mixture in popular fiction of prurience and piety was still very

---

[1] The Evangelical horror of the theatre is nicely shown by the Methodist John Styles in his *Essay on the Stage* (1806), where he argues that 'in the choice of a wife, a gentleman should peremptorily reject every female who has been five times at a Theatre in the course of the last two years of her life'. (p. 37)

much in evidence, though the balance at least was somewhat shifted. Charlotte Dacre had briefly kept the old conventions alive: *The Libertine* (1807), for example, a tirelessly thorough catalogue of seductions by male and female voluptuaries ending predictably with a barrage of sententious moral lessons, includes the time-honoured situation of a licentious father nearly raping his own lost child. But fashionable literature in general now followed the format of writers like Mrs Brunton: in her *Self-Control* of 1811 the prurient content is fairly low, merely two abduction attempts in the first volume, another and more elaborate in the third, and lengthy scenes in which a devilish handsome rake is just held at bay by a virtuous, resourceful but half-enamoured heroine; while the prurience is subdued, the improving piety is laid on very thick, with numerous little sermons about the necessity in affairs of the heart for prudence and self-control and about the perils of imprudence. More serious, however, for the literary puritan was the disturbing popularity of a new and, as he saw it, far more dangerous school of writers. The Satanic School of poetry, we saw in a previous chapter, of Byron, Shelley, Leigh Hunt and their followers, seemed to many at this time to threaten the stability of the nation through its seditious ideas on politics, religion and morality.

To this new threat conservative opinion reacted with violent and universal vehemence, and thanks to the Government's discriminating use of the Stamp Act radical opinion was debarred from making adequate retort. The press was now more hostile than ever before or since to the expression of anything that might be considered subversive, blasphemous or immoral, and in the prevailing mood of political emotionalism the one charge denoted usually the others. If even the dedicated Tory Walter Scott could be accused of immorality, [250] one can appreciate the harsh treatment meted out to radicals like Shelley and Leigh Hunt. The latter, for example, was butchered by *Blackwood's* in October 1817 for his innocuous *Story of Rimini*: 'His poetry is that of a man who has kept company with kept-mistresses . . . with him indecency is a disease. . . . For him there is no charm in simple seduction; and he gloats over it only when accompanied with adultery and incest.' (II, 40) Even Keats, because of his association with Leigh Hunt, was reviled for his 'lubricity'. And so it was hardly surprising that *Don Juan*, when it began to appear in 1819, received a torrid reception. The consulting board of its publisher, on examining the manuscript, though friends of Byron, were unanimous in advising its suppression; and in fact the earliest cantos appeared without author's or publisher's imprint. In the event the reviews damned the immorality of Cantos I and II. Of the twenty-two reviews I have seen up to the end of October 1819, a few were unconcerned by their moral tendency,[1] and the Hunts' *Examiner* not surprisingly defended it; but the great majority of reviewers attacked them, and mostly in very vehement terms.

To *Blackwood's* (August 1819), it appeared 'in short, as if this miserable man, having exhausted every species of sensual gratification—having drained the cup of sin even to its bitterest dregs, were resolved to shew us that he is no longer a human being, even in his frailties;—but a cool unconcerned fiend, laughing with detestable glee over the whole of the better and worse elements of which human life is composed.' (V, 513) In a more moderate vein the *New Monthly* complained: 'A certain degree of fleeting reputation may be acquired by ministering to the fashionable follies and corruptions of the age; but no British poet can obtain a universal and permanent fame, excepting by the devotion of his muse to the interest of truth and justice, and the delineation of examples conducive to social happiness and virtue.' (XII, 78)

By the beginning of the 1820s alarm at the 'fashionable follies and corruptions of the age' had become so general that the extreme prudery of these moral conservatives was much

[1] Two very early reviewers, in the *Statesman* and *Morning Herald*, were untroubled by the moral issue; but they had clearly not had time to study the Cantos with any care.

more representative of middle-class opinion than the Bowdlers had been a dozen years before. Indeed, with the passing of time, with the growing threat of a revival of impure literature, the Bowdlers' mentality was now extremely common. In February 1821 a *Blackwood's* writer sharply spanked them for erecting themselves 'into a sort of *soi-disant* "Holy Family" '. (VIII, 513) But by October and Jeffrey's encomium in the *Edinburgh* they were on their way to becoming a national institution.[1] Jeffrey rejoiced that in the *Family Shakespeare*:

> Mr. Bowdler has not executed his task in anything of a precise or prudish spirit; that he has left many things in the text which, to a delicate taste, must still appear coarse and reprehensible; and only effaced those gross indelicacies which every one must have felt as blemishes, and by the removal of which no imaginable excellence can be affected . . . as what cannot be pronounced in decent company cannot well afford much pleasure in the closet, we think it bitter, every way, that what cannot be spoken, and ought not to have been written, should now cease to be printed. (XXXVI, 53)

Jeffrey's panegyric came at the peak of pre-Victorian prudery. Gratitude to Bowdler for making it possible to put Shakespeare 'into the hands of intelligent and imaginative children' was still being expressed, by Swinburne of all people, as late as the 1890s. [251] But not many enthusiasts of the *Family Shakespeare* after the 1820s would have gone as far as Jeffrey, further in fact than Thomas Bowdler himself, in claiming that the original text should be excluded even from adults' study in their closet. Within a year or so, as it happened, the strict prudery of Jeffrey was in decline. The turning point appears to have been 1822. In that year the level of prudery reached its maximum intensity as *Adonais*, an open declaration of war against the reviews, was followed by the alarming prospect of *The Liberal*, an unholy

---

[1] There were still zealots, however, who felt that the Bowdlers were too permissive. The Rev. J. R. Pitman prefaced his more strictly expurgated *School Shakespeare* (1822) with the complaint that few of the plays in the *Family Shakespeare* were 'sufficiently purified from coarse and profane expressions'.

alliance of Hunt, Byron and Shelley uniting not merely to write poems but practical journalism. In the event, however, Shelley suddenly died and the *Liberal* survived only four numbers. Anxious puritans could relax a little, and the volume of prudery declined, at first sharply, and then gradually. [252]

7 This is not to say, however, that the battle for literary purity was over. In 1825, for example, the spirit of Fashion was still sufficiently strong not only in Vanity Fair but throughout the middle classes for Harriette Wilson's *Memoirs* to enjoy large sales and a great deal of public interest, and for some of the newspapers to reprint sizeable extracts with scant attempt to justify their prurience. In the same year, moreover, and for several years to come the section of society not converted to the cause of militant purity could find titillation in the detailed reports of crim. con. actions in most of the major papers and in the prurient scurrility of such specialist scandal-sheets as *John Bull* and *The Age*. But though there were still many pockets of resistance to the advancing code of purity the battle was well in hand. *Don Juan*, it is true, had enjoyed considerable sales, but it was effectively Fashion's last anti-puritan fling for another forty years: until it was revived by Swinburne and others in the more permissive years of the 1860s it was in a state of virtual eclipse—either ignored or under severe attack. Even in 1825 the signs were very clear. John Blunt Freeman in a poem called 'Fashion' rejoiced in Byron's death and looked confidently to the restoration of literary decency:

> Yet long did Fashion in her train engage
> This bard of rank, obscenity and rage.
> Since Death his mighty head in dust has laid,
> May virtue call oblivion to her aid. [253]

In poetry, the novel and the drama the puritan could now regard the scene with the greatest satisfaction. In February 1826 the *Spirit and Manners of the Age* remarked that in the last five or six years poetry had been free from demoralizing influences 'more than one mighty but erring spirit have been swept into eternity; and most of the bards who remain to us, strike the harps of harmlessness and innocence, and many even those of piety.' (I, 105) By 1824 Keats, Shelley and Byron were all dead, and Hunt, at loggerheads with his brother and struggling with debts, had shot his bolt as a poet: the Satanic School of poets had left the field to such pious, moral and conservative writers as Barton, the Montgomerys and Mrs Hemans. In August of 1826 the *Liverpool Repository of Literature* was gratified by the present moral status of the novel: the increasing popularity of fiction it attributed partly to a relaxation of Evangelical hostility, and chiefly to the improved ethical quality of the novel—the new dignity it had attained especially through Scott. There were still writers who might shock the rigid puritan: Bulwer Lytton, for example, with the voluptuous passions of *Falkland* (1827) or the genial laxity here and there in *Pelham* (1828). But the open or covert prurience of earlier writers was now much less in evidence: the new literature of Fashion, the 'Silver Fork' school, was given very chaste foundations in such novels as Susan Ferrier's *The Inheritance* (1824), Mrs Gore's *Theresa Marchmont* (1824), and most of all in *Tremaine, or the Man of Refinement* (1825) by Robert Plumer Ward. The theatrical tastes of the age showed a similar improvement. It is true that puritan influence did not extend so far as lengthening ballet-dancers' skirts or abolishing *tableaux vivants*, but over straight drama, serious or comic, the public kept a most censorious watch: [254] it was perhaps the only period in theatrical history where the public was even more fastidious than its official guardian, the Lord Chamberlain. Finally, for all the nervous fears of middle-class alarmists, there was the impressive general chastity of proletarian literature. Because of the rapid increase in literacy (the reading population grew from about one and a half million around 1780 to seven or eight million around 1830) [255] and because of technical innovations in paper-making and printing that made literature much cheaper to buy, the working class constituted a vast new market of inexperienced readers. But thanks in part to the efforts of the Society for the Suppression of Vice and more especially to the increasing respectability of the more prosperous working class, here as in bourgeois literature literary decency had largely won the day against the allurements of fashionable permissiveness.

II 1830–1870

Early-Victorian Decorum

8 A writer in *Fraser's* (January 1851), surveying the popularity of lubricious literature in France and its consequent social dangers, remarked: 'It is not without a sentiment of national pride that we recognize the honest purpose and healthful tone which uniformly characterize the works of our most popular writers. Without prudery and without cant, they neither wound Delicacy nor shock Reverence. The scissors of Bowdler are not needed now. And the reason, we venture to believe, is that the people itself has become more delicate and more reverent.' (XLIII, 76) This national pride in the year of the Great Exhibition was by no means an empty boast. Popular literature for the past twenty years, for all the ignorant sniping of alarmist commentators, had grown increasingly moral in tone. There were admittedly a few writers like G. W. M. Reynolds, Thomas Frost and William Leman Rede, and some translators from the French, purveying semi-pornography in the cheap press and penny dreadfuls. But two recent explorers in this area have been impressed by its general level of decency, [256] particularly after the attacks by alarmists in 1847—in the 1850s Reynolds was markedly more decorous, and an attempt to revive the working classes' earlier interest in French literature by republishing Dumas, Hugo and Sue completely failed. An editorial in the *Family Herald* emphasized vigorously the respectability of the penny papers: 'there is no penny paper extant which professedly deals in obscenity or private slander.

The people is a moral censor, and publicity is the guarantee of decorum. Certain advertisements, even of the morning and evening papers, would destroy the circulation of any penny paper in London.' [257]

Middle-class literature was even more uniformly chaste. There was nothing openly indecent in the way of Reynolds or Frost, and precious little that was even equivocal. The more scrupulous reader, it is true, might take offence at the levity with which certain writers dealt with sexual situations: the amusing encounter, for example, in Marryat's *Peter Simple* (1834) between the naive hero and a prostitute (ch. 4); or the mildly risqué bedroom scene in *Gilbert Gurney* (1836) by Theodore Hook (I, 223ff); or the occasional ribaldry in R. H. Barham's *Ingoldsby Legends*, which began to appear in 1837. But such humour was never at all outrageous, and indeed could scarcely afford to be. For in the thirties there was still enough fastidiousness surviving from the nervous years before for even Dickens to be subjected to both censorship and censure: the publishers of his operetta *The Village Coquettes* (1836), fearing that young ladies in boarding-schools might be shocked by such lines as 'A winter's night has its delight,/Well warm'd to bed we go', insisted on bowdlerization; and the *Eclectic Review* (April 1837) professed to find even in *Pickwick* 'some jokes, incidents, and allusions, which could hardly be read by a modest woman without blushing'. (n.s. I, 353) Surtees' Jorrocks was too coarse in the 1840s for either his publisher Colburn or the general public, and it was only in the more relaxed years of the 1850s that he became a national institution.[1] There was admittedly a good deal of coarseness in the comic and scandal papers of the thirties and early forties: the Vanity Fair mentality in society was catered for in Hook's

---

[1] Colburn was reluctant to publish *Handley Cross* in 1843, and in the 1854 edition we can perhaps see why: there is, for example, a passage where Jorrocks is mocked by a pretty woman for falling off his horse (' "Hut! he's always on his back that old feller" ') and retorts ungallantly, ' "Not 'alf so often as you are, old gal!" ' (p. 107); this is absent from the edition of 1843, and also more surprisingly from that of 1891.

John Bull, Charles Westmacott's *The Age*, Barnard Gregory's *The Satirist* and Renton Nicholson's *The Town*. But Henry Mayhew, as editor of *Figaro in London* (1835-9) led the way to a purer comic journal in which satire could exist without scurrility and humour without equivocal suggestion. With the coming of the even more successful *Punch* in 1841 (of which Mayhew was one of the co-founders) the trend was firmly established. Thackeray's comment on the difference between the old papers and the new shows both the improved decorum of comic writing after 1840 and the genial relaxation of the voice of prudery that had accompanied it: humour is a satyr, he writes, 'But we have washed, combed, and taught the rogue good manners. . . . Frolicsome always, he has become gentle and harmless, smitten into shame by the pure presence of our women and the sweet confiding smiles of our children.' [258]

The voice of prudery in the 1840s was much more muted than in the previous decades. Every year that passed distanced further the days when powerful writers seemed to be conspiring against the nation's moral stability. The reading public could now not only trust its writers to work within the limits of decorum but was sufficiently relaxed to accept a certain degree of enlargement of these limits. Charlotte Brontë's *Jane Eyre*, for example, in 1847 presented its readers with a passionate young heroine quite unlike the conventional milksop stereotype, and showed a fair amount of candour in its treatment of sexuality. But up to June 1848 out of well over thirty reviews only a couple were really shocked and a few more somewhat startled; the rest were almost wholly favourable. After June 1848, however, with the publication of Anne Brontë's *Tenant of Wildfell Hall*, a reaction set in, and *Jane Eyre* in retrospect, and later even *Shirley* and *Villette*, were stigmatized by a number of reviewers and readers for their coarseness and indelicacy. [259] The alleged brutality in *The Tenant of Wildfell Hall* and *Wuthering Heights*, which were believed to be by the same author as *Jane Eyre*, the poor reputation of the Brontës' publisher, the political climate of 1848, a year of revolutions, the alleged vulgarity and ill-breeding of all the Brontës, and later the discovery that they were in fact women, all help to explain this turnabout in favour. We should note also by way of qualifying my remark about the relative relaxation of prudery in the 1840s that simply to count the early reviews of *Jane Eyre* is to make the voice of prudery seem more relaxed than indeed it was.

For there was a great deal of early Victorian moral squeamish-ness that received no visible expression: many prudes, for example, especially in the lower-middle and upper-working classes, were still hostile to all novels, even those that were much less daring than *Jane Eyre*. The Rev. Dismal Horror, a young Dissenting minister in Samuel Warren's *Ten Thousand a Year* (1841), preaches on the sad example of Miss Snooks, who had kept a circulating library in the neighbourhood—having visited a theatre on Thursday, she became ill on Friday and died on Saturday; most of the women in the congregation make solemn vows never again to read a novel or see a play (I, 155) The traditional prudery of Dissent was reinforced, one can easily appreciate, by the lazy and uneducated prudery of philistinism. *The Family Herald*, for instance (10 August 1850), launched a stupidly vicious attack on Shakespeare, picturing him as 'revelling in luxurious imagery, and dancing in dirt and drollery. . . . Shakespeare is fit for the very lowest society. There are none so immoral, none so irreligious, none so profane, none so unprincipled, that they may not take pleasure in his ideal creations.' (VIII, 236) The more educated reaches of society could display the same kind of sanctimonious fastidiousness as this penny journal. The *Christian Observer*, for example, true to its Evangelical heritage, declined to examine *Jane Eyre* in 1847, as it explained a decade later: 'Having little taste for this style of literature, the widespread temptation did not extend to ourselves, and we felt no difficulty in refusing to have anything to say to the books, especially after learning, from the report of more voracious readers, that the story was tinged, to say the least, with offences against delicacy, and that their tendency was, to speak most charitably, of a questionable character.' [260]

9 This degree of submerged squeamishness must not be forgotten when we talk of a relaxation in mid-nineteenth century prudery. But such a relaxation there clearly was. As England entered the 1850s it could glory in the purity of its literature, rejoice with the writer I quoted in *Fraser's* in the honest purpose and healthful tone which uniformly characterized its most popular writers. The writers themselves were in general happy to accept the limitations of family literature. Thackeray, it is true, occasionally chafed at his restrictions, as in the famous Preface to *Pendennis* (1851) praising and envying the outspokenness of *Tom Jones*. But he was fundamentally content (two years later he was attacking Fielding for indecency), and his true position is shown in the *Roundabout Papers*: 'I am thankful to live in times when men no longer have the temptation to write so as to call blushes on women's cheeks, and would shame to whisper wicked allusions to honest boys.' [261] The reader's trust in the writers of his literature was the more complete in the 1850s with the emergence of Charles Edward Mudie and W. H. Smith as unofficial national censors. Mudie, a part-time hymn-writer and lay-preacher, took great pains that no work entered his by now truly gigantic circulating library which might offend the eye of modesty; and the devout Methodist W. H. Smith was on his way to securing a book-selling monopoly on all the important railway lines of the country in which he ruthlessly excluded all indelicate books and papers. These unofficial censors were at times unduly squeamish, overresponsive to their more susceptible readers. But we should not allow the occasional excesses of mid-century prudery to distract us from its general relaxation: Michael Sadleir, for example, is quite wrong to take the ludicrous censorship inflicted on Trollope of all people by Longman's reader in 1856 as typical of the fifties. [262] The dominant mood was liberal enough for responsible writers to be able to take certain risks. Mrs Gaskell's *Ruth* (1853) and the story of Marian Erle in Mrs Browning's *Aurora Leigh* (1856) are both a case in point.

These two sympathetic studies of a fallen woman were inevitably strong meat, for all their cautious compromises, to those especially sensitive about the blush on a maiden's cheek. And women themselves, through defective education and ingrained subordination, were especially likely to be fluttered by anything unconventional and daring. It was 'women infinitely more than men' whom Mrs Gaskell found to be shocked by *Ruth*; it was women who complained to Mrs Browning that after reading *Aurora Leigh* they had never felt pure again. [263] But it is clear that this prudish response was very far from typical of the readers of these two books. Mrs Browning's injured ladies did not prevent her from feeling that 'freedom from convention really was growing when she heard of "quite decent women taking the part of the book in a sort of effervescence"'. [264] And Charles Kingsley assured Mrs Gaskell that

> . . . among all my large acquaintance I never heard, or have heard, but one unanimous opinion of the beauty and righteousness of the book, and that, above all, from real *ladies*, and really good women. If you could have heard the things which I heard spoken of it this evening by a thorough High Church fine lady of the world, and by her daughter, too, as pure and pious a soul as one need see, you would have no more doubt than I have, that whatsoever the 'snobs' and the bigots may think, English people, in general, have but one opinion of 'Ruth' and that is, one of utter satisfaction. [265]

That Kingsley was not exaggerating over-much the general response to *Ruth* is borne out by a study of the reviews. Mrs Gaskell's letters would appear to give him the lie: 'I had a terrible fit of crying all Saturday night at the unkind things people were saying . . . About *Ruth* one of your London libraries (Bell I believe) has had to withdraw it from circulation on account of "its being unfit for family reading" and *Spectator, Literary Gazette, Sharpe's Magazine, Colburn* have all abused it as roundly as may be.' [266] Whilst appreciating Mrs Gaskell's pain at receiving a number of indignant letters and protests, at being banned by a library, and having the last volume of the book burned by a couple of zealous fathers, one must note the element of self-pitying distortion here. The four reviews she mentions were part of twenty-two I have seen published in 1853. Thirteen were wholly adulatory. *Sharpe's Magazine* (15 January) did indeed abuse the book roundly in prudish terms ('we must protest against such a book being received into families' n.s. II, 126); but this was one of the only two of its kind (the *Christian Observer* was the other), though one should add that the *Dublin University Magazine* was a little uneasy in its attitude. The other three reviews mentioned by Mrs Gaskell were anything but squeamish. The *Spectator*, like the *Critic*, objected to the book's sentimental distortions; *Colburn's New Monthly*, like the *Athenaeum* and the *Westminster*, criticized it for failing to face the moral issue squarely from embarrassment with the subject. And the *Literary Gazette* brutally exposed both these weaknesses in the book. Six reviewers then were, in different degrees, anticipating W. R. Greg's well-known complaint [267] that Mrs Gaskell had been too timid, making Ruth fall through a purely technical offence and sentimentalizing her as both an immaculate saint and a properly penitent sinner. Much the same complaint was made by a number of critics three years later about Marian Erle in *Aurora Leigh*, though the majority, as with *Ruth*, wrote panegyrics about her nobility of character. This time, in 1856, there was no hostility at all to the choice of fallen woman as subject; though three reviews were troubled, particularly the *Dublin University Magazine*, by the *Clarissa*-like circumstances in which Marian is drugged and raped in a brothel.

The Beginnings of a Counter-trend

10 But if the reception of *Ruth* and *Aurora Leigh* illustrates a relaxation in prudery in the 1850s, what of Meredith's legendary misfortunes in 1859 with *The Ordeal of Richard Feverel*? Mudie's Library, having ordered 300 copies and

assured Meredith's publishers that the book seemed destined
for success, were shortly afterwards panicked into banning it
by 'urgent remonstrances of several respectable families who
objected to it as dangerous and wicked and damnable'.
Meredith's reaction was natural and to some extent quite
justified: 'There are grossly prurient, and morbidly timid
people, who might haply be hurt, and with these the world is
well stocked.' [268] But what is significant about the twenty-
five reviews of *Richard Feverel* that I have seen is not their
prurience and timidity: seventeen were quite unbothered by the
novel's sexual candour, seven were uneasy about its suitability
for young girls, but only one, again the *Dublin University
Magazine*, really morbidly squeamish. What is interesting about
the reaction to Meredith's novel is that it reflects a heightened
sensitivity on the subject of immorality. In the last two or
three years of the fifties, as we saw in the previous chapter, the
Great Social Evil and the divorce courts offered alarming
evidence of the state of the nation's morals. So it is not
surprising that Meredith's flippant and rather cynical treatment
of his hero, especially his intrigue as a married man with the
courtesan Mrs Mount, should arouse a certain hostility, a
heightened degree of prudery: nobody could have brought the
charge of levity against Miss Brontë, Mrs Gaskell or Mrs
Browning. And as England entered the 1860s, with pretty
horsebreakers focussing her marriage and prostitution problems,
with religion assailed by controversy and scepticism, with
Darwin seeming to justify a relapse into animal amorality, with
such a nexus of worrying factors, the moral conservative
was increasingly sensitive to what he considered moral
cynicism.

This fact emerges clearly from the reception in 1860 of
George Eliot's *Mill on the Floss*. *Adam Bede* in 1859, despite for
its time a certain amount of frankness in its treatment of Hetty
Sorel's seduction, had received almost universal approval: of the
twenty-three reviews that I have seen only the *North British* (on
the prominence given Hetty's sin) and the *Saturday Review* and

Examiner (on the depiction of her childbirth) showed any reservations. But in the case of the *Mill* of the twenty reviews I have seen only half accepted the tenor of the story without question. It is hard to interpret the hostility of the others except as a reaction against the writer herself. *Adam Bede* had been published pseudonymously, but the *Mill* was the acknowledged work of Marian Evans, a freethinker and more especially for many people an exponent of free love. Hence the malice in October of the *Quarterly Review*: 'if we are to accept the natural moral of this story, it shows how coarse and immoral a very fastidious and ultra-refined morality may become.' (CVIII, 496) And hence the objection even of more temperate critics to the philosophy the book appeared to advocate, its apparent reduction of man and woman to the level of mere animals: 'She evidently estimates all the natural safeguards which position, duty and feeling in a refined and delicate nature can impose as utterly inadequate to defend her against the approaches of physical passion. She enthrones physiological law so far above both affections and conscience in point of *strength*, that she represents Maggie as drifting helplessly into a vortex of passion, and rescued at last only by the last spasmodic effort of a nearly overpowered will.' [269]

11 An alarm about the nation's morals, arising largely from the resurgence in society of fashionable laxity, was producing a sensitivity about the morality of literature. But a sensitivity about the morality of literature, arising largely from the resurgence in fiction of fashionable laxity, was in turn contributing to the alarm about the nation's morals. Not long after the attacks on *The Mill on the Floss* the *Record* explained that the most important cause of society's immorality was 'the mischievous and impure character of a large portion of the current literature. The majority of the novels of the present day, and many of the biographical volumes, contain passages of the worst character. Vice is dressed out with attractive decorations. We are favoured with a series of assignations,

elopements, seductions, and every kind of indecency.' [270] It is hard to share the *Record*'s simple faith in literature as an agent of moral change, but certainly a good deal of the popular fiction of the 1860s shows a renaissance of blatant amorality that reflected the loosening manners in fashionable society. Fashion for the first time in forty years was once more having a fling. The French were often blamed for the new laxity in literary tastes. In Emma Robinson's *Madeleine Graham* of 1864 the corrupt young anti-heroine justifies her intention to marry for money without rejecting the man she loves: 'In almost all the French novels—and everybody reads them now, and thinks them so amusing—the wife has a lover, too, that she greatly prefers to the husband. And the sympathies of the reader are expected to go with her and with the lover.' (II, 122) But in fact there had been a steady flow of homegrown fast novels about marriage and adultery ever since the Divorce Act of 1857. In the first three years of the sixties, for example, there was a minor flood of novels taking bigamy as their theme, and usually holding up the erring woman for sympathy and admiration.[1] There was also a steady growth in fast novels about the courtesan. In 1864 a book appeared called *Anonyma, or Fair but Frail*, written probably by Bracebridge Hemyng, Mayhew's expert on prostitution. This was the first of a very successful series of similar novels by such writers as W. S. Hayward, E. L. Blanchard and Augustus Mayhew: the series concentrated largely on portraits of horsebreakers, often supposedly factual, as with *Skittles* and its successor *Skittles in Paris*, *Agnes Willoughby*, *Mabel Gray* and *Cora Pearl*. Their tone, spicy but largely quite unerotic, very much in the style a century earlier of de Vergy, is caught in one of the earliest titles: *Annie, or the Life of a Lady's Maid: Comprising a Full Description of all the Curious Occurrences,*

---

[1] See, for example, Miss Braddon's *Aurora Floyd*, Lascelles Wraxall's *Only a Woman*, the anonymous *Clinton Maynyard*, and *The Law of Divorce* by a Graduate of Oxford. For those who liked their sensations factual, but for whom the press reports were inadequate, there were now specialist journals like the penny paper *The Divorce News and Police Reporter*.

Intrigues, Amours, and Expedients of Fashionable Gay Life amongst the Aristocracy (1864).

12 The spirit of Fashion was cracking up the strict and uniform decorum of early Victorian literature. But serious writers too were now impatient with old restrictions. Sexual themes began to assume a quite new dominance in literature. Adultery and bigamy were used to titillate in the fast novel, but amongst serious writers the problem of marriage was given sober and candid scrutiny: in Meredith's *Modern Love*, for example, in Mrs Norton's *Lost and Saved*, in Charles Reade's *Griffith Gaunt*, in Mrs Lynn Linton's *Sowing the Wind*, and in Trollope's *He Knew he was Right*. The prostitute and the courtesan were used to titillate in the fast novel, but amongst serious writers the fallen woman was given sympathetic and candid discussion: in Mrs Houstoun's *Recommended to Mercy*, for example, in Meredith's *Rhoda Fleming*, in Felicia Skene's *Hidden Depths*, and in Mrs Craik's *Parson Garland's Daughter*. Sometimes the writer's enlargement of his freedom went too far. In 1866, only a few years after the attacks on even George Eliot for reducing man to the level of animals, it was not a propitious time for Swinburne in *Poems and Ballads* to sing of quivering flanks, kisses that sting, and bare throats made to bite. For the sado-masochism of some of the poems Swinburne was attacked more savagely than any writer since *Don Juan*. But revolt was in the air and even Swinburne was not without support among reviewers. The *Reader* and *The Sunday Times* were admittedly obtuse,[1] and the *Examiner's* picture of him as an Old Testament prophet rather beside the mark. But the sensible defences in *Fraser's* and the *Westminster* exhibit a definite movement from the conventional reticence of the past. Some indeed of the new

---

[1] Cf. Ruskin's well-known testimonial, quoted Doughty, 'I consent to much, I blame, or reject nothing. I should as soon think of finding fault with you as with a thundercloud or a night-shade blossom. All I can say of you, or them, is that God made you, and that you are very wonderful and beautiful.' (*op. cit.*, p. 490)

generation of young writers were rebelling quite aggressively against the constraints their elders had found congenial. One can hardly imagine Tennyson defending *Poems and Ballads*, like James Thomson in the *National Reformer* (23 December 1866), even without having read it, on the grounds that 'the condition of our literature in these days is disgraceful to a nation of men: Bumble has drugged all the higher powers, and only the rudest shocks can arouse them from their torpor.' (p. 403) One can hardly imagine Dickens prefacing a book as his protégé Wilkie Collins, in that same year, prefaced his novel *Armadale*: 'Estimated by the clap-trap morality of the present day, this may seem a very daring book. Judged by the Christian morality which is of all time, it is only a book that is daring enough to speak the truth.' Even the most notorious of the attacks on *Poems and Ballads*, by John Morley in the *Saturday Review* (4 August 1866), shows a reaction against the old decorum:

> If he were a rebel against the fat-headed Philistines and poor-blooded Puritans who insist that all poetry should be such as may be wisely placed in the hands of girls of eighteen, and is fit for the use of Sunday schools, he would have all wise and enlarged readers on his side. But there is an enormous difference between an attempt to revivify among us the grand old pagan conceptions of Joy and an attempt to glorify all the bestial delights that the subtleness of Greek depravity was able to contrive. (XXII, 145)

In fact there were new pressures in society to support the old decorum, to keep literature suitable for a Sunday school miss of eighteen. In the sixties the size of the fiction-reading public was notably increased, primarily by the rise of the shilling magazine and the huge expansion of Mudie's Library,[1] and with novels now more than ever being published first in a periodical and

---

[1] Between 1852 and 1862 Mudie had added nearly 960,000 volumes to nis library, of which 416,706 were fiction: he estimated that each book was read on average by at least thirty people and novels considerably more.

later as a book, there was a dual form of censorship on any authorial immodesty: in a few years Leslie Stephen, as editor of the *Cornhill*, was to caution Thomas Hardy, 'Remember the country parson's daughters. *I* have always to remember them', and Edmund Gosse to define 'Mudieitis' as the condition of fear in the writer that his work 'will be unpalatable to the circulating libraries, that the wife of a country incumbent . . . may write up to headquarters and expostulate'. [271] The size of the fiction-reading public and the pressures on literary decorum were further increased by two other contemporary developments. One was the virtual eclipse of the old puritan hostility to the novel. In October 1866 the *London Quarterly Review* noted, 'We can well remember the time when novel reading was regarded, especially among Methodists and Evangelical Dissenters, as a grave error, hardly consistent with the maintenance of a Christian profession. Now the very opposite of this is the case, and *Lady Audley's Secret*, *Aurora Floyd* or *East Lynne* may not infrequently be found lying on drawing-room tables, from which in a former generation *Old Mortality* or *The Heart of Midlothian* would have been rigidly excluded.' (XXVII, 101) Such a reader might enjoy the moralistic sensations of Miss Braddon or Mrs Wood but very possibly not be ready yet for the increasing candour of serious novelists. The same might be true of another new reader, the ex-proletarian just embarking on the intelligentsia's literature after an upbringing on the half-educated sentimental pieties of the penny magazines. Articles like the *Family Herald*'s diatribe on Shakespeare in 1850, or the naive didacticism of stories by Pierce Egan Jr. in the *London Journal* or by J. F. Smith in *Cassell's Illustrated*, would be slim preparation for the ethical shocks of the novelists of the sixties.

But despite these pressures to sustain the old decorum the fashionable novel continued on its way, continued to reject the inhibitions of the past. More and more it was accused of being polluted by French influences. In *From Olympus to Hades* (1868) Mrs Forrester complains:

There is no doubt that the literature of the day is veering round to the false sentimentality and prurient style of thought that has so long stimulated the sated palates of our warmer-blooded neighbours over the water. We are beginning rather to like the notion that we have 'wild, passionate, wilful hearts' that won't be controlled by rules or laws, by decency or order. . . . We are beginning, perhaps almost imperceptibly to ourselves as yet, to think of marriage as a certain vulgar necessity, and to look on a real, hearty conjugal love as exceptional and ill-bred. (III, 186–7)

In the following year *Formosa*, one of the courtesan novels in the series begun by *Anonyma*, was performed at Drury Lane in a play version by Dion Boucicault. And again the cry was raised about the influence of the French, that London had followed the Parisian fashion for theatrical harlot heroines. A few moral conservatives raised a storm, but *Formosa* continued to draw packed and enthusiastic houses. Fashion had made huge inroads into early Victorian prudish scruples. Indeed in February of this year George Augustus Sala, addressing his middle-class would-be fashionable audience in *Belgravia*, asked:

Are there any prudes in England at this epoch? I doubt it, I gravely doubt it much. The decline of prudery in this country dates from the day when ladies allowed men to smoke in their presence, and to talk slang and stable (they are sometimes slangy and stably in conversation themselves), and to admit the existence of such creatures as 'pretty horsebreakers'. Your prude of the old school would never have dreamed of permitting men to do anything of this kind. Cheap newspapers, the Court for Divorce and Matrimonial Causes, the frequency of foreign travel, with the confession of one's brother of Sunday evening visits to Mabille, and the Porte St. Martin during the vogue of such *décolleté* pieces as *La Biche au Bois*, may all have had something to do with the decline of that virtuous squeamishness which once led English ladies to avert their eyes from the statues on the sculpture gallery of the British Museum, to banish casts of Danneker's Ariadne and Kiss's Amazon from their drawing rooms, and to speak of the capital of Holland as 'Amster-ahem!' It has become a very free-and-easy country indeed, this England. (VII, 562)

Sala's generalization is patently absurd: as he well knew, there were plenty of prudes in England at this epoch. It was also in 1869 that Francis Newman, writing on the Great Social Evil, argued the nation desperately needed stricter literary controls and furiously attacked any one who might accuse him of being prudish: 'With eight thousand harlots in London alone, what utter nonsense is such talk! It is clear that many of us are early and profoundly corrupted: no one can tell how small a spark may cause explosion.' [272] But Sala was clearly right to point to a general relaxation in prudish scruples. Kathleen Tillotson, it seems, has been misled by the minority voice of outraged conservatives, when she argues that the 1860s were more squeamish than the 1840s, that 'twenty or thirty years later, *Jane Eyre* and *Mary Barton* would have met with far more opposition'. [273] There was indeed more prudery voiced in the 1860s. But it was often in fact a reaction to the growing laxity of attitudes in both society and literature, or the response of an older generation not yet in tune with the shift in tastes: a reflex in each case aggravated by the emergence of a much wider and in some ways more inexperienced reading public. All these factors are observable in Mudie's occasional fits of panic, in Thackeray's timorous editorial interference with Trollope and Mrs Browning, [274] or in Dickens' aversion to Charles Reade's *Griffith Gaunt* of 1866. The last example is particularly instructive. In a well-known letter to Wilkie Collins, Dickens explained that part of Reade's novel he found 'extremely coarse and disagreeable'. [275] Dickens, however, was behind the times. Some of the reviewers criticized *Griffith Gaunt*, though in much less squeamish terms, for dabbling in impropriety. But far more were either unconcerned or moved to forthright praise. The *Daily Telegraph*, the *Spectator*, the *Saturday Review*, the *Illustrated London News*, and the *Illustrated Times* all spoke with but one voice: 'We cordially commend the book to our readers, and offer our thanks to Mr Reade for a courageously conceived, courageously written and honestly exhilarating story.' [276]

In fact this 'courageous' story, like most of the controversial literature of the sixties, was not particularly daring. And in the last three decades of the century writers were to call for greater freedom than Reade's in their discussion of sexual themes. They were prepared to tolerate, perhaps support the movement for social purity, but they were not prepared to let militant prudery rule the roost in literature. If a chaste literature had not produced a chaste society, a responsible slackening of literary decorum was unlikely to precipitate any very great disaster. If anything it would be likely to do good, to focus moral problems, to educate and arouse the general public to take action. Ironically even the militant puritans would in some respects relax the restraints of prudery: their ventilation, for example, from 1869 onwards of the Contagious Diseases issue was inevitably to help the cause of candour. In 1851 *Fraser's* had rejoiced that Bowdler's scissors were no longer needed. By 1869 according to the O.E.D. the word 'bowdlerize' had entered the language and with purely pejorative connotations. As far as modern literature was concerned, for some puritans as well as the liberal-minded and fashion-conscious, Bowdler's scissors by now were no longer wanted—which marked a significant change in social attitudes.

III 1870–1900

The Struggle for New Freedoms

In May 1870 a writer in *Temple Bar* had an interesting variation on the anecdote with which I began this chapter: 'An old lady told Scott that the advance in propriety in her time had been so great, that the works she had perused in her youth without a blush she re-read in her old age with consternation. The middle-aged person of today has a precisely opposite tale to tell. In his youth he bought the novels of Sir Edward Bulwer Lytton with a certain fear and trembling. They now lie overtly upon his table, and are rapidly passing into the domain of the Sunday

Library.' (XXIX, 178–9) Another indication of the relaxed state of prudery in the opening years of the seventies is the reception of Rossetti's verse-collection of 1870. One can hardly imagine a poet of the previous generation treating sexual relations with the candour of 'Nuptial Sleep'. Still less can one imagine him writing about a prostitute as Rossetti does so candidly and tenderly in 'Jenny'.

> Your silk ungirdled and unlac'd
> And warm sweets open to the waist,
> All golden in the lamplight's gleam . . .

We remember best of course Robert Buchanan's famous attack on these poems in 'The Fleshly School of Poetry' in the *Contemporary*. But this attack, prompted more by professional jealousy than moral indignation, was in response to the critical adulation and the extensive sales Rossetti's collection had enjoyed. Of the seventeen reviews I have seen only the *Quarterly* adopted Buchanan's position. And most of them gave particular praise to 'Jenny'.[1] One of these, in *Tinsley's Magazine* (March 1871) shows the prevailing liberal climate:

> The fact that this poem has been accepted for what it is—a noble work of art, and that no voice has been raised against the situation taken for treatment, shows pretty conclusively that the outcry raised against some poetry of our day has not been the result of mere squeamishness on the part of the public, but the natural and proper stigma of ignoble work. English readers and critics have shown that they are alive to the beautiful adaptabilities of subjects once tabooed, provided the treatment be worthy of the matter, and the matter, however sad, worthy of the treatment. (VIII, 158)

The progressive liberalization of the intelligentsia noted by this writer was underpinned on a less serious level by a fashionable laxity. In 1870, for example, theatre-goers were offered three quite separate, almost simultaneous, and highly

[1] Oddly enough one of the few reviewers who did not approve of 'Jenny' was John Skelton in *Fraser's*, who had defended Swinburne passionately four years earlier.

successful productions of a French play called *Frou Frou* by
Meilhac and Halévy (not surprisingly there was a legal tussle
over the copyright of this valuable piece of property). The full
title of the pirated version, *Frou Frou, or Fashion and Passion*,
indicates the flavour of the play: it is the story of a frivolous
Parisian wife, the daughter of a roué in the demi-monde, who
elopes with her lover only to return home in penitence and die.
Plays such as this, it need hardly be said, had little intrinsic
merit, but they did at least familiarize audiences with the
treatment of sexual themes, and in this way help prepare the
way for the problem dramatists of the eighties. In a similar way
the fast novel was an ally of Hardy and other novelists. On
another level the relaxation in prudery was supported by the
candour of social purity propaganda. On 26 February 1870
an old-fashioned writer in the *Saturday Review* complained that
'a free and unembarrassed talk goes on between men and
women about contagious diseases, prostitution and the
Mordaunt scandal. It is the strangest possible reaction from
the mincing prudery of the typical English miss.' (XXIX, 278)
Increasingly in the seventies, and more especially in the
eighties, the press, pulpit and general society were prepared to
discuss the Social Evil question with a hitherto unknown
frankness.

There were still limits, however, for poets, novelists and
dramatists to observe. It was permissible, for example, to
discuss venereal diseases in a pamphlet or an article, but it was
quite unthinkable in a work of family literature. Throughout
the 1870s writers inched their way to greater freedom, but
they were prevented from making large advances by the
timorous and often philistine resistance of a vocal body of
prudery. Wilkie Collins in the preface to *Jezebel's Daughter*
(1880) expressed his frustration in very forthright terms: 'there
are certain important social topics which are held to be forbidden to the English novelist (no matter how seriously and
how delicately he may treat them), by a narrowminded
minority of readers, and by the critics who flatter their

prejudices.' In fact the critics were less a problem to the writer than the unofficial censors, the magazine editor or library proprietor, who were indeed often nervously responsive to minority opinion. In 1883, for instance, George Moore's *A Modern Lover* was well received by the reviewers but banned by Mudie after he had received complaints from 'two ladies in the country'. In 1885, however, a blow was struck for freedom. Moore decided to by-pass Mudie's by having *A Mummer's Wife* published by Vizetelly in a single volume at six shillings, less than a fifth of the normal three-decker price. In the same year Vizetelly consolidated this publishing revolution and opened the flood-gates of cheap translations from the French by issuing Zola's *Pot-Bouille*, *La Curée*, *L'Assommoir*, *Germinal*, and *Thérèse Raquin*. Another literary event of 1885 seemed to be a harbinger of progress. Richard Burton began to publish, in an expensive, limited edition, his mammoth translation of the *Arabian Nights*. Although he declined to expurgate the obscenity in these stories and in fact incorporated a lot of pretty gratuitous erotic information in his commentary, he was acclaimed almost universally by the critics (some of whom indeed complained that the book should have been made available to the general public), and was knighted shortly afterwards.

Also in 1885, however, there was a publication which was to blight much of the progress being made. The publication was W. T. Stead's 'Maiden Tribute' series in the *Pall Mall Gazette*. Nobody could accuse Stead of being squeamish in publishing these articles. His sensational revelations, coupled with the yet more lurid publicity on newspaper placards, gave his journal the nickname in Fleet Street of 'The Dirt-Squirt'. And up to a point the influence of these articles was distinctly anti-prudish: in a sense they represented a triumph for sexual frankness. Yet paradoxically one result of Stead's outspoken freedom from prudery was a new form of unofficial literary censorship. The alarm for the nation's morals that Stead occasioned stimulated the foundation of the National Vigilance Association, a body of militant puritans acting as watchdogs of public morals. Worried by the effects on the public of what they considered pornographic works, and especially worried in this respect by the influence of the French, they quickly marked out Vizetelly as a target for their attack. Their campaign against immoral literature led to the passing, in May 1888, of a motion in the Commons calling for the enforcement and, if necessary, strengthening of the statutes on obscenity and pornography. After the debate two of its instigators wrote to the press, and the latter with few exceptions endorsed everything they said, some calling specifically for Vizetelly's prosecution. In October the trial took place, Vizetelly being charged with publishing pornographic foreign works, principally *La Terre* (for which Zola had three weeks earlier been awarded the *Légion d'Honneur*). Vizetelly made the tactical error of pleading guilty, and his conviction and fine brought universal approval from the press. Next year he was prosecuted again, for publishing Flaubert, Bourget and de Maupassant. He again pleaded guilty, was this time sentenced to imprisonment, and once more the press endorsed the verdict.

It might seem possible to explain the papers' hostility to Vizetelly and Zola in Wilkie Collins' terms, as journalists flattering the prejudices of a narrowminded minority. But in fact it was much more a response to a quite new situation. In the first place, Zola for the English represented a challenge they had not encountered, except briefly perhaps with Swinburne, since the days of Byron and *Don Juan*. Their hostility was not a sign that they had suddenly grown more prudish but an indication that their sensibility was under a new degree of strain. [277]

Like Byron seventy years before, Zola could easily be seen as both salacious in his depiction of indecent details and cynical, morbid, and nihilistic in his general view of life. But his affront to traditional notions of propriety was only half the story. What perhaps alarmed the middle classes more was the huge increase in proletarian literacy that had followed the Education Acts. [278] The literature of this vast, new, inexperienced reading public could not be censored by magazines and reviews, which they did not read, nor by circulating libraries, to which through the revolution in publishing they had no need to subscribe. The law seemed the only answer. As one newspaper put it in a perhaps forgiveable manifestation of paternalism: 'There is nothing likely to be of more injury to the morals of the people than the free publication of cheap editions of works which pander to prurient tastes . . . the law should protect the masses against their own weakness, for they will buy deleterious literature if it be put cheaply in the market and sold without restriction.' [279] The press, then, could not wholly be blamed for their emotionalism; nor, in the light of the huge sales Vizetelly rather injudiciously boasted and the fact that he twice pleaded guilty to his charges, could they wholly be blamed for misjudging the purity of his motives as a publisher.

In 1893, however, when Zola was invited to England by the Institute of Journalists in his capacity as Président de la Société des Gens de Lettres, press comment was very different: Zola was, in the words of the *Spectator* (30 September) 'A Delicious Celebrity'. (LXXI, 427) Prudery had so far waned that active hostility among the respectable reading public was being replaced in some quarters by tolerance, in others by curiosity, and in others by active appreciation. In March 1891 H. D. Traill had written an article for the *National Review* on 'The Abdication of Mrs. Grundy'. Traill's announcement was at this time somewhat premature. For it was in this month that a private, unlicensed performance of Ibsen's *Ghosts* stimulated an hysterical orgy of abuse. The foremost prude on this occasion was the *Daily Telegraph*, whose theatre critic, Clement Scott, ironically was to lead three years later its anti-puritan attack on 'Prudes on the Prowl'. In a famous editorial (14 March) the *Telegraph* claimed that *Ghosts* was a picture 'of an open drain, of a loathsome sore unbandaged, of a dirty act done publicly, of a lazar-house with all its doors and windows open'. (p. 5) As with Zola, so with Ibsen, the attack was on two fronts: on his alleged salaciousness, his picture, for example, of a mother conniving at the incestuous affair of her venereally diseased son; and on his alleged decadent morbidity and nihilism, his cynical treatment of the ideals of love and honour on which society was based. *Ghosts*, it must be said, was for the Victorians peculiarly strong meat: even in the half of Europe that acclaimed Ibsen as a genius it had had to wait two years before any theatre was willing to stage it. But the hysteria was by no means universal: there were many critics prepared to defend the play, and even those who attacked it did so often less from primness than from philistine laziness and incompetence. (Ibsen technically as well as morally was an excessive challenge for many reviewers, who were sometimes mere theatrical newsmen.)

Traill's celebration of the end of Mrs Grundy was not altogether misplaced. The fact emerges more clearly when we consider the relative broadmindedness, compared with earlier decades, that was shown to less shocking and less technically unconventional plays than *Ghosts*. Two months after the Ibsen *furore* Boucicault's *Formosa*, which had shocked some people including *The Times* in 1869, was revived at Drury Lane, and thus afforded an opportunity to assess the change in the public's attitudes. 'Nowadays,' said *The Times* (28 May 1891) doing so, 'it is certain, a play which was no more audacious than *Formosa* would excite little remark. . . . the public now see with unconcern pieces of a much more corrupting tendency.' (p. 14) By the following year the relaxation in prudery was even more apparent. *Tess of the D'Urbervilles*, with its uncompromising affirmation of the purity of its heroine, was surprisingly well received. Of the twenty reviews I have seen twelve showed no embarrassment whatever at Hardy's moral challenge, six showed some uneasiness. But only two were downright squeamish: the *Saturday Review* (16 January 1892) thought Hardy had told 'an unpleasant story in a very unpleasant way'; (LXXIII, 74) and the *Quarterly* in April could find little pleasure for a wholesome-minded reader in 'this

clumsy tale of boorish brutality and lust'. (CLXXIV, 324)
Two years later George Moore's *Esther Waters*, on a somewhat
similar theme, was received so favourably by press and public
that the *Spectator* (2 June 1894) was moved to criticize this
'outburst of such uncritical enthusiasm'. (LXXII, 757) And
Hubert Crackanthorpe, surveying the change between Vizetelly's imprisonment and Zola's visit to England, could
remark that 'Mrs Grundy is becoming mythological . . . the
roar of unthinking prejudice is dying away'. [280] The major
authors were beginning to treat sexual themes with much more
freedom than before: Hardy, Gissing, Moore, Meredith and
Mark Rutherford, for example, produced in successive years,
Tess, *The Odd Women*, *Esther Waters*, *The Amazing Marriage* and
Clara Hopgood. Minor writers, like John Oliver Hobbes and
G. S. Street could make adultery a subject for wry comedy, or,
like Kipling, du Maurier and Henry Harland treat fallen
women with an unmoralistic, tender amusement. And the fast
novel had given way to the Fiction of Sexuality, which made it
look quite tame in retrospective comparison. Rhoda Broughton,
who had been thought somewhat improper in the 1860s,
reflected, 'I began my career as Zola, I finish it as Miss Yonge;
it's not I that have changed, it's my fellow countrymen'. [281]
    In some of this fiction the exploration of sexuality was on a
pretty theoretical level. In the 1880s and 1890s, for example,
people were increasingly willing to consider the weaknesses of
the present marriage system. Mona Caird's attack on it in the
Westminster of August 1888 produced a correspondence in the
Telegraph of 27,000 letters and a controversy lasting two whole
months. The debate was frequently joined by outspoken
advocates of free love, like Karl Pearson and Grant Allen, and
these extremists received a remarkably low-keyed critical
response. We can chart this growing freedom of discussion
through a group of similar novels. In each a pure, young,
idealistic heroine persuades her reluctant lover to forego
marriage for free love, but there is a difference. In Olive
Schreiner's *Story of an African Farm* (1883) the heroine pays

for her action with a very painful death; in William Barry's *The New Antigone* (1887) she is struck down by remorse, but allowed to live by her author—in a convent; in Frank Frankfort Moore's *I Forbid the Banns* (1893) she repents in time for a happy marriage with her lover; and in Grant Allen's *The Woman Who Did* (1895) she dies, but she dies quite un-repentant—a noble martyr and example for humanity. The last of these novels, for all its idiocy of argument and ab-surdities of style, went through twenty editions in a year.

With other writers the examination of sexuality was of a rather more radical kind. In Lucas Malet's *The Wages of Sin* (1890) and Iota's *The Yellow Aster* (1894) for example, we find two lady novelists making very tentative but nonetheless genuine attempts to explore woman's sexual nature; and in George Egerton's *Keynotes* (1893) and *Discords* (1894) we find a quite thorough-going essay in the rehabilitation of the flesh, an assertion of the pure animality of woman as against the prurience and hypocrisy of the repressive current code. Not surprisingly this kind of fiction aroused more opposition than the other. In March 1895 a writer in the *Westminster Gazette*, calling himself 'The Philistine', launched an onslaught on the Sex Mania of the New Fiction. He meant by this not the advocacy of free love in *The Woman Who Did* but the alleged morbid eroticism of works like *Keynotes*: 'there is all the difference in the world between a serious proposition for the reconstruction of society put out with gravity as expressing the author's profoundest convictions, and these probings of the problem of sex which characterize the new fiction'. [282] In the next month James Ashcroft Noble made a similar attack in the *Contemporary* on 'this persistent presentation of the most morbid symptoms of erotomania' (LXVII, 493). And *Reynold's News* (21 April), like a number of other papers, followed suit: 'what does all this perpetual discussion of sex mean? Wherefore this constant analysis of the passions? How comes it that the novels of today are filled with nothing but sex, sex, sex?' (p. 1)

Where had this sudden burst of puritanism come from? In

the first place the articles of 'The Philistine' and Noble had anticipated two important, simultaneous events. One was the publication of Max Nordau's *Entartung* in translation, with its thesis that all characteristically modern art showed a disease, decadence and degeneration that threatened the human race. The other, and more important, was the trial of Oscar Wilde. Almost overnight a violent reaction set in to the permissive trend, and especially the decadent excesses of the last few years. 'Whatever may happen,' *Reynold's News* (5 May) commented during Wilde's trial, 'it is certain that this whole case has stamped as pernicious the kind of literature with which Wilde's name is closely identified. That literature is one of the most diseased products of a diseased time. Indeed, so far as English writers are concerned, we do not know where we should find all the worst characteristics of our decadent civilization— its morbidity, its cold, heartless brilliance, its insolent cynicism, its hatred of all rational restraint, its suggestiveness —more accurately mirrored than in the writings of Oscar Wilde.' (p. 1) The hysterical reaction against aestheticism, the fiction of sexuality, and other symptoms of sex mania in literature, was partly the product of a sudden fear about the country's moral health, a fear that Fashion and sexual liberalism had gone very much too far. 'It is quite extraordinary,' commented the *Review of Reviews* (June 1895) 'to discover how virtuous so many people have become the moment vice is locked up. It is edifying indeed to read some of the articles in the current periodicals, but we can only regret that their appearance should have been delayed until the chief offender had been safely laid away in Pentonville.' (XI, 538) But the abrupt *volte-face* also came, as this writer and others indicated, from a fear by the press that perhaps *they* had gone too far: 'A doubt whether the pace has not been made "too hot" for the public, and consequently for profit, is showing itself in Janus-faced articles, and a general "Please, sir, it wasn't me, sir," resounds from the Press and the critics.' [283]

Indeed perhaps Wilde was the catalyst as much as the cause

of a change in literary fashions. Perhaps the real reason why 'The Philistine' and Noble met with such response was that they were articulating a fairly common view. When *Jude the Obscure* appeared a few months after the Wilde trial, H. G. Wells in the *Saturday Review* (8 February 1896) suggested that public tastes had already deserted the cause of sexual frankness before the Wilde affair. *Jude* appeared, he wrote, by an unfortunate coincidence 'just at the culmination of a new fashion in cant, the cant of "Healthiness" ':

> It is now the better part of a year ago since the collapse of the 'New Woman' fiction began. The success of *The Woman Who Did* was perhaps the last of a series of successes attained, in spite of glaring artistic defects, and an utter want of humour or beauty, by works dealing intimately and unrestrainedly with sexual affairs. It marked a crisis. A respectable public had for a year or more read such books eagerly, and discussed hitherto unheard of topics with burning ears and an air of liberality. The reviewers had reviewed in the spirit of public servants. But such strange delights lead speedily to remorse and reaction. The pendulum bob of the public conscience swung back swiftly and forcibly. From reading books wholly and solely dependent upon sexuality for their interest, the respectable public has got now to rejecting books wholly and solely for their recognition of sexuality, however incidental that recognition may be. And the reviewers, mindful of the fact that the duty of a reviewer is to provide acceptable reading for his editor's public, have changed with the greatest dexterity from a chorus praising 'outspoken' purity to a band of public informers against indecorum. . . . They out-do one another in their alertness for anything they can by any possible measure of language contrive to call decadent. (LXXXI, 153)

In fact, whether the Wilde affair was cause or catalyst of the change in fashion that Wells describes, Wells' indictment of press and public is both too cynical and severe. By February 1896, when his review was published, *Jude the Obscure* was already selling very well and critical hostility was far from universal—of the seventeen reviews that I have seen five were disturbed by the indelicacy of some of its details, but only four were really abusive and eight were whole-heartedly favourable. And the next year saw two interesting reversals of previous triumphs of prudery. In 1889 Vizetelly had been imprisoned for publishing Flaubert and Bourget; in 1897 Oxford University invited Bourget to lecture on Flaubert. In 1891 *Ghosts* had been hysterically vilified; in 1897 Queen Victoria went to see it during the Jubilee celebrations.

Nevertheless in the last four years of the century the demand for 'Healthiness' that had emerged in 1895 continued to dominate the literary scene. Some of it was by no means wholly prudish. A critic in 1896 showed the late-Victorian sensitivity to the irreverent candour of the naturalistic novel: 'as if lack of reticence and want of decorum were the hall-mark of power and life, and not the brand of vulgarity and poverty of mind'. But he also had no time for 'the immoral prudery that will not face the facts of human nature itself, and falsifies them to the young'. [284] Much of the call for 'Healthiness', however, especially among the half-educated philistines of the lower middle class and the variety of old-fashioned sentimental intellectuals, reflected a timorous narrow-mindedness about both literature and society. On 31 December 1898 in a symposium on the modern novel and morality in *Great Thoughts*, a smug and priggish journal designed for the lower orders, John Clifford exhibited a not uncommon attitude to naturalistic writers:

They do not recognise the injury that is done to the man by staining the *imagination* through and through with these evil pictures. To paint a man puling and whining because he has fallen in love with another man's wife and cannot marry her, is bad Art and bad ethics combined. Such a novel . . . gives the rein to passion, and imperils the man, the home, and the State. The story of a manly love for a pure girl, battling against a thousand odds and conquering a thousand difficulties, is a healthy diet for our ethical fibre, a consecration of the home, and a pledge of stability to the State, but the pictures of illicit and debasing love do infinite harm.

They haunt the mind; they suggest capitulations to desire; they become goads to evil; they overturn the very foundations of morality. (p. 224)

The sad feature of the dying years of the century, is that the literary field was left open very largely to just this kind of prude. The impetus of the first half of the nineties was now almost entirely spent: stagnation was everywhere. Some of this stagnation in the aftermath of the Wilde affair was fairly understandable. Before the scandal, for example, Fisher Unwin had agreed to publish *Love's Coming-of-Age* by Edward Carpenter, but afterwards, with an eye on Carpenter's pamphlet *Homogenic Love*, Unwins like other publishers felt obliged to turn it down. In October 1898 Havelock Ellis' book on sexual inversion was prosecuted successfully for obscenity. The Recorder of London dismissed the suggestion that it was a scientific work, claiming that it was impossible for anyone with a head on his shoulders to open it without seeing this was a pretence and a sham; and Massingham, the editor of the *Mail*, who had been preparing to defend it, swung round violently to reject it as 'worthless as science even if the science it professes to advance were worth studying'.[1] This sensitivity about homosexuality, though regrettable, was only to be expected. So too was the sensitivity about the decadent movement, even though with the eclipse and demise of its principal figures and journals it was patently in decline. It is sad, however, to see how prim the drama had become. Quite soon after the Wilde affair it was apparent that the 'problem plays' and 'sex plays', which had begun to discuss the more important human issues, were already fading away. Pinero was almost the only dramatist in the last years of the century to flutter prudish scruples; and the limits of theatrical

---

[1] Havelock Ellis, *My Life*, pp. 309–10. As with the Vizetelly trial the papers could not wholly be blamed for misjudging Ellis' intentions: his case was incompetently presented, with no medical evidence given in support even by himself. It was brave as well as perceptive for a number of journals, notably the *Sketch*, the *Saturday Review*, *Reynold's News* and the *Review of Reviews* to come out in his defence.

liberalism were clearly exposed when Shaw's *Mrs Warren's Profession* was eventually given an unlicensed private performance in 1902 (even J. T. Grein and William Archer, Ibsen's principal champions, were among those who found the play offensive). [285] It is sad too to see how prim the novel was becoming: the fiction of sexuality was soon a thing of the past, Hardy and the other major writers losing interest, the flashy purveyors of titillation turning to new literary fashions. W. J. Dawson in his contribution to the *Great Thoughts* symposium on the novel and morality (11 February 1899) rejoiced complacently that 'The sex novel has already had its day. For a time it was widely read because it was a novelty. It has long ceased to be a novelty, and it is rapidly ceasing to be read. There has been a swing back of the pendulum towards romance'. (p. 316) It was only in fact when the Victorian age was over that the pendulum swung again, that the novelist, dramatist and poet once more put the puritan under pressure, once more began to enlarge the limits of their discussion of sexual issues.

10

The Rise and Fall of
the Madonna

I GROWTH

1 IN THE SECOND HALF of the eighteenth century an enthusiasm for the genteel education of young girls swept through the middle classes, from the upper regions of affluence and position down to, and indeed sometimes beyond, the very brink of the working classes. 'Every village in the neighbourhood of London,' complained the *Sentimental Magazine* in July 1773, 'has one or two little boarding schools, with an inscription over the door: "Young Ladies Boarded and Educated". The expense is small and hither the blacksmith, the ale-house keeper, the shoemaker, etc. sends his daughter, who from the moment she enters these walls becomes a young lady.' [286] The kind of education these young ladies received soon came under heavy attack from preachers and moralists, who argued that sound instruction in ethics and domestic usefulness, which were the basis of good motherhood and happy, ordered homes, was being sacrificed for the acquisition of superficial, genteel accomplishments, like painting, music, foreign languages, deportment and elocution. Dr James Fordyce in his famous *Sermons to Young Women* (1765), discussing the rage for boarding schools, asked what their pupils mostly learned there, except 'to dress, to dance, to speak bad French, to prattle much nonsense, to practise I know not how many pert conceited airs, and in consequence of all to conclude themselves Accomplished Women! I say nothing here of the alarming suggestions I have

heard as to the corruption of their morals.' (3rd edn I, 25) When Thomas Marriott had made much the same charge a little earlier in his verse essay on *Female Conduct* (1759), he had claimed that very few before him had touched his subject in prose, and none in verse, excepting 'some few small sketches'. (p. XVIII) But within a few years the fashion for boarding schools was matched by a stream of 'courtesy books' in the line of those by Marriott and Fordyce, works on female education aimed at grounding middle-class aspirations to gentility on a foundation of solid moral values, at forming good women rather than mere fine ladies.

Not that the moralists were against polite accomplishments as such. On the contrary, these were an important part of a woman's grace and charm. The full title of Marriott's book was *Female Conduct: being an Essay on the Art of Pleasing, to be practised by the Fair Sex, before and after Marriage.* Women, however, were to pursue the art of pleasing not to establish their credentials to Fashion, but to exert a moral influence on their families. The *locus classicus* of eighteenth century thought upon this matter, and surely one of the 'few small sketches' Marriott had in mind, is a passage in Thomson's 'Autumn' (1730):

> To teach the lute to languish; with smooth step,
> Disclosing motion in its every charm,
> To swim along and swell the mazy dance;
> To train the foliage o'er the snowy lawn;
> To guide the pencil, turn the tuneful page;
> To lend new flavour to the fruitful year,
> And heighten nature's dainties; in their race
> To rear the graces into second life;
> To give society its highest taste;
> Well-ordered home man's best delight to make;
> And, by submissive wisdom, modest skill,
> With every gentle care-eluding art,
> To raise the virtues, animate the bliss,
> Even charm the pains to something more than joy,
> And sweeten all the toils of human life:
> This be the female dignity and praise. (lines 594–609)

A woman's artistic accomplishments were meant to sweeten the toils of life, to give society order and taste, and to make virtue both attractive and influential through its charm. But to be fully effective in bringing comfort, harmony, and moral improvement to society they needed to be grounded on principled conduct and to be balanced with the skills of domestic economy. Without this ethical and practical basis, it was argued, artistic accomplishments were not only ineffective but often positively harmful, encouraging frivolity and vanity in their possessors and giving them a very doubtful moral influence on their admirers. Moreover, claimed the moralists, all too frequently the lack of this two-fold basis in young ladies' education quite extinguished all their power to please. Their time and energy were dissipated in the frivolities of Fashion, in a preoccupation with dress, dancing and card-playing, with ceaseless visiting, idle talk and gossip.

The responsibility for this lack of moral discipline, this inattention to household duties, was not difficult to determine: 'For whatever perverts the passions of their daughters, or intoxicates their fancies with giddiness and pride, dazzles their rising minds with the glare of fashion, or inflames their tender affections with fictitious desires, may be traced with certainty to the pernicious and ill-judged tenderness of mothers.' [287] 'Ill-judged tenderness' in fact was a more gentle criticism than was commonly levelled at England's mothers. The lack of guidance they gave their offspring was attributed more often to their own devotion to worldly pleasures and genteel posturing: 'Would to heaven,' complained Dr Fordyce in some remarks on the importance of domestic economy, 'that of this science many mothers would teach their daughters but the common rudiments; that they were unfashionable enough to educate them to be fit for any thing beyond mere show! (I, 226) But if England's mothers were to blame, so too were the moralists themselves. For poets and 'courtesy book' writers rarely recognized the contradictions latent in their views of the Art of Pleasing. They preached the need for female education to be based on firm morality, and yet we find even one of the most sensible of them counselling girls to practise guile and insincerity, to conceal from men, for example, any evidence of unfeminine qualities such as robust health or an informed intellect. [288] They preached the need for female education to be based on domestic usefulness, and yet we find at the centre of their idealization of women, in, for example, Thomson's talk of woman's 'winning softness', a celebration of feminine fragility and helplessness:

> In them 'tis graceful to dissolve at woe;
> With every motion, every word, to wave
> Quick o'er the kindling check the ready blush;
> And from the smallest violence to shrink
> Unequal, then the loveliest in their fears;
> And, by this silent adulation soft,
> To their protection more engaging man. (*loc. cit.*, lines 79–85)

With masculine egotism cloaked in a protective, sheltering solicitude, feminine egotism was led to express itself in a quivering sensibility, in counterfeiting a delicate, physical fragility, in cultivating a modish, self-centred listlessness or self-indulgent posturing romanticism. To be helplessly fretful over a sick canary, to be melted to tears by the latest poem or novel, was not only easier but often more profitable with men than the exercise of energetic duty.

Contemporaneously with the growth of 'courtesy books' arose a school of novels which gave short shrift to this kind of affected sensibility. These were forthright works of propaganda, written for women and usually by women, stressing the mother's educational responsibilities to her children, many of them with self-explanatory titles like *The Exemplary Mother* (1769) by Maria Susanna Cooper, the anonymous *Twin Sisters, or the Effects of Education* (1789), *The Errors of Education* (1791) by Mrs Eliza Parsons, or Mrs Jane West's *The Advantages of Education* (1792). In the last of these, a frank piece of didacticism, more of a tract than a novel, we are shown an astonishingly perfect mother, a paragon of prudence, wisdom, self-control, modesty and dignity, who comes home from abroad to find her daughter tarnished, but not yet corrupted, by the education she has received in a fashionable boarding school. The daughter is systematically re-educated by her mother, first to reject the blandishments of fashionable vanities and then to discipline her tendencies to immoderate sensibility, the emotional excesses of an abortive and misguided love-affair. In 1796 Mrs West delivered another sermon about the dangers of false refinement and romantic emotionalism in *A Gossip's Story*, a tale with interesting similarities to Jane Austen's *Sense and Sensibility*, written two years later. One can appreciate the anxiety of moralists at this time at the elevation of feeling over moral sobriety and duty. In August 1798 the *Anti-Jacobin Review* published a cartoon which included a figure of Sensibility in a cap of liberty, weeping over a dead robin and trampling on a crowned and severed head: the implicit argument, as J. M. S. Tompkins notes, was clearly to the effect that over-indulged feelings loosened the bonds of moral constraint, destroyed the sense of proportion, and induced a self-centred callousness of heart. (*op. cit.*, p. 111)

2 Certain kinds of fashionable sensibility moreover seemed yet more dangerous to the health of English society, encouraging women, it was alleged, to forsake traditional notions of religion and morality for subversive new ideas. The vogue, for example, enjoyed by Rousseau's *Nouvelle Héloise* and Goethe's *Werther* in the last quarter of a century produced a succession of books warning fashion-conscious readers of their peril.[1] In the panic of the 1790s, particularly after 1797, when moral reform seemed England's only protection from subversion and

[1] For an engaging account of an advocate of the merits of the *Nouvelle Héloise* being barred the house by an outraged father see *The Early Diary of Frances Burney 1768–1778* ed. Annie Raine Ellis (1889) I, 290–2. For attitudes to Rousseau and to *Werther* generally see Utter and Needham, *op. cit.*, pp. 126–7; Tompkins *op. cit.*, p. 84.

revolution, moralists were very sensitive to the dangers of insidious demoralization. Hannah More in her *Strictures on the Modern System of Female Education* (1798), which was in its eighth edition by the following year, called for women's influence 'to raise the depressed tone of public morals, to awaken the drowsy spirit of religious principle, and to re-animate the dormant powers of active piety . . . at this period, when our country can only hope to stand by opposing a bold and noble unanimity to the most tremendous confederacies against religion, and order, and government, which the world ever saw'. (I, 4–5) But in this hour of greatest need the women of England seemed in danger of becoming the dupes of fashionable folly. John Bowles in his *Remarks on Modern Female Manners* (1802) claimed that

> Of all the dangers to which this country is now exposed, great and manifold as they are, not one, perhaps, has so destructive a tendency, as the disposition which manifests itself among the fair sex, particularly in the higher circles, to sacrifice decency at the shrine of fashion, and to lay aside that modesty, by which the British fair have long been pre-eminently distinguished. He must have a very superficial knowledge of human nature; he must be consummately ignorant of the structure of the social machine; who does not see, in this disposition, a much more formidable enemy than Buonaparte himself, with all his power, perfidy, and malice. (p. 11)

With this background in mind we can understand why in 1806 Mrs West should devote the longest of her *Letters to a Young Lady* to a comprehensive attack on 'Absurdities and Licentiousness among Women of Fashion'; we can understand too the significance in *Leonora* of that year by Miss Edgeworth of the contrast starkly drawn between on the one hand the fashionable vanities and emotional affectations of the heroine's closest friend, and more especially the dangerous ideas on religion, marriage and motherhood she had derived from French and German sensibility (*Werther* is her favourite novel), and on the other the infallible good sense and impeccable ethics of the heroine's paragon mother.

Amidst the prevailing suspicion of revolutionary ideas feminist works like Mary Wollstonecraft's *Vindication of the Rights of Woman* (1792) seemed utterly pernicious to the moralists: Hannah More's *Strictures* indeed were intended in some measure as an antidote to that book (see I, 68–72). But if Miss More had troubled to read the *Vindication*, which apparently she did not, [289] she would have found a good deal of common ground. For despite the revolutionary flavour of the title Mary Wollstonecraft's book was less a treatise on women's rights than a rambling discussion of the social factors inhibiting women from playing their vital role at a critical time, their role as virtuous mothers. Some of the remedies she offered, such as the liberation of women from educational, professional and electoral inequalities, were anathema to conservative moralists. But her diagnosis, her attacks on fashionable dissipation and fashionable sensibility, for example, was extraordinarily similar to that given six years later by Hannah More. Ironically too Miss More's own stance had more than a touch of feminism, at least compared with the masculine condescension of earlier moralists. The poets and 'courtesy book' writers of the previous generation had seen woman as a polisher of manners rather than as a reformer of morals. Now the emphasis had changed under the pressure of Evangelicalism and political anxiety. Accordingly what man now wanted in his wife, argued Miss More, was not 'winning softness' so much as ethical maturity. 'It is not merely a creature who can paint, and play, and dress, and dance; it is a being who can reason and reflect, and feel, and judge, and act, and discourse, and discriminate; one who can assist him in his affairs, lighten his cares, sooth his sorrows, purify his joys, strengthen his principles, and educate his children.' (I, 107) The poets too were changing their views of the ideal woman very considerably, stressing increasingly, as in Wordsworth's 'She was a phantom of delight' (1804), not woman's power to charm so much as woman's power to strengthen:

The reason firm, the temperate will,
Endurance, foresight, strength and skill;
A perfect woman nobly planned,
To warn, to comfort, and command;
And yet a spirit still and bright
With something of angelic light.

3 Preaching the necessity for women to conform to the new
ideal, moralists were disturbed to find for the next three decades
that, though they were making headway, the old style of
fashionable education continued still to flourish. In 1831, for
example, the anonymous author of *Females of the Present Day*
repeated Hannah More's accusation about the rage for Fashion
running through society at a time when there was 'confusion
and disorder in every rank and degree of life'. Instead of being
'employed in averting the storm which now threatens us'
female education seemed only 'to serve the purpose of vanity,
and to comply with the dictate of fashion';[1] instead of training
girls to be virtuous mothers and efficient homemakers it seemed
designed to produce only self-indulgent slaves to affected
sensibility and helpless, genteel, domestic ornaments, Mrs
Ellis' *Women of England* (1838) was based on the premise that

> . . . the women of England are deteriorating in their moral
> character, and that false notions of refinement are rendering them
> less influential, less useful, and less happy than they were. . . . By
> far the greater portion of the young ladies (for they are no longer
> women) of the present day are distinguished by a morbid
> listlessness of mind and body, except when under the influence of
> stimulus, a constant pining for excitement, and an eagerness to
> escape from everything like practical and individual duty. (pp.
> 15–17)

But if many had ignored the call to moral duty, still many
more were answering. For Mrs Ellis' book went through

[1] Pp. 5, 182, 14. The immediate source of the writer's fears for England's
safety seems to have been the French September Revolution of 1830.

sixteen editions between 1838 and 1841, and she followed up her success with *The Mothers of England* and *The Wives of England* (both 1843), and *The Daughters of England* (1845).

Propagandist novels on the subject of good motherhood were also frequently best-sellers. In the very popular *Amy Herbert* (1844), for example, by Miss Sewell we have a similar format to that of Mrs West's *Advantages of Education* fifty years before: Amy, well brought up by a perfect mother, is contrasted with the ultimate tragic frivolity of her badly mothered cousins. And in *Emilia Wyndham* by Mrs Marsh, of 1846, the advantages of Emilia's education by her mother are contrasted with the unfortunate upbringing given her husband by his, and still more the near-disastrous upbringing given Emilia's friend: 'Such was the effect of the evil passions and prejudices of that deformity of nature—that most fatal and mysterious form of evil—*a bad mother!*' (II, 30)

Emilia Wyndham is very like the education novels of the previous century. But in one respect, the emphasis given to the heroine's duties as a wife, the difference is significant. For by this time moralists, novelists and poets were insisting increasingly on women's function as the tutelary angels of their husbands. It was the wife's part by the inspiration of her purity to save her husband from the perils of sensuality, from the dehumanization of the cash nexus, from doubts about the moral and spiritual reality of man. It was the wife's part through the warmth of her affection to shelter her husband from the psychic pressures of the age, the stress of new ideas and technological changes—to give him the comfort and security he had enjoyed, or found wanting, in his mother as a child. And it was the wife's part through this purity and affection to offer her husband a complement or substitute for faith, a confirmation of God's existence or at least a quasi-religious outlet for doubt-inhibited emotions. It was natural that this changing emphasis in the feminine ideal should lead to an extension of the Angel Mother image.

II ASCENDANCY

4 When the hero of Thackeray's *Esmond* protests that Lady Castlewood 'is as pure as an angel', her repentant husband assenting describes her in earlier years 'when she used to look with her child more beautiful, by George, than the Madonna in the Queen's Chapel'. (p. 140) For the Victorian idealist frightened by sex, devoted to motherhood, and troubled by religious doubts the Virgin Mother, as a feminine archetype, combined immaculate sexual purity, perfect motherly love and a vehicle for pent-up religious emotions.

It might be thought that such a metaphor, in an age of often bigoted controversy, might be subject to accusations of impiety. But in fact even the most frigid Evangelicals were prepared to countenance its use. *The Mother's Mission*, a story published in 1858 by the Religious Tract Society, was admittedly somewhat cautious: the brother of the triumphant mother heroine (who is in truth repellently and almost insanely over-protective with her children) tells her, 'I feel tempted to appropriate to you an angel's salutation to the favoured one of old, and to say, "Blessed art thou among women".' (p. 238) Much more remarkably the heroine of Emma Worboise's *Father Fabian, the Monk of Malham Tower* (1875), who delivers much of the novel's violent invective against Roman Catholicism and especially its Mariolatry, is yet herself described from her first appearance as having a sad and beautiful 'Madonna-like face'. (p. 54) By this time Madonna was a not uncommon sobriquet for women. In November 1830 we find *Fraser's* making fun of the poet Alaric Watts for calling his wife Madonna (II, 492), and in 1854 evidence that some people thought it irreverent—Wilkie Collins in *Hide and Seek* has the heroine's adoption of that name defended at some length. (I, 110–1) But there was no hint of absurdity or impiety when in the late 1850s the devout Elizabeth Barrett Browning applied the name to the well-known writer on womanhood, Mrs Jameson, or when in the 1860s a young clergyman called Story bestowed it on the novelist Mrs Oliphant, or when in the 1870s Robert Louis Stevenson and G. H. Lewes frequently used it with their loved ones, Mrs Sitwell and George Eliot. [290]

Wilkie Collins' heroine, like it seems the wife of Alaric Watts, [291] had a distinct facial resemblance to the Madonnas painted by Raphael; and clearly, as the remark I quoted from *Esmond* indicates, the visual element played a large part in the identification of women as Madonnas. Julia Margaret Cameron, for example, the pioneer camera-portraitist, made numerous Madonna studies in the 1860s of her favourite model, her parlourmaid May Hillier, and from these the latter became known locally as Mary Madonna. [292] It could be argued in fact that the models used by Raphael had very much an English style of beauty. Hippolyte Taine at any rate was much struck by it in the sixties: 'The fair maiden—lowered eyes, blushing cheeks, purer than a Raphael Madonna, a kind of Eve incapable of a Fall, whose voice is music, adorable in her candour, gentleness and kindness; one is moved to lower one's eyes respectfully in her presence. . . . the perfect flower of England.'[1] And in 1884 George Barlow began a collection of poems called *An English Madonna* with a lament that he lacked the power of Raphael to convey the beauty of his beloved to posterity:

> A new Madonna-face thou hast. Our skies and waters
> See faces fair as those of old Italia's daughters
> Whose dark sweet pure eyes gleam
> Forever through the might of Raphael . . .

There is a clear connection then between visual appearance and the currency of the image of the Madonna. But this

---

[1] *Op. cit.*, p. 56. I should point out that this style was not to everybody's taste. The forthright Mrs Trollope in *Uncle Walter* (1852) much prefers the irregular features of her heroine 'so rich in expression, so stamped with intelligence' to 'the incontestable insipidity of Raphael's Madonnas'. (I, 40)

currency was by no means dependent on any accident of national physical types. Neither Mrs Oliphant nor George Eliot, by the wildest stretch of imagination, could have been confused with one of Raphael's models. In the case of the former, as with the heroine of her novel *Madonna Mary* (1867), the sobriquet may have originated 'perhaps with some faint foolish thought of Petrarch and his Madonna Laura' (I, 18); but with George Eliot there is no question it was the moral, rather than the literary or artistic, resonance of the name that was predominant. The first lines of *Middlemarch* (1872), for example, compare Dorothea's beauty with that of the Blessed Virgin as she appeared of old to Italian painters, and Ladislaw's German painter friend regards her as 'the most perfect young Madonna I ever saw'. (I, 290) But the point of the comparison lies in Dorothea's moral beauty, her inspirational quality, as for example, when Lydgate rides away after meeting her thinking 'This young creature has a heart large enough for the Virgin Mary'. (III, 361) It was this element rather than the physical which established the currency of Madonna imagery. Indeed one can argue that the English physical type, the figure of soft, pure modesty that moved Hippolyte Taine to reverence, was itself largely a product of the moral propaganda broadcast from the 1790s onwards. In the first half of the century, for example, we find a Madonna hair style in vogue, literary heroines characterized by softness, simplicity and innocence having their hair parted on their temples 'a la Madonna'. [293]

5 It was not in short facial lineaments or hair-styles that caused men to apply the Madonna image to their loved ones, it was the moral qualities of purity and love that lay behind them. In an early poem 'Isabel' Tennyson panegyrized his mother as 'The queen of marriage, a most perfect wife':

> the world hath not another
> (Tho' all her fairest forms are types of thee,

And thou of God in thy great charity)
Of such a finish'd chasten'd purity.

Quite naturally, in celebrating the comfort and inspiration of
her perfect love and purity he was led to talk of 'locks not
wide-dispread/Madonna-wise on either side her head'. In a
slightly later poem 'To Rosa' (1836) Tennyson panegyrized
his early love Rosa Baring, and the fact that he found in her
the same kind of inspiring moral qualities is implicit in the
reference to her 'madonna grace of parted hair'. [294]
Thackeray, on beginning *Pendennis*, wrote of his mother: 'I look
at her character, and go down on my knees as it were with
wonder and pity. It is Mater Dolorosa, with a heart bleeding
with love'. [295] We can appreciate then his rapture in the
novel at the reunion of Pen and Helen: 'What passed between
that lady and the boy is not of import. A veil should be thrown
over those sacred emotions of love and grief. The maternal
passion is a sacred mystery to me. What one sees symbolised in
the Roman Churches in the image of the Virgin Mother with
a bosom bleeding with love, I think one may witness (and
admire the Almighty bounty for) every day.' (p. 19)

One of the greatest attractions of Roman Catholicism for
converts was clearly the emphasis it gave to the Virgin Mother.[1]
This attraction it seems was often less doctrinal than psychological. A Tractarian curate on the brink of Rome in *Yeast*
indicates the Virgin's protective motherly powers for men
beset by doubt: "Would you have me try to be a Prometheus,
while I am longing to be once more an infant on a mother's
breast? . . . . Will you reproach me, because when I see a soft
cradle lying open for me . . . with a Virgin Mother's face
smiling down all woman's love about it. . . . I long to crawl
into it and sleep awhile?" (p. 64)

The Catholic convert Coventry Patmore, in a note on the

---

[1] It was an attraction too for the unconverted: see, for example, Leslie
Stephen's excited remark on the birth of his first child, 'As for a mother and
child in the attitude of a Madonna, I can only say that the sight goes some
way to reconcile me to papists'. (Noel Annan, *op. cit.*, p. 65)

Virgin Mary, indicates her powers as a symbol of immaculate sexlessness for men who reverenced feminine purity: 'All who approach womanhood in holy awe and belief in her perfection and with the mystic passion of refusal which is the first motion of love, believe in, love, and worship thee.' [296] Despite the sexual mysticism of some of *The Unknown Eros* poems Patmore's celebration of married love remained always on the passionate but unerotic level of *The Angel in the House*; his projected but unfinished *Marriage of the Blessed Virgin* (1876–8), a celebration of Joseph's 'mystic passion of refusal', his acceptance of a purely virgin union with his wife, was if anything a more ascetic casting of his pre-conversion views.

It was this kind of Catholic asceticism that led some anti-Papists to reject the Madonna as an image of sexual perfection. Kingsley, for example, an eminent advocate of the Angel Mother ideal, advised a young clergyman on the point of becoming a Romanist to 'look at St Francis de Sales or St Vincent Paul's face—and then say, does not your English spirit loathe to be such a prayer-mongering eunuch as *that*? God made man in His image, not in an imaginary Virgin Mary's image.' [297] In a similar way Charlotte Brontë, another adherent to the ideal of motherly womanhood, rejected any suggestion of Mariolatry. In *Shirley* Robert Moore tells Caroline Helstone, 'My mother was a Roman Catholic; you look like the loveliest of her pictures of the Virgin: I think I will embrace her faith, and kneel and adore' (II, 317); and he is rebuffed for his pains. The reason is clear from Charlotte Brontë's use of the Madonna image in this novel, in *The Professor*, and in *Villette*, her application of it not to her heroines but to women of a statuesque, frigid and bloodless kind of beauty. [298] It is clearest of all perhaps in her poem 'Apostasy', where a dying woman refuses to revert to the faith she has given up for love:

> Point not to thy Madonna, Priest,—
> Thy sightless saint of stone;

> She cannot, from this burning breast,
>   Wring one repentant moan. . . .

> 'Tis my religion thus to love,
>   My creed thus fixed to be;
> Nor death shall shake, nor priestcraft break
>   My rocklike constancy!

Other non-Catholics, less repelled by Papist theology and asceticism, had none of this difficulty in accepting the Madonna as a figure of ideal womanhood. In George Eliot's *Felix Holt* (1866) the troubled hero draws comfort from the beauty of his beloved, looking up at her quite calmly, 'very much as a reverential Protestant might look at a picture of the Virgin, with a devoutness suggested by the type rather than by the image: an inspiring beauty who makes a great task easier to men.' (II, 39) In her *Legends of the Madonna* (1852) Mrs Jameson claimed that where others saw only pictures or statues of the Virgin she saw the prospect 'of the coming moral regeneration, and complete and harmonious development of the whole human race, by the establishment, on a higher basis, of what has been called the "feminine element" in society'. (p. xix) The working-class radical Gerald Massey in a poem called 'Woman' also prophesied a new world of moral purity to be brought about by the feminine element:

> She is the natural bringer from above;
> The Earthly mirror of Immortal Love;
> The chosen Mouthpiece for the Mystic Word
> Of Life Divine to speak through; and be heard
> With human Voice, that makes its Heavenward call
> Not in one Virgin Motherhood, but all.

> Unworthy of the gift how have Men trod
> Her pearls of pureness, Swine-like in the sod,
> How often have they offered her the dust
> And ashes of the fanned-out fires of lust;
> Or, devilishly inflamed with the divine,
> Waxed drunken with the Sacramental wine. . . .

Our coming Queen must be the Bride of Heaven;
The Wife who will not wear her bonds with pride
As Adult doll with fripperies glorified;
The Mother fashioned on a nobler plan
Than Woman who was merely made from Man. [299]

Massey's simplistic millennialism might seem not unsimilar
to that which had been rebuked a number of years earlier by
George Eliot. Discussing 'Silly Novels by Lady Novelists' in
the *Westminster* (October 1856) George Eliot had ridiculed one
novel of that year called *The Enigma*, whose simple solution to
the problem of the existence of evil was made plain from the
very first page: 'The spirited young lady, with raven hair, says,
"All life is an inextricable confusion," and the meek young
lady, with auburn hair, looks at the picture of the Madonna
which she is copying,—and—"There seemed the solution of
that mighty enigma".' (n.s. X, 450) But in fact George Eliot
herself saw the Madonna as a kind of answer to the problem of
evil: she was thoroughly captivated by the ideal of woman
represented by the Virgin. In Dresden the following year she
went back again and again to see Raphael's Sistine Madonna;[1]
and in *Scenes of Clerical Life* (1858) she introduced her very first
literary heroine with the words 'She was a lovely woman—Mrs
Amos Barton; a large, fair, gentle Madonna.' (I, 24) Her absorption in the Virgin feminine type is most manifest in
Romola. At one point she juxtaposes a chapter called 'The
Unseen Madonna', referring to a purely religious, processional
image, with a chapter called 'The Visible Madonna', a
description of Romola's work among the starving and the sick:
' "Bless you, Madonna! bless you!" said the faint chorus, in
much the same tone as that in which they had a few minutes
before praised and thanked the unseen Madonna.' (II, 146)
Later a drifting boat by chance takes Romola to a secluded,
plague-ridden village, where her mysterious arrival and her

[1] Other Comtists besides George Eliot were much taken by the Virgin:
Frederic Harrison put a large copy of the Sistine Madonna in his Comtist
school along with the busts of great men of all ages.

immediate action of nursing a Jewish baby presents an astonishing picture for a young boy looking on:

> Romola certainly presented a sight which, at that moment and in that place, could hardly be seen without some pausing and palpitation. With her gaze fixed intently on the distant slope, the long lines of her thick grey garment giving a gliding character to her rapid walk, her hair rolling backward and illuminated on the left side by the sun-rays, the little olive baby on her right arm now looking out with jet-black eyes, she might well startle that youth of fifteen, accustomed to swing the censer in the presence of a Madonna less fair and marvellous than this. (II, 403–4)

Not surprisingly the boy concludes that Romola is literally 'the Holy Mother, come to take care of the people who have the pestilence'.

It need hardly be said that in the character of Romola there is a good deal of self-indulgent fantasy-projection: George Eliot at the time of writing, like her heroine, was a childless 'mother', looking after Lewes' children like Romola with Tito's. There is a good deal too of self-indulgent religiosity, the sentimental residue of a lost religious faith. But there is also in *Romola* the rigorous self-mortification of humanist idealism: 'You are right in saying that Romola is ideal,' George Eliot told a correspondent, 'I feel it acutely in the reproof my own soul is constantly getting from the image it has made. My own books scourge me.' [300] George Gissing might have described *Workers in the Dawn*, his novel of 1880, in somewhat similar terms. On one level it is a fantasy distortion of the facts of Gissing's life: Golding, the autobiographical hero, is tied in marriage to a dehumanized and dehumanizing slut, yet ennobled by his chaste love for Helen Norman, a 'sweet and placid-faced Madonna'. (III, 171) On another level, however, it is the study of inadequate idealism, of Golding's failure to live up to Helen's ethical directives, to follow her example of self-sacrificial goodness.

Helen's rarefied, sentimentalized goodness in fact was

becoming somewhat exceptional by the eighties amongst writers of Gissing's quality. With greater realism in the novel the old ideals were beginning to look as false as the former fictional conventions. 'Whatever comes next,' Edmund Gosse claimed in 1890, 'we cannot return, in serious novels to the inanities and impossibilities of the old well-made plot, to the children changed at nurse, to the Madonna-heroine and the godlike hero, to the impossible virtues and melodramatic vices'. [301] Gosse was not entirely right; for the madonna-heroine, though much less common, was still in evidence in the nineties. Sometimes she was prominent in rather unlikely places, as, for example, in the Fiction of Sexuality. In 1881 Ruskin had pronounced, 'All beautiful fiction is of the Madonna. . . . And all foul fiction is *lèse majesté* to the Madonna and to womanhood.' [302] One wonders how he would have described George du Maurier's *Trilby* (1894), where the heroine, an immoral little waif almost submerged in sin, who at one point is explicitly dissociated from the image of the Virgin (I, 241–2) is yet finally remembered for 'that good smile like the Madonna's, so soft and bright and kind!' (III, 170) One wonders if Ruskin would have been shocked by *A Yellow Aster*, Iota's controversial study of female sexual frigidity, where the heroine awakens to womanhood through the painful joys of motherhood, to be described as 'the figure of a new Madonna, before whom the whole world must kneel and rise up to call her blessed'. (III, 196) One wonders finally what Ruskin would have made of Grant Allen's *The Woman Who Did*, a fervent attack on marriage which is yet soaked in Madonna-worship: when the heroine refuses to renounce free love for marriage she is pictured as 'a lonely soul, enthroned amid the halo of her own perfect purity . . . like one of those early Italian Madonnas, lost in a glory of light that surrounds and half hides them' (p. 102); when her defiance of social custom brings her misery she has 'the beauty of a broken heart, of a Mater Dolorosa, not the round-faced beauty of the fresh young girl' (p. 156); and when her sufferings reach a climax she draws comfort from a portrait of the Virgin, which for her is 'no mere emblem of a dying creed, but a type of the eternal religion of maternity. The Mother adoring the child.' (p. 234) Even for a sexual iconoclast like Allen the cult of the Madonna had by no means had its day.

III DECLINE

6 Just how vigorous and widespread the Madonna cult had been is rather difficult to judge. One wonders how many even of the middle classes, let alone society at large, shared the views of the sexual idealists, how many of the people who bought a quarter of a million copies of *The Angel in the House* in forty years and seventeen editions of *The Princess* in just thirty, really understood or believed what Patmore and Tennyson were preaching. To a large extent, it seems certain, the ideal was given purely nominal assent: a mere convention, not a deeply felt conviction.

The Victorian woman, we saw in an earlier chapter, was often a slave to conventional opinion; a timid creature who saw everything in the wide world through the coloured glasses of the proprieties, whose intellectual horizons rarely stretched beyond the patterns of the antimacassars and doylies she seemed to be endlessly making, whose interest in ethics seemed to go no further than dutifully reading uplifting works and casting languishing looks at the curate. Significantly in July 1863 the *Christian Remembrancer* describes the years which saw the first flowering of Madonna idealism as

A time when the charge against young ladies was a marked love of sermons and a too exclusive devotion to the persons that preached them; then they were the subjects of tender ridicule for a fantastic refinement . . . then it was interesting and an attraction, at least to seem to live in ignorance of evil; then they felt it good taste to shrink from publicity, and submitted to the rules of punctilio and decorum as if they liked them. Those were the days when the red coat was not unreasonably jealous of the academic gown, when dash was not the fashion, when the ordinary gaieties of life were entered into not without a disclaimer, and an anxiety to assert an inner preference for something higher and better, fuller of heart and sentiment, satisfying deeper instincts. (ns. XLVI, 209)

With many women the new feminine ideal was more a question of fashion than of faith. Mrs Sandford in *Woman in her Social and Domestic Character* (1831) indicates the danger of incomplete sincerity, of women finding the patronage of charities, the distribution of bounty among the poor, the cultivation of a delicate spirituality, merely a charming and elegant posture: 'Simplicity, too, may be more becoming than ornament; and beauty seldom loses any thing by Madonna tresses and a sombre robe.' (p. 124)

With some indeed the adoption of the current style in womanhood, like the current style in hairdressing, was less conventionalism than rank hypocrisy. Rosalia St Clair in *Fashionables and Unfashionables* (1827) describes a young girl at her morning toilet:

Young as was Julia Carlingford, for she had not yet completed her nineteenth year, her incessant devotion to fashionable follies, late hours. and the indulgence of evil passions, had robbed her fine features of the first early freshness of youth, and art was sometimes called in to remedy the defect. On this morning however she resolved to assume the interesting languor of fatigue and delicate health . . .

Arrayed in a morning dress of plain muslin, with an unpretending Brussels lace cap, underneath which her fine flaxen locks were arranged in the true Madonna style, she proceeded to the morning sitting room of Lady Carlingford . . . (I, 55–6)

To some extent writers on women were themselves to blame for this insincerity: Mrs Sandford, for example, like the eighteenth century 'courtesy book' writers before her, at times tends to talk of religion as though it were some kind of superior cosmetic. In any event, the middle classes' expanding affluence and luxury in the second half of the century, the resurgence of the spirit of Fashion, demonstrated clearly the conventionalism and hypocrisy latent in the vogue of the Madonna.

In 1851 Florence Nightingale complained, 'Women, don't consider themselves as human beings at all, there is absolutely no God, no country, no duty to them at all, except family'. [303] The previous year John S. Smith in *Social Aspects* had painted a very different view: his heart bled 'to see the intercourse between child and parent not one of confidence and love, but of cold politeness and reserved fear; to see the children removed away to some far apartment as a nuisance, necessary but unpleasant, and only permitted the parlour on sufferance, when they are trotted out to exhibit the mamma's taste in dress to an admiring, but inwardly ridiculing, company. And yet this is now becoming a very general case.' (p. 53) Smith exaggerates, but he appears to have spotted a trend: so soon after the huge sales of Mrs Ellis and her colleagues, at the very time when the Madonna image was becoming most current, the ideal of motherhood was being attacked by Fashion. In the upper-middle classes the child tended to be looked after increasingly by servants in the nursery, while the mother was free to enjoy the new found pleasures of greater affluence, more especially entertaining, visiting and dressing (it was said a fashionable lady was never 'at home' except when she sent out cards to announce the fact). 'Society', lamented Mrs Lynn Linton at the end of the 1860s, 'has put maternity out of fashion, and the nursery is nine times out of ten a place of punishment, not of pleasure, to the modern mother.' Nevertheless, she claimed, women were still hypocrites enough to adopt the conventional posture: 'If they hold a child in their arms, they are Madonnas, and look unutterable maternal love though they never saw the little creature before, and care for it no more than for the puppy in the mews.'

These attacks by Mrs Lynn Linton on the revolt against motherhood were part of a series of broadsides in the *Saturday Review* she aimed at 'The Girl of the Period'. The contemporary girl, she complained, was in fact an even more distressing aberration from the feminine ideal than the contemporary mother: 'The Girl of the Period is a creature who dyes her hair and paints her face, as the first articles of her personal religion—a creature whose sole idea of life is fun; whose sole aim is unbounded luxury; and whose dress is the chief object of such thought and intellect as she possesses. Her main endeavour is to outvie her neighbours in the extravagance of fashion.' [304] Again John S. Smith in *Social Aspects* seems to have spotted the trend very early: he asks in 1850, as though Dr Fordyce, Hannah More, Mrs Ellis and all the other moralists of the previous ninety years had never written, what was the tendency of the present system of female education but 'to create a class of brilliant, luxurious, gay-coloured butterflies—to produce a race of nondescripts, such as are now beginning to appear in society: accomplished, yet ignorant; fashionable, yet vulgar to the core; eye-dazzling but heart-sickening; a race who are entitled to the name of 'fine girl', or 'elegant creature', but who can never, without mockery, bear the hallowed name of woman'. (pp. 82–3) By the 1860s the 'fine girl' was quickly becoming the 'fast girl'. With the upper classes getting both more affluent and less prudish the fashionable young lady often reacted sharply against early-Victorian etiquette, particularly where her success in the marriage mart seemed threatened by the loose charms of pretty horsebreakers: 'Aping the demi-monde, talking slang, turning dressing for society into undressing, reading the worst of the French novels, and discussing freely with men questions which are not for mixed debate, our young women it would appear, have lost all that native modesty which was our moral strength, our glory and our pride'. [305] Fast girls of this type were of course a small minority—the great bulk of middle-class womanhood still behaved with strict decorum—but they were a very significant minority. For their behaviour was an overt expression of an increasing moral laxity beneath society's surface decorum. The lower-middle class girl could not enjoy in fact the luxury and permissiveness of fashionable society, but she could enjoy it in fantasy, in the fast novels of Ouida and her colleagues. In these novels she could revel in highly coloured pictures of fashionable vice, and yet keep in touch with the proprieties through the writers' nominal morality, their frequent diatribes against the immorality they depicted, their genuflections through their virtuous heroines towards the Madonna ideal.

The Ouida child-Madonna heroine, ostensibly a figure of redemption amidst the debauchery of Fashion, illustrates in fact how Fashion had perverted the Madonna, making her simply a vehicle for moral claptrap and religiosity. The process of perversion had been gradual. In *Ellen Middleton* (1844) by Lady Georgiana Fullerton we find Alice, an authentic, idealized Madonna child, who passes from ignorance to maturity through her sufferings in marriage. In *The Morals of Mayfair* (1857) by Mrs Edwards the rot is setting in: we have again a completely innocent ingenue Madonna, brought up, as Ouida's heroines were often to be, in wild seclusion by the sea; but the author's main interest is in the glamorous vice of 'the frail daughters of fashion' with which she is contrasted. In *Strathmore* (1865) by Ouida the evolution is complete: the religiose panegyrics about the child-Madonna's purity take second place to the irresistible sexual voluptuousness, desperate godlessness, ruthless cruelty, intellectual brilliance, and social pre-eminence of the evil, serpent-like adulteress Marion Vavasour and the Byronic superman Strathmore. The latter is responsible for the death of the child-madonna's mother, herself a childlike Madonna figure; adopts her in remorse, renouncing the fatal Marion; falls in love with her as she grows up, and is ultimately redeemed in scenes of affecting piety. Even the evil Marion, who has lost her beauty and social status, is inspired by the child-wife's innocence to devote herself, in the Order of St Vincent de Paul, to tending the poor and suffering deep in the pestilential swamps of the great western forests. Four years after *Strathmore* was published

Lawrence Lockhart in *Doubles and Quits* professed himself sadly destitute of the technical jargon used by most novelists in descriptions of their heroines: 'Pathetic eyelashes, Madonna mouths, married brows, swimming eyes, impossible combinations of non-existing tints, and the mysterious terms of physiognomical architecture—these are machineries I know not how to work.' (I, 67) The heroine he was mocking was not the authentic Madonna of Tennyson and Thackeray, but the phoney Madonna of the fast novel, the heroine who in fact was signalling the decline of the true ideal.

7 The decline, however, was not simply due to the resurgence of the spirit of Fashion. It was due also to the growth of feminism and a more liberal view of sex, an increasing appreciation in the later decades of the century that the Madonna ideal was no longer appropriate to society's needs. In the forties and fifties, as we saw in a previous chapter, the sexual idealist was often in favour of a degree of female emancipation, recognizing, for example, that reforms in women's education were likely to produce more mature and enlightened mothers: he was not alarmed therefore by the creation of Queen's College, Bedford College, the London Collegiate School and Cheltenham College in the years between the appearance of *The Princess* and *The Angel in the House*. By the seventies, however, the success of these and other ladies' colleges and the foundation of Girton and Newnham were helping to cause a growing feminist militancy that worried the idealist: woman's domestic role, it seemed, was being threatened by the feminists' demands for equality with men. In 1871 Mrs Samuel Carter Hall expressed a common anti-feminist view: 'It is no exaggeration to say that "those who rock the cradle rule the world". The future rests mainly with the mother; foolish are all who strive for the enactment of laws that would deprive her of her holiest rights, to try a wild experiment by which, under the senseless cry of "equality", women would be displaced from the position in which God has placed them since the beginning of the world,

for all Time, and for Eternity.' [306] In a similar way in the following year Ruskin scathingly attacked 'the enlightened notion among English young women, derived from Mr. J. Stuart Mill,—that the "career" of the Madonna is too limited a one, and that modern political economy can provide them, as the *Pall Mall* observes, with 'much more lucrative occupations than that of nursing the baby".' [307]

In one sense the anti-feminist disquiet was misplaced. The feminists were often firm believers themselves in woman's domestic role: 'No one,' said Emily Faithfull, one of their representatives, in 1863, 'disputes that household management and the nurture of children are good true womanly work. No one wants to take women from homes where there are home duties to perform.' [308] Even the more extreme feminist attacks on marriage in the 1890s were often based on premises close to those of the traditional idealist: 'We shall never have really good mothers until women cease to make their motherhood the central fact of their existence. The woman who has no interest larger than the affairs of her children is not a fit person to train them.' [309] Fears of a feminist threat to the mother ideal, if misplaced in this respect, were, however, well grounded in another. The conservatives saw rightly that the feminists' influence was out of all proportion to their numbers and that this influence was corroding the old unquestioned faith in womanly deference. The New Woman on the lines of a Sophia Jex-Blake, an Octavia Hill, or a Millicent Fawcett was in a tiny minority, but like the fast girl she was an overt indication of an underlying trend, a trend towards a relative independence in young women from the traditional narrowness of their lot and a rejection of the traditional pedestalization of their virtue.

In 1881 Oscar Wilde published a sonnet called 'Madonna Mia', an extravagant example of this traditional pedestalization:

> A lily-girl, not made for this world's pain,
>   With brown, soft hair close braided by her ears,

And longing eyes half veiled by slumberous tears
Like bluest water seen through mists of rain:
Pale cheeks whereon no love hath left its stain,
Red underlip drawn in for fear of love,
And white throat, whiter than the silvered dove,
Through whose wan marble creeps one purple vein.
Yes, though my lips shall praise her without cease,
Even to kiss her feet I am not bold,
Being o'ershadowed by the wings of awe.
Like Dante, when he stood with Beatrice
Beneath the flaming Lion's breast, and saw
The seventh Crystal, and the Stair of Gold.

In 1889 Gladstone was rather more moderate in his remarks on the dangers to women inherent in political enfranchisement: 'it would trespass upon their delicacy, their purity, their refinement, the elevation of their whole nature'. [310] Few young women in fact were in favour of enfranchisement, and most would profess agreement with the Gladstone view of feminine delicacy, purity and refinement. But a great many of them were now becoming very impatient with the old-fashioned definition of these qualities, the definition so vividly pictured in Wilde's 'Madonna Mia'. 'The newspapers were still forbidden,' Mrs Peel recalled from her girlhood in the eighties, 'and the novels were tried out by Aunt Markey, and if in one otherwise innocuous, she found something not fitting our budding minds, she clipped the pages together and bade us not undo them. Did we obey her? We did not.' [311]

The popularity of books like *The Heavenly Twins* (1893) by Sarah Grand illustrated the new restlessness in young women. In this story of two women married to wretched husbands we have almost an inversion of the old-time education novel: one wife governed by traditional views of womanly deference has her sufferings ended only in death, the other brought up on J. S. Mill's *The Subjection of Women* casts her husband off. A book like this may not perhaps have won many women to militant feminism, but it did focus a common feeling amongst

them that they should have more freedom to determine their
own lives. The following year saw 'The Revolt of the Daughters',
a voluminous correspondence in the public press on a young
girl's right to shape her destiny, to make her own decisions free
from the proprieties of the etiquette books, on her right to have
a latchkey and to know the facts of life. Mrs Lynn Linton's
contribution to the 'Tree of Knowledge' controversy was brief:
'I deprecate the public discussion of the whole subject. I think
it indecent and unnecessary. There are certain things which
belong to the secret life of the home, and to drag these out
into the light of day is a violation of all the sanctities, all the
modesties of one's existence.' [312] Mrs Linton unquestionably
spoke for a large body of traditional opinion; but she and her
supporters were slipping well behind the times, and another
large body of opinion was delighted with the new young girl's
impatience with the inhibitions of the past. A writer of the
nineties remarked without too much exaggeration: 'The girl
of today, with her fine physical development, her bright
cheery nature and her robust contempt for all things small and
mean, is an immense improvement on the girl of yesterday. She
has a vigorous contempt for all forms of softness; her mind and
character are strung up to a firmness of which a sentimental
heroine of fifty years ago would have been ashamed.'
[313]
   With a more open mind the young girl was likely to be
sympathetic to more liberal views of sex, to question man's
assumption that preserving purity was woman's peculiar duty,
to perhaps appreciate the naturalness of feminine passion. In
this respect the success of novels like *The Heavenly Twins* had
been prepared to some extent by the fast school. For one thing
the latter showed that even their kind of etherealized child
Madonna could sometimes fall from grace, could prefer
adultery to a loveless marriage (usually, however, her honour
remained inviolate, either through a timely death as in *The
Morals of Mayfair*, or a timely divorce as in Ouida's *Moths*). For
another, they combined sometimes their etherealized Mario-

latry with a healthy kind of earthiness which the more orthodox Madonna worshipper called voluptuousness. Mrs Oliphant, for example, was much offended by a passage in Annie Thomas' *Called to Account* (1867) describing the perfect taste of a fallen woman's room, a room in which besides a Madonna portrait there was also 'a ruby, velvet shrine, composed of a pedestal and curtains for the glorious goddess who is grander and more perfect in her mutilated beauty than anything else the world has seen in marble—a nearly life-size copy of "Our Lady of Milo" '. [314] It was just this kind of gesture to sexual amorality that helped to kill the orthodox Madonna. By the nineties a new generation of young women had arisen; unimpressed by prudish restraints; prepared to listen to ideas that were anathema to the earlier idealists; interested in, if not convinced by, the arguments of advocates of free love or the rehabilitation of the flesh. The Madonna had declined partly because it went out of fashion, it declined also because it became out-of-date.

Ironically, one should note by way of postscript to her history, her image often survived the sexual revolutionaries' iconoclasm. The heroine of Grant Allen's *The Woman Who Did* is, as we have seen, a case in point. More remarkably there is a poem by Havelock Ellis called 'Notre Dame de la Place Blanche', whose central figure is the complete antithesis of the traditional Madonna's protective motherly purity: solid and sensual, joyously amoral

> . . . with coquettish tender eyes she greets
> And takes the arm of the slender lad she meets,
> And looks down on him with her queenly grace. [315]

Most remarkably of all there is another poem by Ellis on the joys of observing a woman urinate (a somewhat uncommon sexual preference formed by Ellis in an aptly ironic Victorian way, through his very close attachment in childhood to his mother): [316]

My lady once leapt sudden from the bed,
  Whereon she naked lay beside my heart,
  And stood with perfect poise, straight legs apart,
And then from clustered hair of brownish red
A wondrous fountain curve, all shyness fled,
  Arched like a liquid rainbow in the air,
  She cares not, she, what other women care,
But gazed as it fell and faltered and was shed.

Familiar acts are beautiful through love:
  A picture that no painter ever wrought,
  Nor poet knew to weave within his dream,
Is more than Virgin throned with saints above,
  Only sweet woman made as Nature sought,
  And yet Life's symbol of joy's golden stream.

The poem is called 'Madonna'.

11

The Fortunes of the Magdalen

I GROWTH

1 IN THE SECOND HALF of the eighteenth century society began to concern itself with the harlot's progress. In March 1751 a letter in the *Rambler*, followed a month later by another in the *Gentleman's Magazine*, argued the need for a rescue home for penitent prostitutes. Nothing materialized immediately, but the topic was kept alive in the following years by woeful pictures of the prostitute's plight in a few short stories in the journals and especially a novel of 1754, *The Sisters*, by a young clergyman William Dodd. In 1758 the writer of the letter to the *Rambler*, a London silk-merchant Robert Bingley, decided the time had come for action and, with remarkable speed considering the unprecedented nature of the project, collected over £3,500 in subscriptions, secured appropriate premises, furnishings and staff, and received the first inmates in his Magdalen Home. The Home very quickly flourished, largely through the attraction of its public chapel services: its preacher was William Dodd, now exercising his novel-writing talents in highly affecting sermons. [317] Until his disgrace in 1774 and subsequent execution for forgery, the glamorous Dodd enjoyed such crowded congregations, the Home was obliged to request the public not to come to the chapel more than half an hour before service.

The burden of Dodd's refrain was that the whore was normally a daughter of wretchedness. She did not fall into sin, as was commonly supposed, through lust but through seduction or destitution, her youthful, generous innocence corrupted, perhaps ravished, by the guile of a deceiver, or her virtue sold to keep body alive when her parents had died or deserted her. She did not live, as was commonly supposed, a life of carefree indolence and luxury but ravaged by remorse, ill-treatment, privation and disease until, her beauty blasted, her body wrecked, her conscience haunted by fear of Heaven's wrath, she sank into an early and unwept grave. This highly-coloured fusion of squalor and sentimentality was designed, of course, to soften the hearts of potential benefactors, to make each prostitute seem a poor little middle-class girl longing to return to good society. But good society, in fact, though prepared to shed a tear at the harlot's plight, was usually unwilling to take her back. In the novels of the day, for example, with a few exceptions like Goldsmith's *Vicar of Wakefield* (1766) and Hugh Kelly's *Memoirs of a Magdalen* (1767), the fallen woman of any breeding was irredeemably lost. In this fiction notes J. M. S. Tompkins, 'A servant or a shopkeeper's daughter may retrieve her virtue and make some honest man happy; she is even justified in hiding her past if her present resolve is honest. But all the Magdalens of gentle blood are tragic; their delicacy forbids compromise or concealment; they languish in a settled melancholy and descend, elegantly penitent, to the family vault.' (*op. cit.*, p. 153) In 1781 Robert Bage was scathing about this elegant penitence, the belief that even where women were not to blame for their defloration, as in rape, a melancholy death was nevertheless *de rigueur*. In his novel *Mount Henneth*, Bage has a naive Persian girl refuse an honourable marriage because she has read in English novels that to be raped, as she has been, is to be irretrievably tainted: 'women who have suffered it, must die, or be immured for ever; ever after they are totally useless to all the purposes of society . . . all crimes but this may be expiated; no author has yet been so bold as to permit a lady to live and marry, and be a woman after this stain.'[1]

[1] 1824 edn., p. 161. Bage himself, in the figure of Kitty Ross in *Barham Downs* (1784) was shortly to be so bold.

If the fallen woman's rehabilitation was often made impossible by the cult of elegant penitence, in some ways the magdalen's friends had only themselves to blame. The constitution of the Magdalen Home was genuinely humane, but its propaganda often encouraged a mawkish sentimentality that far from softening the heart achieved effectively the reverse. The sermons and poems of Dodd, still more the series of novelettish penitent histories allegedly, but most improbably, written by the inmates of the Home, helped to foster a species of self-indulgent, complacent philanthropy more moved by maudlin fiction than stirred by magdalen fact. A poem of 1795, *Matilda; or the Dying Penitent* by a bachelor clergyman, George Richards, is very much in this line—a loving description in lachrymose couplets of a magdalen's terrible sufferings and contrition, ending with her final ascent on angel's wings to heaven, A novel of the following year, *The Farmer of Inglewood Forest* by Elizabeth Helme, is a much more repellent example; in this case the penitent Emma's sufferings and confessions being described not only with exaggerated sentiment but with naked pharisaism and blatant prurience. Even the humane writer sometimes seemed in league with the cult of elegant penitence. Mrs Opie in *The Father and Daughter* (1800) seems to believe that fallen women should be rehabilitated through their 'perseverance in a life of expiatory amendment' (2nd edn., p. 191); but instead of restoring her heroine to society she kills her off for the sake of an edifying pathos. One questions how many converts this enormously popular novel in fact secured for the magdalen's cause: the *Critical Review* (May 1802), for example, construed its moral simply as exhibiting 'in the most affecting point of view the misery consequent upon the illicit indulgence of the passions'. (XXXV, 114–15)

2 By this time the French Revolution had offered additional reasons for not restoring the fallen woman to good society. In the nervous years of the 1790s a partly hysterical and partly

rational anxiety about the morality of the masses caused the bourgeoisie to become very sensitive to the question of sexual example. The fallen woman in consequence was more likely than ever to be ostracized, either through emotional revulsion or through society's desire to show its detestation of her crime and to protect its young people from her contaminating influence. A punitive treatment of the penitent was a product then of a general sexual fear. It was a product too of a special fear that, at this very time when sexual decency was so vital, marriage seemed to be in new and serious danger—threatened by the dangerous libertarian ideas propounded, for example, by Godwin's *Political Justice* (1793) and Mary Wollstonecraft's posthumous *Wrongs of Woman* (1798) and by the dangerous laxity shown to female frailty in such fashionable foreign literature as Rousseau's *Nouvelle Héloise* or Kotzebue's *The Stranger*. The result was a stream of novels warning women not to be seduced from their wifely duties. In 1798 Charles Lloyd's *Edmund Oliver* has a misguided young lady, a Godwinian exponent of free love, die insane and unregenerate. In 1799 Mrs West's *A Tale of the Times* complemented her earlier *Advantages of Education* by showing here not the rewards of good motherhood but the dire consequence of bad—in this novel the mother is technically unfallen, yet driven to her grave by remorse at having listened to the Godwinian views on marriage of her lover. In a similar way, Elizabeth Hamilton's *Memoirs of Modern Philosophers* (1800) and Mrs Opie's *Adeline Mowbray* (1804) show young women paying for their heresies in early, edifying deaths. In 1806 Mrs West argued that the true magdalen did not in fact wish to be restored to good society but 'to avoid the hazard of falling into new transgressions, and the contumely attending the past. . . . Turn thee, backsliding daughter, turn to the cool sequestered vale of life, and thy troubled day may yet have a peaceful close.' [318] In the light of the change in sexual attitudes of the previous decade one can ascribe Mrs West's resistance to the idea of a rehabilitated penitent not to sentimental pharisaism but to an austere, frightened, but genuine humanitarianism. In these years the sentimental picture of the magdalen was becoming progressively less common, but it was still too common for the peace of mind of a number of anxious moralists. In 1809 William Hale delivered a broadside against the misguided sentimentality of many rescue workers in his *Address to the Public upon the Dangerous Tendency of the London Female Penitentiary*. In 1812 he returned to the attack, arguing as before that the romantic view of the prostitute was not only impractical but positively dangerous, in that it encouraged young people into sin:

> The most amiable of our youth have been taught to consider harlots as subjects of pity. Instead of viewing their conduct as the result of voluntary and awful depravity, they have considered it as the effects of dire necessity. They have been taught to believe, that harlots were once virtuous females, who were seduced in an unguarded hour; and that after they were forsaken by their betrayers, they were driven sorely against their will, by inevitable consequences, to prostitution; and that in this state they were doomed, under a horrid necessity, to continue, or perish with hunger in the streets. [319]

By now the Evangelicals were becoming very involved in rescue work, and with few exceptions they were influenced less by Bingley's humane example at the first Magdalen Home than by Biblical denunciations of the harlot. The prostitute was now not the daughter of wretchedness nor the elegant penitent, but a recalcitrant sinner to be won to repentance with severity and discipline: instead of a comfortable Home she was offered bleak houses of correction in which, with cropped hair, drab uniforms and hard, tedious labour, she might win her way to piety.

About this time a tract was published called *An Address to the Unfortunate Female*. Unfortunate indeed if she were cast on the mercies of such a priggish, hard-hearted philanthropist as this writer. 'Most assuredly', she is told,

. . . we are not forbidden to offer you encouragement. Tears and moanings, it is true, unattended with reform, avail nothing; it is also true, that though the reform be complete and permanent, its existence may be questioned by many whose esteem you are most anxious to recover; and some traces of degradation may be visible, some springs of sorrow be kept open, till you cease to live. To flatter you with the exhibition of a prospect unbeclouded by your past folly, were unjust and inhuman. Such comfort as we can safely administer, we most cheerfully invite you to accept. However faint the ray that shines forth from the stormy cloud, it is your duty with grateful promptitude to accept the relief which it affords you. (pp. 4–5)

Having accepted this cheerful comfort the unfortunate female is told to apply to an asylum to be helped to return to virtue, but she is also told at the same time not to expect this return to be easy. The asylums are 'incapable of admitting all who would welcome and appreciate their advantages. Yet make the trial— you may be successful, and if not, in the absence of every better provision, you ought to feel that the lowest workhouse in the kingdom is a scene of luxury, in comparison, not only with your degraded tenements, but with the most splendid mansion occupied by the sons and daughters of dissipation.' (p. 5) As a final gesture of encouragement the outcast is warned that she may despise the 'humble effort' made on her behalf: 'and, certainly, our fears exceed our hopes. We are almost persuaded to say, "let them alone; in vain you remonstrate, in vain you beseech; their consciences are seared, they are past feeling; they are twice dead".' (p. 7)

3 By the accession of Queen Victoria, the Religious Tract Society had issued five hundred million tracts directed at the rescue of fallen women. With many along these lines one can understand why the rescue movement was still making little headway; for its propaganda was no more effective with the public than with the prostitute. It needed funds, co-ordination and expertise, and to obtain these it needed the backing of

society. For twenty years, however, the claims of the magdalen had been buried in near oblivion: buried, as we saw in an earlier chapter, by society's concern for the nation's morals, its revulsion at feminine impurity, its prudish and often conscience-ridden evasion of an unpleasant and intractable problem. It was not until the first years of Victoria's reign that the magdalen began to emerge once more from the shadows. Between 1839 and 1844, for example, there was a sudden burst of books on prostitution by doctors, social workers and divines; and, more important, novelists and poets, with a much wider readership, were once more taking up the issue. After the years of silence many of these writers found the subject difficult, even painful, to discuss, as they stressed in prefatory statements or revealed implicitly in cautious or embarrassed ambiguity of treatment, but at least the problem was once more receiving public ventilation.

Dickens' first sketch of the prostitute in 'The Pawnbroker's Shop' of 1836 shows just this kind of reticence. It shows also embryonically, that as the writer returned to the problem of William Dodd and his contemporaries, the need to soften the public's heart, he returned also to their methods, to a combination of squalor and sentimentality in the portrait of the outcast:

> In the next box is a young female, whose attire miserably poor, but extremely gaudy, wretchedly cold but extravagantly fine, too plain bespeaks her station in life. The rich satin gown with the faded trimmings, the worn-out thin shoes, and pink silk stockings, the summer bonnet in winter, and the sunken face, where a daub of rouge only serves as an index to the ravages of squandered health never to be regained, and lost happiness never to be restored, and where the practised smile is a wretched mockery of the misery of the heart, cannot be mistaken.

The sight of a young gentlewoman and her mother pawning some little trinkets, a sight that awakens some remembrance of her past, changes her whole demeanour; and as they involuntarily shrink from her, she retreats, covering her face with her hands and bursting into tears. [320] Nancy in *Oliver Twist*, of the following year, reveals the same cautious ambiguity, but the squalor and pathos are developed much more fully. The coarse, tawdry, gin-swilling slut of the earlier scenes becomes a figure of Sunday school piety in her meetings with Rose Maylie, and she dies holding up to Heaven 'A white handkerchief—Rose Maylie's own'. (p. 441)

Giving the magdalen a pious death was not the only method of demonstrating sympathy. In the same year as *Oliver Twist*, the unsentimental Captain Marryat in *Snarleyyow* showed a reformed prostitute, another Nancy, leading a perfectly happy and rehabilitated life, and one year later Bulwer Lytton in *Alice* broke with precedent by restoring finally to happiness his repentant fallen heroine. Thackeray in fact was openly contemptuous of Dickens' sentimentality: 'Bah! What figments these novelists tell us! Boz, who knows life well, knows that his Miss Nancy is the most unreal fantastical personage possible; no more like a thief's mistress than one of Gesner's shepherdesses resembles a country wench.' [321] But from his attacks on Nancy in *Catherine* (1839–40) we can see that Thackeray had missed the point, confusing her with Harrison Ainsworth's glamourized trollops in *Jack Sheppard*. Marryat's broadmindedness and Bulwer's courage were very well in their way, but it was Dickens' squalor and sentiment that would most move society to action: squalor to shame its conscience, sentiment to pluck on its heartstrings. To have left Nancy simply a coarse, gin-swilling slut would have aroused no pity amongst the fastidious (even so, one recalls Melbourne's disgust at the 'low debasing view of mankind' in the novel [322]). But to have her respond to Rose Maylie's kindness with the tearful, hand-clasping words: 'Oh, lady, lady! . . . if there was more like you, there would be fewer like me,—there would—there would!' (p. 368), though not perhaps good literature was certainly excellent propaganda.

In the 1840s it was Dickens' blend of squalor and pathos, not Thackeray's call for accuracy, that was followed. Thomas

Miller, for example, in *Godfrey Malvern* (1842) follows a grisly picture of 'those poor young creatures whose faces you never see for many years together, whose hollow coughs, sunken eyes, painted cheeks, and fevered lips, death soon gathers into his great garner' with a sentimental plea: 'A kind word, or a kind action, may call the penitent tear to their cheeks—may strike some slumbering chord, which, though out of tune, has still sweet music in it—may drive the memory back to happier days, and to reflections which in the end may lead them, though fallen, into some other Eden! where the flaming sword is quenched by the tears of the angel who keeps watch at the gates.' (II, 360) He returns from this to the squalor of the brothel, a sordid picture of fights, robbery, drunkenness and disease, and then reverts once more to sentiment with another tearful plea. The sudden lurch from one tactic to another is yet more strongly marked in Froude's *The Lieutenant's Daughter* (1847): the melodramatic pathos of the opening scene, a fallen woman's suicide upon her parents' grave, abruptly gives way for the bulk of the novel to a realistic description of the bawd-and-brothel milieu of upper-class debauchery from which she came, until this in turn gives way at the end to a sentimental pleading.

The magdalen's suicide was by now a common theme. William Bell Scott in 'Rosabell', a poem written in 1837, sought to move his reader's pity and conscience at the drowned girl's unregenerate condition:

> And hearts as innocent as hers
> As blindly shall succeed, shall take
> Leap after leap into the dark,
> Blaspheming soul and sense at once,
> And every lamp on every street
> Shall light their wet feet down to death. [323]

In Thomas Hood's 'Bridge of Sighs' (1844) the drowned magdalen was the occasion of a yet more aggressive attack upon society's indifference:

> Alas! for the rarity
> Of Christian charity
> Under the sun!
> Oh! it was pitiful!
> Near a whole city full,
> Home she had none!
> Picture it—think of it,
> Dissolute man!

More typically, the squalor and despair of the prostitute's end were transformed by divine forgiveness. A. B. Richards, for example, in *Death and the Magdalen* (1846), dwells on the dying prostitute's reception into heaven before delivering his last belligerent broadside, 'Proud ones! do ye hear?' (p. 11) Most typically of all, despite Thackeray's protest that whores did not 'die white-washed saints, like poor Biss Dadsy in *Oliver Twist*', [324] the prostitute was given a tear-soaked death-bed surrounded by loving, generous-hearted women: Esther in Mrs Gaskell's *Mary Barton* and Alice Marwood in *Dombey and Son* are perfect illustrations. These two women, Esther and Alice, are indeed in every way very typical of the magdalen of the period. In their sudden, brief appearances, always at night, dressed in wet, shabby clothes, suffering from hunger, cold, poverty and loneliness, and above all from a haunted self-disgust which makes them liable to tears at the slightest gesture of kindness, they exhibit splendidly the forties' characteristic blend of distressing squalor and pleasing sentiment.

II ASCENDANCY

4 The fifties opened with this same pattern. In 1850 Kingsley's picture in *Alton Locke* of two young women forced onto the streets to support a sick friend stressed the squalor of the prostitute's life, and Dickens' portraits of Martha Endell and Little Em'ly in *David Copperfield* put the emphasis on sentiment. W. R. Greg's famous article in the *Westminster* (July 1850) was

a masterly fusion of the propagandist's tactics. In accents that must have made William Hale turn in his grave, Greg insisted that while the unknowing world imagined the prostitute revelling in vice, dead to all shame, wallowing in mire because she liked it, in all but the most exceptional cases she fell not through lust or greed but through an unfortunate love affair or from economic necessity, in all but the most exceptional cases she lived not amidst the luxuries of sin but in remorse, despair, privation, brutality and disease until an early death took her trembling to damnation. Propaganda of this character may have been crude but it was certainly effective. For the 1850s saw an explosion of interest in the rescue of fallen women.

In September 1848 the *Quarterly Review* had surveyed ruefully the limitations of missionary endeavour in this area: 'a certain number of feeble institutions creep on from year to year, offering scanty accommodation, languishing under the shade of narrow means or a burden of debt, unable for want of room or funds to carry out any efficient system of discipline or classification, and conducted on most imperfect principles'. (LXXXIII, 361) But the tide was turning at that moment. In the first place, rescue work was attracting numbers of dedicated laymen to its service. In 1847, for example, Dickens had begun his work at Urania Cottage, a refuge for homeless women, his involvement being a model of energy, good sense, patience and generosity. In 1848 Gladstone, who as an undergraduate had solemnly vowed to devote a tenth of his income to the reclamation of prostitutes,[1] began the night walks he was to make at least once, and often three or four times, a week for the following forty years, looking for fallen women who would accept his offer of aid and shelter. In the fifties some of the pre-Raphaelites, not content with stirring public interest with such pictures as Millais' *Virtue and Vice*, Rossetti's *Found* and Hunt's *The Awakened Conscience*, tried to reclaim prostitutes they

---

[1] Gladstone eventually spent an estimated £80,000 on this work: see Deacon, *op. cit.*, pp. 28–9.

met while looking for models. More important, rescue work was now enjoying the momentum and professional expertise of the mid-century religious revival. The late 1840s saw a new High Church commitment, notably in the foundation of the first of the Anglican Sisterhood's magdalen homes, and a new Evangelical commitment stimulated by Lieutenant Blackmore's London by Moonlight Mission. And in the early 1850s this involvement was given a more systematic programme: in 1851 a Church Penitentiary Association was formed to co-ordinate High Church rescue work, followed in 1853 by the Society for the Rescue of Young Women and Children, the first of three large Evangelical societies.[1]

In 1857, the year of Dr Acton's classic book on prostitution, a real breakthrough began at last to be made with the general public. In May there was a spate of leaders and letters on the prostitution problem in *The Times*; in September the sedate *Punch* shocked its more narrow-minded readers with John Leech's famous cartoon 'The Great Social Evil'; and by the end of October press coverage of the magdalen was becoming quite extensive. The immediate source of much of this new interest was the effort being made by the vestries of St James and St Marylebone to clear their streets of prostitutes and to establish reformatories for such women as wished to enter them. But the deep-lying cause was the cumulative growth of literary propaganda through the fifties. In 1857, besides this press activity, there were two novels published indicating the change that had come over the image of the magdalen. One was the anonymous *Magdalen Stafford*, the other Charles Miller's *Magdalene Nisbet*, neither of them in any way about prostitution, but each illustrating the novelist's growing choice of the name of Magdalen for his heroines. The trend went back at least to Mrs Oliphant's *Magdalen Hepburn* (1854) and continued through

---

[1] It should be said that some of the new homes were as harshly disciplinarian as the worst of the earlier penitentiaries. Felicia Skene in her *Penitentiaries and Reformatories* (1865) and her novel *Hidden Depths* (1866) fiercely attacked the lack of enlightenment still common.

Caroline Mary Smith's *Magdalen Havering* (1861), Wilkie Collins' Magdalen Vanstone in *No Name* (1862) and Shirley Brooks' Magdalen Conway in *Sooner or Later* (1868), at least as far as Averil Beaumont's *Magdalen Wynyard* (1872). The vogue enjoyed by the name of Magdalen then was almost exactly contemporaneous with that enjoyed by the sobriquet of Madonna, a coincidence that appears less remarkable when we consider the nature of the literary propaganda about the prostitute in the fifties.[1] In 1850 the fallen woman in fiction was a wretched wanderer of the night, a figure of squalor and pathos. By 1853 she was establishing herself as a feminine archetype almost equal to the Madonna, almost equally motherly, pure and inspirational. From representing the antithesis of the Victorians' purity ideal the magdalen was fast becoming an essential constituent of it: after the years as taboo she was quickly becoming totem.

5 We can see the new image emerging in that typical outcast of the forties, Esther in *Mary Barton*. Mrs Gaskell pleads for compassion for Esther not only on the grounds of her squalid misery and tearful penitence but because of the intensity of her love for her dead child; 'Her voice rose again to the sharp pitch of agony. "My darling! my darling! even after death I may not see thee, my own sweet one!" ' (I, 253) In *Lizzie Leigh*, her story for *Household Words* in 1850, Mrs Gaskell explores this theme once more, the fallen Lizzie being haunted by guilt at the death of her little girl: ' "if I go to heaven, I shall not know her—I shall not know my own again—she will shun me as a stranger".' (I, 65) It was a rich vein to be tapped: to present the fallen woman as a loving mother aroused compassion for her sufferings, perhaps forgiveness for her sins, whilst at the same time glorifying the maternal impulse, its unquenchable strength

[1] I am not suggesting, of course, that the use of the name Magdalen necessarily implied the author's special sympathy for the prostitute: it may, for example, in the case of Mrs Oliphant, have been merely an unconscious reflection of a change in society's attitudes.

and redeeming powers in even wretched and tainted women. By *Ruth* (1853) the integration of magdalenism and mother idealism was virtually complete. Lizzie Leigh had at length been saved physically and spiritually by the unstinted love of her mother. Ruth is an orphan, but after her fall she is saved from suicide and inspired through hardship by merely remembering 'the gentle, blessed mother, who had made her childhood's home holy ground'. (I, 289) More especially, she is given a purpose in living and a new moral and personal maturity through becoming a mother herself: 'The child and the mother were each messengers of God—angels to each other.' (III, 127)

For the next twenty years there was to be an ideal magdalen in literature who complemented the Madonna. Sometimes she would be, like Ruth or Marian Erle in Mrs Browning's *Aurora Leigh* (1856), an ingenuous girl brought to maturity and saintliness through the birth of a bastard child. Sometimes, like Ruth or Helen Langton in Mrs Houstoun's *Recommended to Mercy* (1862), she would care for the sick and unhappy, inspiring them, in Biblical terms, to arise and call her blessed. [325] She would, in short, be a type of Angel Mother. Wilkie Collins' *The New Magdalen* (1873), for all its title, had a heroine very much of this description. Mercy Merrick had fallen further, perhaps, than some magdalens, to the level of common whore and gaolbird, but once reformed she evokes an identical response amongst the sick: 'They kissed the hem of her black dress; they called her their guardian angel, as the beautiful creature moved among them, and bent over their hard pillows her gentle compassionate face.' (I, 51)

The source of this idealization of the prostitute lies deep in Victorian sexual thinking. It arose partly, we have seen, as a technical ploy to win compassion for the outcast whilst at the same time vindicating the holy name of motherhood, a ploy that slid easily to excess in such a highly emotional age. It arose partly, it seems clear, from a degree of pious sentimentality, an Evangelical confidence in the omnipotent power of Grace to elicit spiritual regeneration: the midnight suppers of the Rev. Baptist Noel in the sixties, where he offered free tea, toast and salvation to all interested prostitutes, were often accused of being governed by this approach. It arose partly, it seems obvious, especially amongst men, from a species of romantic projection: Labouchere noted, perhaps not without some justice, that Gladstone managed 'to combine his missionary meddling with a keen appreciation of a pretty face. He has never been known to rescue any of our East End whores, nor for that matter is it easy to contemplate his rescuing any ugly woman, and I am quite sure his conception of the Magdalen is of an incomparable example of pulchritude with a superb figure and carriage.' [326] It arose above all, I think, from the Victorian idealist's need to believe in the perfect purity of womanhood, to believe that ultimately, whatever sinful man might do to stain her, woman's natural character was that of the Madonna.

It arose also, surprisingly enough, to a certain degree from fact. In such an emotional age, when prostitutes at Urania Cottage were deeply moved by Dickens' extremely sentimental *Appeal to Fallen Women*, [327] it is perhaps less surprising on reflection that the real-life magdalen sometimes conformed to her literary image. Acton, for example, talks of an untypical but fairly common class of gentle, retiring prostitutes:

> above all, they are notable for the intensity of love with which they will cling to the sister, the mother, the brother—in fact, to anyone 'from home' who, calling, still cherishes some respect and regard for them. The sick man is safe in their hands, and the fool's money also. There is many a tale well known of this nursing and watching, and more than will do so could tell of the harlot's guardianship in his hour of drunkenness. I have seen the fondest of daughters and mothers amongst them. [328]

If we consider the power of a remembered mother over her fallen daughter a little implausible in Ruth and Helen Langton, we should note a description quoted by Acton of

Baptist Noel's technique at a midnight meeting. For a long time, it seems, he aroused little interest in his audience, but then

> As by an afterthought, he mentions that, since their last meeting, some mother has sent him a photograph of her daughter, beseeching him to seek that lost one in this company. In an instant the sealed-up fountains are opened, and strong emotion replaces real and feigned indifference. They who heard unmoved of Divine love and human help are touched and shaken by the voice of a weeping mother. Some sob audibly in their tempest of awakened memory. Tears run down the cheeks of many. It seems as though every fallen daughter were asking: 'Is it my mother? Is it my picture?'
> [329]

If we consider somewhat implausible the transition of Rhoda Somerset in Charles Reade's *A Terrible Temptation* (1871) from a flagrantly immoral horsebreaker to an angel wife and mother and itinerant lay-preacher, we should note the spectacular conversion a few years earlier of Laura Bell, a celebrated courtesan, who gave up her calling for marriage and shortly became a fervent revivalist preacher, considered by some to be almost as brilliant as Spurgeon. [330]

By the time of Reade's novel in fact the approximation of real and fictional magdalens had become even closer through a progressive modification in the literary archetype. The reasons for the magdalen's fall, for example, were now less coloured by special pleading. Mrs Gaskell with Ruth and Mrs Browning with Marian, over-anxious to win their readers' sympathy, had made their heroines fall respectively by a rather unlikely moral idiocy and a rather sensational case of rape in the Clarissa Harlowe style. In the same year as *Ruth*, Sarah Whitehead in *Nelly Armstrong*, though idealizing equally her heroine's post-redemption qualities, was much more candid about her initial fall from grace, the product of egotistical giddiness and vanity (she also incidentally, unlike Mrs Gaskell, made her heroine resort to prostitution). Henry Jebb in *Out of the Depths* (1859) was yet more uncompromising: his Mary Smith falls not through implausible naivety or rape but through a very human mixture of conceit, sexual inclination and a partially genuine love for her seducer—she recognizes in fact that she was more to blame than he. Jebb's vivid description of her decline to a common street-walker was too much for many of his reviewers, even the more favourable complaining that such material belonged more in a rescue worker's manual than in a work of general fiction.

This new realism was a natural outcome of the greater frankness about prostitution after 1857. So too was another and more radical kind of realism, in the style of Dr Acton, the appreciation that the squalid life of a prostitute like Mary Smith was really rather exceptional. The characterization of Mrs Mount, a successful courtesan, in *The Ordeal of Richard Feverel* (1859) is a good example of this new objective treatment of the harlot. Again the reviewers were rather disconcerted by this realism (even those who singled out the scenes with Mrs Mount for special praise sometimes did so in a somewhat muddled, contradictory manner [331]); and they were still occasionally rather uneasy in the sixties and seventies when books like *Recommended to Mercy* and *A Terrible Temptation* gave frank, objective pictures of life in the demi-monde with quite immoral but perfectly likeable horsebreaker figures. After the appearance in 1871 of a coarse and common little baggage like Rhoda Somerset, Wilkie Collins' heroines looked a little old-fashioned: Mercy Merrick in *The New Magdalen*, who loses her virtue like Marian Erle through drugs and rape, and Simple Sally in *The Fallen Leaves* (1879), a greater moral idiot even than Ruth, are throwbacks to the magdalen of the fifties.

In one respect, however, Mercy Merrick is unquestionably a new magdalen compared with most of her predecessors: she ends happily married to an Evangelical clergyman. Ruth had ended a deeply lamented corpse, which again reflected her creator's over-anxiety to secure her readers' sympathy, and which ironically left Mrs Gaskell open to the charge of being hard-hearted. The *New Monthly*, for example (February 1853), was completely misled in its summary of *Ruth* by Mrs Gaskell's unfortunate ambiguity over the rehabilitation of the fallen: 'For Ruth herself never to be cleansed of her one error . . . for which, it appears, according to writers of the stamp of the authoress of *Mary Barton*, there is no atonement here below, nothing remained but death'. (XCVII, 198) Subsequent writers unfortunately were often over-cautious in the manner of Mrs Gaskell; but others, in tune with the general reduction in prudery and the new, more objective view of the harlot's progress, were willing to give their magdalens happy endings: Mrs Craik, for example, in *A Life for a Life* (1859) and *Parson Garland's Daughter* (1867), Reade in *A Terrible Temptation*, Collins in *The New Magdalen*, and Gissing in *The Unclassed* (1884).

By the time of *The Unclassed* rescue work among fallen women had undergone a remarkable transformation compared with the situation half a century earlier. The change was due in part to society's growing liberation from the sexual fears of the past, partly to the literary propaganda we have examined and partly to the increasing candour and charity shown towards prostitutes after 1869 through the efforts of the Campaign against the Contagious Diseases Acts. In 1882 and 1883 the abolitionists released a flood of material to greet the report of the Commons' Select Committee on the Acts and Parliament's subsequent decision to suspend them; and this successful agitation did much to nourish the magdalen's cause. In 1885 in the *Fortnightly Review* Lady Jeune, describing the rescue worker's former difficulties, rejoiced that 'Now the long-desired change has come, and for the moment a great deal of the sympathy and charity in England is being lavished on homes and penitentiaries for raising and rescuing the fallen. That numbers of women have been rescued and restored to a respectable life, and have regained a position in the world that fifteen years ago seemed impossible is a fact.' (n.s. XXVIII, 672) Later that year the cause was given yet more momentum by Stead's Maiden Tribute revelations. The Salvation Army in particular, whose previous rescue work had been largely abortive, made great capital from both the articles and the subsequent Armstrong case (in which it was much involved): a new and elaborate National Scheme was quickly announced for the Deliverance of Unprotected Girls and the Rescue of the Fallen; and soon the Army was busily organizing rescue brigades, holding midnight meetings and founding magdalen homes. In 1889 the first number of *The Deliverer* appeared, a monthly devoted to reporting on its progress in this area.

Also in 1889, however, there was a controversy in the *Daily Telegraph* which supplies a different perspective to this chronicle of success. On 22 March Robert Buchanan, deploring the decline in current values, plaintively asked,

> . . . if it is not possible, in the face of the grievous social peril— the threatened loss of a Feminine Ideal—for some few men, knights errant in the modern sense, but full of the old faith, the old enthusiasm, to remind the world, in the very teeth of modern pessimists, of what woman has been to the world, and of what she may yet become; to keep intact for our civilisation the living belief which sanctified a Madonna and a Magdalen. (p. 5)

On 2 April in reply to the intervention of some sceptics he reaffirmed that the votaries of chivalry found 'in the *Ewigweibliche* an abiding temple; on its threshold, kneeling prone, the Magdalen; in its inmost shrine, typical and supremely spiritual, the Madonna'. (p. 3) Buchanan's remarks indicate the proximity in status to the Madonna that the magdalen had gained in the creed of the sexual idealist. But they indicate too that, at the very moment when the prostitute was at last receiving the charity she deserved, the ideal of the magdalen, like that of the Madonna, was falling increasingly out of favour. Upon examination, we shall find, the decline of the magdalen ideal, like its ascendancy, stemmed from sources very similar to those that shaped the fate of the Madonna.

III DECLINE

6 Just how vigorous and widespread the magdalen cult had been is difficult to determine. One wonders how many readers of a magdalen novel really accepted its ethical implications, and how many in fact merited William Bell Scott's reproach in 'Rosabell':

> We sit beside the winter fire
> Or on the garden bench to read
> Her story, pleased if it be told
> With art and some sweet pathos, such
> As flatters us to feel.

In the year this was written, in March 1837, *Blackwood's* claimed of *The Father and Daughter* that it would endure 'till pity's self be dead' (LXI, 409), but one questions whether Mrs Opie would have enjoyed such success (ten editions by 1844) if her heroine, as in stage adaptations of the novel for working-class audiences, had ended happily married to her seducer. [332] There was, in short, in Victorian, as in eighteenth century England, a good deal of pharisaism disguised as sentimentality in readers' attitudes to the sufferings of the penitent. In the *Westminster* (April 1853) G. H. Lewes complained:

> The circulating libraries have furnished, and will continue to furnish, abundance of sickly sentimentality on this subject, wherein heroines strive to atone by consumption and broken hearts, for their lapse from virtue; or, if they do not take this 'rose-pink' turn, present a frigid and barren morality under which the luckless maiden, if her mind be very much set upon re-entering the Eden of respectability lingers through the remainder of her life under a deadly weight of patronage and encouragement, 'her sincere repentance and subsequent good conduct' being like a badge of infamy perpetuating the memory of her shame: a scarlet letter flaming upon her breast, attracting every eye; until one wonders how any being can be found able to live under such a restoration to social amnesty! (n.s. III, 476)

Lewes was dissociating *Ruth* from this purely nominal sympathy for the magdalen, but one questions again whether Mrs Gaskell would have enjoyed her success if she had been less ambiguous about restoring the fallen to good society.[1] In *Rhoda Fleming* (1865), Meredith attacks the principle of making an 'honest woman' of the fallen regardless of her emotional situation, but it might have better served the magdalen's cause if Ruth, Marian Erle and other penitents had not been so much praised by their creators for idealistically refusing the face-saving marriage. Perhaps the most blatant examples of a purely nominal compassion for the fallen are in the adultery novels of the sixties. In the immensely popular *East Lynne* (1861), for example, by Mrs Henry Wood, after hundreds of pages of lacerating penitence and suffering the errant wife is comfortably packed off to heaven with the forgiveness of her husband (in one of the many theatrical versions she and her dead little boy are enthroned on a golden cloud).

Since *East Lynne* first thrilled its readers at a time when Baptist Noel's Midnight Meetings campaign was receiving a good deal of public interest, one is tempted to infer that much of this interest was fairly superficial. The *Saturday Review* (1 February 1862), discussing the prostitute's emergence as 'one of the most interesting classes in English society', certainly did so: 'The fast man makes love to them; the slow man discusses them; the fashionable young lady copies their dress; the Evangelical clergyman gives them tea, toast and touching talks at midnight; and the devout young woman gives herself up to the task of tending them in some lovely and sequestered retreat, while they are resting between the acts of their exhausting lives'. (XIII, 125) That the Midnight Meetings soon faded from public notice, that the *Magdalen's Friend*, a journal for rescue workers which burst into being in 1860,

---

[1] In 1874 she was still being misinterpreted. A writer in the *Cornhill Magazine* (February 1874) remarked approvingly, 'Pure in her inmost soul as she is, Ruth is not allowed to conquer that social ostracism which is the ban of all who sin'. (XXIX, 203)

was defunct only four years later, was due partly, I suggested in
an earlier chapter, to society's disillusionment with the
intractable nature of the prostitution problem and the small
amount of progress being made. But it was also true that by the
mid-sixties for many people the magdalen had gone out of
fashion and been replaced by a new image of the fallen woman.
The resurgence of the spirit of Fashion attending the expansion
in middle-class affluence, which hastened the decline of the
Madonna, demonstrated also the conventionalism and hypocrisy
that had been latent in the cult of the magdalen. In Edmund
Yates' *Land at Last* (1866) the heroine, a fallen woman, notes
the new style in fashionable literature:

> There was a great run upon the Magdalen just then in that style
> of literature; writers were beginning to be what is called 'out-
> spoken'; and young ladies familiarised with the outward life of the
> species, as exhibited in the Park and at the Opera, read with
> avidity of their diamonds and their ponies, of the interior of their
> *ménage* and of their spirited conversations with the cream of the
> male aristocracy. A reference to British virtue, and a desire to stand
> well with the librarian's subscribers, compelled an amount of
> repentance in the third volume which Margaret scarcely believed
> to be in accordance with truth. The remembrance of childhood's
> days, which made the ponies pall, and rendered the diamonds
> disgusting—the inherent natural goodness, which took to eschewing
> the crinoline and the adoption of serge, which swamped the colonel
> in a storm of virtuous indignation and brought the curate safely
> riding over the billows—were agreeable incidents, but scarcely, she
> thought, founded on fact. (II, 112–13)

The most notable example of this new style in literature is
Anonyma (1864) and the series that it spawned, a series of mildly
salacious tales of pretty horsebreakers. Some of them, purport-
ing to be portraits of actual women, like Skittles, Agnes
Willoughby and Mabel Gray, inevitably ended with their
subjects still enjoying their heedless lives of sin. But most of
them, as Yates noted, paid lip-service to the cause of British

virtue. Anonyma, for example, after running through a variety of lovers, reforms utterly, becomes very devout and gets engaged to a clergyman; the heroine of *The Soiled Dove*, on the other hand, also of 1864, atones for her depravity with a squalid, miserable death. Another illustration of Fashion's new fusion of prurience and moral conventionalism is the cult of the beautiful demon, the irresistibly attractive and cataclysmically wicked enchantresses of G. A. Lawrence, Miss Braddon, Ouida and their followers, who usually finished in either an extraordinary show of penitence or a most fittingly wretched death. In *Puck* (1870) Ouida for once gave a very unglamorous picture of the courtesan (modelled, it seems, on the real-life Cora Pearl), claiming in censorious tones that the chief reason for her eminence 'was that this woman was so entirely harmonious with her time, so utterly its true daughter in rapacity, in licentiousness, in egotism, in coarse, hard lust of gold, in dull, dead indifference to anything save gain'. (III, 289) Without accepting all of Ouida's impressive ethical severity about 'an Age which has elected to deify the courtesan' (III, 287), one can see that Fashion had perverted the magdalen ideal in much the same way as that of the Madonna. In the fast novel, in the fashionable play, the courtesan was the complement in moral claptrap and religiosity to the phoney Madonna.

The process of perversion had been gradual. In 1837 Bulwer Lytton was roasted for his play *The Duchess de la Vallière*, a sentimental but quite innocuous study of the moral reformation of Louis XIV's concubine. *The Spectator* (7 January) spoke for most of the critics, and for the general public too (the play lasted only eight nights): 'we cannot pass uncensured the dramatist who calls upon us to sympathize with the woes of a discarded mistress and a disappointed voluptuary. It is the pathos of the stews.' (X, 10) In 1853 we find G. H. Lewes, not the most squeamish of critics, rejoicing in the suppression of another, and far more equivocal, courtesan play :'At Drury Lane, we were threatened with a version of *La Dame aux*

Camélias, but the Lord Chamberlain refused a licence to this unhealthy idealization of one of the worst evils of our social life. Paris may delight in such pictures, but London, thank God! has still enough instinctive repulsion against pruriency not to tolerate them.' [333] Three years later on the appearance of *La Traviata*, Verdi's operatic version of the story, the critics revived the charges they had directed against Bulwer; and with far more justice, for where the Duchess had been haunted throughout the play by remorse for her sins and had finally entered a convent, Verdi's heroine, though worshipped by all around her as an angel destined for heaven, seemed to have no conception of chastity or religion whatsoever. 'It is opposed,' thundered the *Saturday Review* (31 May 1856), 'to all the highest interests of morality to excite our sympathies on behalf of such a character as Violetta, who, while deserving our pity, ought not to be represented in such a way as to excite our admiration and love.' (II, 105) This time, however, the public did not share the critics' scruples, and the opera was a riotous success. Much of its popularity was doubtless solely due to its musical qualities, but some of it, it seems certain, was due to a prurience and sentimentality in its audience, an admiration for the courtesan figure, that had nothing to do with compassion for the magdalen.

Within a few years the *Traviata* story was being shamelessly plagiarized in novels, in, for example, *Nobly False* (1863) by James McGrigor Allan or *Annie, or the Life of a Lady's Maid* (1864). But it was a little longer before the courtesan-heroine became firmly entrenched in the theatre. In 1869 an outraged correspondent provoked *The Times* to an attack on Boucicault's *Formosa*, but the play's success with critics and public showed that London now, like Paris, was pleased by slightly risqué pictures of high-class vice with lashings of moral sentiment. Some of the courtesan plays of the following years in fact neglected to observe the moral conventions: at the end of W. G. Wills' *Nell Gwynne* (1878), for example, the heroine is still the king's mistress having rejected once more her old and faithful lover. But the typical moral ethos is that of *The Pompadour* (1888) by Wills and Sydney Grundy. After a sumptuous picture of the dissolute brilliance of Louis XV's court the play finishes with Pompadour's collapse and death at the rattle of musketry which, she thinks, proclaims the execution by her unwitting order of her own dear, long-lost son. 'Some such *dénouement* as this', commented *The Times* (2 April), 'unhistorical though it may be, was not to be avoided. Dumas's famous axiom, *Tue-la*, as applied to the peccant wife, may be somewhat impracticable in everyday existence, but it is of prime necessity in the case of a dramatic heroine of the Pompadour stamp.' (p. 10) Six years later in *Mrs Warren's Profession*, Shaw created a heroine who was the antithesis of the conventional courtesan heroine: 'I am not a pandar posing as a moralist,' he wrote, 'I want to make an end, if I can, of the furtively lascivious Pharisaism of stage immorality, by a salutary demonstration of the reality.' [334] But as the century drew to a close Mrs Warren remained unknown to the general public, because of the Lord Chamberlain's veto, and Fashion's perversion of what had been the magdalen ideal continued to hold the stage.

7 The magdalen, however, had been outmoded by more than the spread of Fashion. Like the Madonna she had been out-moded too by time, by a growing awareness in the later decades of the century that she was no longer a suitable archetype. As early as 1858 Miss Mulock had attacked the 'exaggerated sentimentalism' with which fallen women were being treated, 'laying all the blame upon the seducer, and exalting the seduced into a paragon of injured simplicity, whom society ought to pet, and soothe, and treat with far more interest and consideration than those who have not erred'. [335] For the compassionate idealist it was a temptation to lay all blame upon the seducer: like the hero of F. W. Farrar's *Julian Home* (1859) to reproach the patron of prostitutes with 'the cry of the souls of which you have been *the murderer*—yes, do not disguise it—the *murderer*;

the cruel, willing, pitiless murderer'. (p. 275) But though natural it was hardly likely to make for effective rescue work: when Baptist Noel talked in the following year of 40,000 prostitutes dying annually 'all murdered by profligate men', [336] one cannot believe he impressed overmuch the well-dressed harlots at his midnight suppers with his grasp of the situation. For the compassionate idealist it was a temptation to exalt the seduced into a paragon of injured simplicity, particularly after 1869 when the agitators against the Contagious Diseases Acts had burnished afresh the prostitute's image as a martyr. But though natural it was again not likely to make for effective rescue work.

In the year 1870, however, there was a significant advance in realism in the literary image of the magdalen. Trollope's *The Vicar of Bullhampton*, for example, though meant chiefly to excite sympathy for the fallen, was also a hard-headed attack on the counter-productive tendencies of well-meaning sentimentality. In it Carry Brattle is no idealized Ruth-figure but a very ordinary and, to begin with at least, not particularly likeable young woman; and the young clergyman Mr Fenwick, though contrasted favourably with the lack of charity amongst the girl's relations, is yet criticized for his self-indulgent softness, his romantic over-involvement: 'Was it a fault in him that he was tender to her because of her prettiness, and because he had loved her as a child? We must own that it was a fault. The crooked places of the world, if they are to be made straight at all, must be made straight after a sterner and a juster fashion.' (p. 256) More impressive than Trollope's unsentimental candour was the delicate tenderness and yet honest sexuality and matter-of-fact realism of Rossetti's 'Jenny', a poem he had started twenty-two years earlier, about a young student's ruminations beside a sleeping whore. The poem demonstrates and evokes not sentimental pity, but as Swinburne puts it, 'the more just and deeper compassion of human fellowship and fleshly brotherhood': the girl is no ruined angel, but one who 'plies her trade like any other trade, without show or sense of reluctance or repulsion'.[1] If her beauty at one point reminds the student of, one infers, a Madonna by Raphael or Da Vinci (ll. 230–40), he never loses sight of her real nature: 'Lazy laughing languid Jenny,/Fond of a kiss and fond of a guinea.' If sentimentality and Madonna idealism seem implicit in 'Poor shameful, Jenny, full of grace', he immediately goes on:

> Thus with your hand upon my knee;—
> Whose person or whose purse may be
> The lodestar of your reverie?

The hard-headed realism of Trollope and Rossetti took some time unfortunately to become common. Indeed in the 1870s even more than in 1858 there was cause to complain that the fallen woman was exalted as a paragon martyr whom society ought to pet and treat with more consideration than those who had not erred. For one thing, in magdalen fiction those who had not erred were often treated with scant respect: 'Vice is continually represented by certain novelists in the most glowing colours,' it was remarked in 1874 with, I think, *The New Magdalen* in mind, 'whilst those in whom virtue is predominant, are supposed to be weak, silly or ugly.' [337] The sentimental adulation of the fallen besides offending possible supporters of the magdalen's cause, was also counter-productive with another class of women who had not erred. 'What is the likely effect,' wrote Mrs Lynn Linton in 1889, 'of all this high-flown idealisation on the mind and principles of the struggling hard-working girl who resists the temptation of the streets, and prefers to vice and champagne, chastity and a crust . . . when she reads of the women whose lives she has been taught to loathe, talked only of as the pitiable victims of

---

[1] *Fortnightly Review* (May 1870) n.s. VII, 570. Another reviewer, in *Tinsley's* (March 1871), pointed out 'the case of the courtesan is taken up and analysed, not from the distant stand-point of a parliamentary or scientific debate . . . but from the near position which only one who has seen the inside of Jenny's own room could assume'. (VIII, 158)

man's brutality, held as themselves free from moral blame, and as the fit objects for admiration and pathetic idealisation, how much easier does that make her own struggle?' A week earlier Mrs Linton had expressed comprehensively a by now very common impatience with the old idealized pathos: 'The Magdalen is a very beautiful theme for art and poetry, but the poor drunken flaunting Professionals are stern facts—the results of poverty and passion combined—and white kid gloves are as much out of place when dealing with them as either art or poetry . . . the present danger is not in over-severity, but in over-petting and sentimentality, in maudlin pity and unjust partiality.' [338]

Another aspect of the magdalen's martyr image that had been proving counter-productive was her tendency in literature to be given a moving death. In 1838 Bulwer Lytton, defending the happy ending, in a loving marriage, enjoyed by the heroine of *Alice*, had claimed it was time to 'do away with the punishment of Death for inadequate offences, even in books'. (III, 324) Often in fact, as we have seen, even genuine idealists continued to have the magdalen die, either through an over-anxiety not to alienate their readers or a desire to inspire them with shame and pity for the outcast. Often, however, the non-rehabilitation of the magdalen seems to have been a self-indulgent wallowing in sentiment: the redeemed heroine of *The Penitent* (1839), for example, is quite arbitrarily murdered by an enemy from her past; the redeemed heroine of *Out of the Depths* dies gratuitously just before her marriage to a worthy man. In Thomas Miller's *Godfrey Malvern* the minor figure of the prostitute Arabella is married off, but the major figure of the hero's discarded mistress is given a *Traviata* death-bed. In Dickens' *David Copperfield* the minor figure of Martha Endell is happily wedded, but the more important figure of Little Em'ly, even in the remoteness of Australia, refuses several good matches to lead a life of penitent spinsterhood. Clearly, as Philip Collins has pointed out, we are meant to admire Em'ly's resolution more than Martha's earthier pursuit of happiness, and Dickens is thus in fiction capitulating to the views on the rehabilitating marriage that at Urania Cottage he had consistently rejected. [339] The complacent reader in cases like these, whatever the ambitions of the writer, was more likely to enjoy an emotional bath than to become an active convert to the magdalen's cause.

By the 1880s the serious writer and the serious reader were fast out-growing this kind of self-indulgence. Besides the prurient pharisaism that delighted in courtesan literature there was also a new liberalism in society about the fallen woman's right to social amnesty. As Henry Arthur Jones' *Saints and Sinners* was performed on its opening night in 1884 the seduced heroine died a Ruth-like penitent death, but public reaction soon forced Jones to put in a happy ending, to have her married off to her honest former fiancé. With *The Middleman* (1889) he needed no prompting (the fallen heroine ends the play happily married to her seducer). And with Pinero's *The Profligate* of that same year the new direction of public taste was once again made plain: in the acted version Pinero was persuaded to change the written text for a happy ending, in this case cutting the death of an erring hero. The new liberalism was very far from universal: Mrs Erlynne in Wilde's *Lady Windermere's Fan* (1892), a fallen woman restored to good society, may seem light years from, say, the heroine of *East Lynne* (the name is perhaps no coincidence), but it is she who accuses Windermere of wanting her 'to retire into a convent, or become a hospital nurse, or something of that kind, as people do in silly modern novels'. [340] A large number of writers were now prepared to have the fallen woman redeem herself in marriage, like Frank Frankfort Moore, for example, in *I Forbid the Banns* (1893) or, far more subtly, and persuasively, Mark Rutherford in *Clara Hopgood* (1896); and some of them like Hall Caine in his immensely successful novel of 1894 *The Manxman* were prepared to have even an adulterous passion end in triumphant happiness. But there were still a lot of silly novelists sticking to the old conventions of convent walls and hospital wards; and a number of writers too, like Pinero and

Jones, who though sympathetic themselves to the fallen woman's cause felt that, human nature being what it was, she had usually no more chance of social restoration than the heroines of *The Second Mrs Tanqueray* and *Mrs Dane's Defence*.

Society was still confused in its views on feminine unchastity. It was, however, unquestionably much more broadminded in general than previously in the century. Jones, for example, in *The Masqueraders* and *The Case of Rebellious Susan* (both 1894) flirts with the idea of a wife's adulterous retaliation against her husband's peccadilloes, in a way that would have scandalized earlier audiences. But though the social climate was confused, it was decided in one respect: it was no longer favourable to the old polarities of apotheosized female purity and vilified female wantonness. In *Ernest Maltravers* (1837) Bulwer Lytton had been a heretic to argue that an ingenuous woman's fall could make, not mar, her virtue (II, 16–18); but Hardy's belligerent affirmation in *Tess of the D'Urbervilles* (1892) that his heroine's fall was 'simply a liberal education' seems to have raised remarkably little heat. In a sense the magdalen herself had shaken the old polarity by assuming many features of the Madonna, but it was this devaluation of virginity, to the level of a technical rather than absolute measure of purity, that finally quashed it utterly. As a new century began there were small but definite hints beneath society's surface decorum of a quite new approach to the question of the relation of the sexes.

12

Epilogue

In December 1832 Samuel Warren contributed a story to *Blackwood's* called 'The Magdalen' which, though of negligible interest in purely literary terms, may help to focus the relevance of the mass of material the reader has been shown. It concerns a beautiful young girl who is so like portraits of the Virgin in appearance that she goes amongst those who know her by the name of 'The Madonna'. She is seduced into prostitution, but is sufficiently redeemed through her agonies of repentance to regain her former Madonna-like beauty. She dies soon after, as she is embroidering on a sampler the words 'Mary Magdalen', and her kindly old benefactor, the narrator, concludes his tale with the vow 'I shall never part with that sampler till I die! —Oh, poor Mary Magdalen!—I will not forget thee!' (XXXII, 911)

Nothing that I have written in this book will make Warren's story a better piece of literature. But I hope it might now be considered a more interesting human document: as a very early specimen of Madonna and Magdalen imagery it is a helpful index of contemporary sexual attitudes and to the treatment of those attitudes in the more lasting and valuable literature of the age. I hope too it might now be considered a more impressive human document. The moral values it upholds might seem foreign, not to say repulsive, to the twentieth century reader and the psychological distortions ludicrous and banal. But seen in historical context, with due allowance given for Victorian psychic difficulties beyond our modern experience, Warren's story and, still more, the work of the great nineteenth century masters, has a genuine moral dignity. The Victorians now are rarely shown the contemptuous incomprehension of a Lytton Strachey, but they still merit much greater understanding than we usually give them. When we consider the absurdities and painful confusions of our own sexual attitudes, our own manifestations of hypocrisy and prudery, our own vanities and cruelties, we have need to hope that the twenty-first century will be more generous to us than we have been to them.

Reference Notes

Reference Notes

1. *The Letters of Edward Dowden and his Correspondents*, ed. E. D. and H. M. Dowden (1914), p. 30
2. Simon Nowell Smith, *Letters to Macmillan* (1967), p. 56
3. A. M. D. W. Stirling, *The Ways of Yesterday* (1930), p. 238
4. *Fraser's Magazine* (June 1838) XVII, 763
5. *Morning Advertiser* (2 June 1859), p. 4
6. John Ruskin, *Works*, ed. E. T. Cook and A. Wedderburn (1903-12) XXII, 222
7. Havelock Ellis, *Studies in the Psychology of Sex* (New York, 1936) I, Pt 1, 34
8. W. T. Whitley, *Artists and their Friends in England 1700-1799* (1928) I, 348-50
9. Sir Henry Cole, *Fifty Years of Public Work* (1884) I, 288
10. 'Parleyings with Certain People . . . With Francis Furini' (1887) in *Poetical Works of Robert Browning*, ed. Augustine Birrell (1929 rev. edn) II, 711
11. Betty Miller, *Browning: A Portrait* (1952), pp. 104-6
12. *Kilvert's Diary*, ed. William Plomer (1938-40) III, 37; II, 358
13. Cf. *The Observer* (27 Aug. 1856), p. 5; and Dr Spencer Thomson, *Health Resorts of Britain* (1860), p. 73
14. Quoted Cyril Pearl, *The Girl with the Swansdown Seat* (1955), p. 230, in a useful section on seaside nudity.
15. Quoted in the *Illustrated Times* (8 Oct. 1864), p. 231
16. A similar pattern is observable in Henry Rider Haggard's *She* (1887), pp. 162f and especially 291f
17. See above, pp. 130-1
18. *New Review* (Jan. 1890) II, 8
19. 'Locksley Hall Sixty Years After' (1886), lines 141-2

20. (W. R. Greg), 'French Fiction: the Lowest Deep', *National Review* (Oct. 1860), XI, 427

21. Tennyson's remarks about this figure are to be found in a poem of 1852, 'Suggested by Reading an Article in a Newspaper'.

22. Grant Allen, 'The New Hedonism', *Fortnightly Review* (March 1894) n.s. LV, 390

23. W. R. Greg, review of Stanley's *Life*, quoted Walter E. Houghton, *The Victorian Frame of Mind 1830–1870* (1957), p. 221

24. Noel Annan, *Leslie Stephen* (1951), p. 14

25. Charles Kingsley, *Alton Locke* (1850) I, 114

26. James Boswell, *The Life of Samuel Johnson*, ed. G. B. Hill (Oxford 1934–64) IV, 219

27. Edward Carpenter, *Love's Coming-of-Age* (1896), p. 43

28. 'The New Hedonism', *loc. cit.*

29. Mark Longaker, *Ernest Dowson* (Philadelphia, 1944), p. 59

30. G. M. Young, *Victorian England, Portrait of an Age* (Oxford, 1936), p. 2

31. Maurice J. Quinlan, *Victorian Prelude: A History of English Manners, 1700–1830* (New York, 1941), p. 108

32. Quoted Margaret Dalziel, *Popular Fiction 100 Years Ago* (1957), p. 94

33. Peter T. Cominos, *The Late-Victorian Revolt, 1859–1895* (unpublished D.Phil. thesis, Oxford 1959).

34. Grant Allen, 'Letters in Philistia', *Fortnightly Review* (June 1891) n.s. XLIX, 955

35. Geoffrey Mortimer, *op. cit.*, pp. 4–5

36. Thomas Carlyle, 'Sir Walter Scott', *Works* (1896–99) XXIX, 49

37. Both illustrations are cited by Gertrude Himmelfarb, *Victorian Minds* (1968), pp. 290–1, to whose discussion I am indebted. For other examples see Houghton, *op. cit.*, pp. 238–9

38. Noel Annan, *op. cit.*, p. 75

39. Coventry Patmore, 'The Angel in the House', *Poems*, ed. Frederick Page (1949), p. 83

40. Hallam Tennyson, *Alfred Lord Tennyson: a Memoir* (1897) I, 329

41. Ralph Wilson Rader, *Tennyson's Maud* (Berkeley, 1963), p. 98

42. Compare, for example, the parallels drawn between England and Rome in Conyers Middleton's *Life of Cicero* (1741) with William Hale, *Considerations of the Causes and the Prevalence of Female Prostitution* (1812), p. 70; John Stores Smith, *Social*

Aspects (1850), pp. 75–6 and 223–4; and *Reynold's Newspaper* (21 April 1895), p. 1

43. The 'Reform or Ruin' chapter in Quinlan, *op. cit.*, is particularly helpful on this subject.
44. *Annual Register* for 1798, p. 230
45. Quoted Houghton, *op. cit.*, p. 55, in a valuable discussion of the Victorian fear of revolution. The italics are mine.
46. Friedrich Engels, *The Condition of the Working Class in England in 1844* (1892 edn.), p. 298
47. *Alton Locke*, the 1862 preface, I, 83
48. See John Killham, *Tennyson and the Princess* (1958), pp. 147–69, where there is an excellent analysis of this article.
49. Philip Magnus, *King Edward the Seventh* (1964), p. 74
50. *The Poems and Plays of Tennyson* (Oxford, 1953), p. 730
51. 'Autumn', lines 65–8, in *The Seasons*
52. *Works* XVIII, 22; quoted by Houghton, *op. cit.*, p. 343, in a most valuable discussion of the Victorian home.
53. The poem 'Sensibility' in *The Works of Hannah More* (1830) I, 175
54. James Anthony Froude, *Thomas Carlyle: A History of his Life in London 1834–1881* (1884), pp. 290–1
55. *The Nemesis of Faith*, p. 103
56. 'Suggested by Matthew Arnold's "Stanzas from the Grande Chartreuse"', *Poetical Works*, ed. Bertram Dobell (1895) II, 370–1
57. Coventry Patmore, *op. cit.*, p. 69
58. Reprinted in Greg's *Literary and Social Judgements* (1877) II, 263
59. *First Principles of Ecclesiastical Truth: Essays on the Church and Society* (1871), pp. 224–5
60. *Young Men and Maidens* (1871), p. 9
61. *Op. cit.*, p. 153
62. Elizabeth Blackwell, *Counsel to Parents on the Moral Education of their Children in Relation to Sex* (2nd edn. 1884), p. 97
63. Anthony Nutting, *Gordon, Martyr and Misfit* (1966), p. 319
64. William Hale White, *The Autobiography of Mark Rutherford and Mark Rutherford's Deliverance* (2nd edn. 1888), p. 9
65. (3rd edn. 1862), p. 3. References will be to this edition, except where otherwise specified.
66. *Op. cit.* (6th edn. 1875), p. 64
67. *Ibid.*, pp. 146–7

68. (11th edn. 1881), p. 105
69. T. L. Nichols, *Esoteric Anthropology* (Malvern, 1873), p. 296
70. *Op. cit.*, p. 13
71. See his *On Marriage; its Intent, Obligations, and Physical and Constitutional Disqualifications, Medically Considered* (1838)
72. *Op. cit.* (6th edn. 1875), p. 188
73. See Culverwell, *op. cit.* and Walker, *Woman Physiologically Considered* (1839)
74. Richard Burton, *Supplemental Nights to the Book of the Thousand Nights and a Night* (1885–8) VII, 439
75. *Op. cit.*, I, Pt. 1, 164
76. T. L. Nichols, *op. cit.*, p. 284
77. Edward Tilt, *Elements of Health, and Principles of Female Hygiene* (1852), p. 183
78. F. W. Newman, *Miscellanies* (1889) III, 279
79. George Egerton, *Discords* (1894), pp. 157, 158
80. Quoted A. O. J. Cockshut, *The Unbelievers* (1964), p. 162
81. *Westminster Review* (July 1850) LIII, 473
82. Arthur H. Nethercot, *The First Five Lives of Annie Besant* (1961), p. 40
83. Elizabeth Longford, *Victoria R.I.* (1964), p. 270
84. Nichols, *op. cit.*, p. 97; H. Arthur Allbutt, *The Wife's Handbook* (1887), p. 5
85. Annie Besant, *An Autobiography* (2nd edn. 1893), pp. 223–4
86. See Tilt, *op. cit.*, p. 269
87. Edward Carpenter, *op. cit.*, p. 66
88. For some good examples see J. A. and Olive Banks, *Feminism and Family Planning in Victorian England* (Liverpool, 1964), pp. 111–13
89. *The Letters of Olive Schreiner 1876–1920*, ed. S. C. Cronwright-Schreiner (1924), p. 217
90. Erna Reiss, *The Rights and Duties of Englishwomen* (Manchester, 1934), p. 41
91. John S. Smith, *Social Aspects* (1850), pp. 91–2
92. *Lord Chesterfield's Letters to his Son* (1929 edn.), p. 66
93. Edmund Burke, *A Philosophical Enquiry into the Origin of Our Ideas of the Sublime and Beautiful* (1757), p. 91
94. (Anne Richelieu Lamb), *Can Women Regenerate Society?* (1844), p. 13

95. Emma Worboise, *Singlehurst Manor* (1869), p. 372
96. The view of the old king in Tennyson's *The Princess* (1847) Pt. V, lines 437–41
97. *Edinburgh Review* (Jan. 1850) XCI, 155
98. *Hansard* (3rd series) CXLIII, cols. 233–4
99. *The Humanitarian* (Nov. 1894) V, 355
100. Geoffrey Best, *Shaftesbury* (1964), p. 25
101. *Sermons to Young Women* (3rd edn. 1766) I, 99–100
102. *Woman as she is and as she should be* (1835) I, 37
103. Quoted Dalziel, *op. cit.*, p. 94
104. *The Princess* Pt. VII, lines 259–60, 283–6
105. *Westminster Review* (Oct. 1887) CXXVIII, 825
106. *The Letters and Private Papers of William Makepeace Thackeray*, ed. Gordon N. Ray (Cambridge Mass., 1945–6) II, 361
107. William Allingham, *Songs, Ballads and Stories* (1877), p. 60
108. Sir Charles Tennyson, *Alfred Tennyson* (1949), pp. 89, 355
109. J. A. Froude, *Thomas Carlyle: A History of the First Forty Years of His Life 1795–1835* (1882) II, 354
110. The Thackeray *Letters* III, 13
111. Rowland E. Prothero, *The Life and Correspondence of Arthur Penrhyn Stanley* (1893) II, 148
112. Betty Miller, *op. cit.*, p. 13
113. Gaylord C. Leroy, *Perplexed Prophets: Six Nineteenth-Century British Authors* (Philadelphia, 1953), p. 88
114. Miller, *op. cit.*, p. 58
115. James L. Halliday, *Mr. Carlyle: My Patient* (1949), p. 3
116. Miller, *op. cit.*, pp. 148–52; Giles St Aubyn, *A Victorian Eminence: The Life and Works of Henry Thomas Buckle* (1958), p. 37f; Prothero, *op. cit.*, II, 72–8, 95–7, 130–1, 139f
117. *The Passing of Victoria: The Poets' Tribute*, ed. J. A. Hammerton (1901), pp. 80–1
118. Derek Hudson, *Lewis Carroll* (1954), p. 57
119. Beatrice Webb, *My Apprenticeship* (2nd edn. 1947), p. 7
120. Miller, *op. cit.*, p. 13
121. Quoted Pearl, *op. cit.*, p. 213
122. J. C. Reid, *Francis Thompson* (1959), p. 22
123. R. L. Stevenson, *Collected Poems*, ed. Janet A. Smith (1950), p. 361
124. J. C. Reid, *Thomas Hood* (1963), p. 70. Disraeli was a notable

example of the love of being petted—see Hesketh Pearson, *Dizzy* (1951), p. 144

125. Miller, *op. cit.*, p. 98
126. Miller, *op. cit.*, pp. 9–10 and *passim*; Oswald Doughty, *Victorian Romantic: Dante Gabriel Rossetti* (1949), pp. 38, 121–2, 256–7
127. John D. Rosenberg, *The Darkening Glass: A Portrait of Ruskin's Genius* (1963), *passim*; Philip Henderson, *The Life of Laurence Oliphant* (1956), *passim*.
128. Quoted Gillian Avery, *Nineteenth Century Children* (1965), p. 91
129. George H. Ford, *Dickens and his Readers* (Princeton, 1955), p. 56
130. *Appreciations and Criticisms of the Works of Charles Dickens* (1911), p. 58. See also Jack Lindsay, *Charles Dickens* (1950), p. 194
131. Edgar Johnson, *Charles Dickens: his Tragedy and Triumph* (1953) I, 44
132. *The Letters of Ernest Dowson*, ed. Desmond Flower and Henry Maas (1967), p. 279
133. Rosenberg, *op. cit.*, p. 162
134. Longaker, *op. cit.*, p. 155
135. Rosenberg, *op. cit.*, p. 203
136. Hudson, *op. cit.*, p. 188
137. Longaker, *op. cit.*, p. 59
138. See Ronald Chapman's biography of Watts, *The Laurel and the Thorn* (1945), p. 67
139. Patmore, *op. cit.*, pp. 89, 180
140. Ray, *op. cit.*, I, 303f; Johnson, *op. cit.* I, 131
141. Arthur Maddison, *Hints on Rescue Work* (1898), preface
142. William Logan, *The Great Social Evil* (1871), p. 104
143. John Thomas, *An Appeal to the Public* (1809), p. 63
144. *England and the English* (1833) I, 370
145. Tennyson's 'Merlin and Vivien', lines 814–15
146. *An Eye for an Eye* (1879) II, 116
147. Quoted Patricia Thomson, *The Victorian Heroine* (1956), p. 122
148. William J. Taylor, *The Story of the Homes* (1907), p. 23
149. 8 Jan. 1858, p. 6
150. *A Regency Visitor: the English Tour of Prince Pückler-Muskau*, ed. E. M. Butler (1957), p. 84
151. Alexander Slidell, *The American in England* (New York, 1835) II, 211–12

152. For a graphic description of the Haymarket in the early 1860s see the *Saturday Review* (June 1862) XIII, 644

153. Mrs C. S. Peel, *Life's Enchanted Cup* (1933), pp. 105–6

154. Ralph Wardlaw, *Lectures on Female Prostitution* (Glasgow, 1842), pp. 93–4

155. There is a useful account of this affair in Giles Playfair, *Six Studies in Hypocrisy* (1969), pp. 98–100

156. (6 Oct. 1860) X, 417

157. Dinah Mulock, *A Woman's Thoughts about Women* (1858), p. 285

158. S. T., *An Address to the Guardian Society*, reprinted in the *Pamphleteer* (1818) XI, 227–8

159. Acton, *Prostitution*, p. 101

160. *Saturday Review* (16 Oct. 1858) VI, 373

161. (20 Oct. 1866) XXII, 42

162. J. A. Banks, *Prosperity and Parenthood* (1954), p. 48

163. Oswald Doughty, *op. cit.*, pp. 253, 343

164. Sigmund Freud, 'Contributions to the Psychology of Love', *Collected Papers* (1924–50) IV, 210

165. W. E. H. Lecky, *The History of European Morals* (1869) II, 283

166. The *Globe* (15 Jan. 1858), p. 1

167. Pearl discusses these cases, *op. cit.*, pp. 210–11

168. *The Daily Telegraph* (13 Oct. 1894), p. 5

169. *Miscellaneous Prose Works* (Edinburgh 1827) III, 516–7

170. von Raumer, *op. cit.*, II, pp. 99, 97

171. Taine, *op. cit.*, p. 95

172. *Op. cit.*, pp. 99, 97

173. Pearl, *op. cit.*, pp. 13, 262–3

174. 'On Cant and Hypocrisy', *Selected Essays of William Hazlitt*, ed. Geoffrey Keynes (1930), p. 353

175. *The Subjection of Women* (1869), p. 167

176. *Edinburgh Review* (June 1831) LIII, 547–8

177. See Playfair, *op. cit.*, p. 31

178. Reprinted in *Readiana* (1887), p. 314

179. *The Letters and Journals of Lord Byron*, ed. Rowland E. Prothero (1898–1904) V, 542

180. Peter Fryer, *Mrs Grundy: Studies in English Prudery* (1963), p. 18

181. The preface to his *Vision of Judgement* (1821).

182. *Oscar Wilde* (1946), p. 261

183. A gruesome example from 1810 is given by Fernando Henriques in his *Modern Sexuality* (1968), pp. 72–3
184. This point has been made eloquently by Ronald Bryden in *The Unfinished Hero and Other Essays* (1969), pp. 184–5
185. Quoted C. W. and Phillis Cunnington, *Handbook of English Costume in the Nineteenth Century* (1959), p. 388
186. John Carleton, *Hyde Marston* (1844) II, 128
187. Quoted C. W. Cunnington, *Feminine Attitudes of The Nineteenth Century* (1935), p. 181
188. Quoted C. W. Cunnington, *The Art of English Costume* (1948), p. 201
189. Jane Taylor, *Essays in Rhyme on Manners & Morals* (1816), p. 145
190. *Op. cit.*, III, 517
191. See Donald McCormick, *The Hell-Fire Club* (1958); George Martelli, *Jemmy Twitcher, A Life of the Fourth Earl of Sandwich* (1962), pp. 44–9 and 56–66; and Betty Kemp, *Sir Francis Dashwood* (New York, 1967), pp. 131–6. Byron's escapades at Newstead Abbey fifty years later were similarly magnified: see Leslie A. Marchand, *Byron* (New York, 1957) I, 173–5
192. *The World* (20 Feb. 1755) III, 675–6
193. Earl of Ilchester, *The Home of the Hollands* (1937), p. 205
194. Quoted Martelli, *op. cit.*, p. 85
195. Loren Reid, *Charles James Fox* (1969), p. 199
196. See McCormick, *op. cit.*, p. 154
197. The letter is quoted in full by Michael T. H. Sadler, *The Political Career of Richard Brinsley Sheridan* (1912), pp. 82–3
198. *Hints, etc., submitted to the Serious Attention of the Clergy, Nobility and Gentry* (1789)
199. Hannah More, *Thoughts on the Importance* (1788), p. 114
200. See Dorothy Margaret Stuart, *Dearest Bess* (1955), pp. 23–35, 40–4, 62–3
201. *Ibid.*, pp. 147–8, 163–4, 166, 184–5
202. Oliver Warner, *A Portrait of Lord Nelson* (1958), pp. 224–5
203. Joanna Richardson, *George IV* (1966), p. 77
204. See Roger Fulford, *Royal Dukes* (1933), pp. 98–100
205. *An Enquiry into the Duties of the Female Sex* (1797), p. 327
206. Quoted C. W. and Phillis Cunnington, *Handbook of English Costume in the Nineteenth Century*, p. 12
207. See Ilchester, *op. cit.*, pp. 142–3

208. *Letters to a Young Lady* (1806) I, 138–9
209. Quoted Muriel Jaeger, *Before Victoria* (1956), p. 72
210. Quoted Maurice J. Quinlan, *op. cit.*, p. 257
211. Quoted Stuart, *op. cit.*, p. 163
212. Quoted Jaeger, *op. cit.*, p. 74
213. 'Aristocracy, Social Structure and Religion in the Early Victorian Period', *VS* (March 1963) VI, 265
214. William Law Mathieson, *England in Transition 1789–1832* (1920), p. 120
215. See E. D. H. Johnson, 'Don Juan in England', *ELH* (1944) II, 144
216. Quoted Mathieson, *op. cit.*, p. 121
217. Joanna Richardson, *The Disastrous Marriage* (1960), p. 192
218. *Edinburgh Review* (June 1831) LIII, 548
219. Quoted Quinlan, *op. cit.*, p. 259
220. *Ibid.*, p. 173
221. *Temple Bar* (May 1870) XXIX, 178
222. 'The Role of the Aristocracy in the Late Nineteenth Century', *VS* (Sept. 1960) IV, 61
223. See W. Gore Allen, *King William IV* (1960), pp. 61–4
224. Quoted O. F. Christie, *The Transition from Aristocracy 1832–1867* (1927), p. 75
225. *England and the English* I, 180
226. Benjamin Disraeli, *Sybil* (1845) II, 289
227. See Roger Fulford, *The Prince Consort* (1949), p. 61
228. Quoted Spring *VS* (March 1963) VI, 267
229. See Acton, *Prostitution* (1857), pp. 99–105
230. Richard Deacon, *The Private Life of Mr. Gladstone* (1965), pp. 80, 95
231. *Pall Mall Gazette* (21 Sept. 1867), p. 11
232. *Saturday Review* (30 Jan. 1869) XXVII, 139
233. Philip Magnus, *King Edward the Seventh* (1964), p. 71
234. Arthur Brinckman, *Notes on Rescue Work* (1885), p. 34
235. Winston Churchill, *My Early Life* (1930), p. 71
236. *Universal Review* (Feb. 1890) VI, 201
237. Quoted Royden Harrison, *Before the Socialists* (1965), p. 27
238. Walter Bagehot, *The English Constitution* (1928 edn.), p. 100
239. Quoted Magnus, *King Edward the Seventh*, p. 108
240. Quoted Playfair, *op. cit.*, pp. 99–100

241. See, for example, an article by the rescue worker Lady Jeune in the *Fortnightly* (Sept. 1885) n.s. XXXVIII, 345–6

242. *Temple Bar* (May 1870) XXIX, 181

243. Quoted Jules Abels, *The Parnell Tragedy* (New York, 1966), p. 324

244. *Fortnightly Review* (Dec. 1885) n.s. XXXVIII, 778

245. *The Letters of Sir Walter Scott*, ed. Herbert Grierson *et al.* (1932–7) X, 96. The date to which the anecdote alludes is given by Noel Perrin, *Dr. Bowdler's Legacy* (1970), p. 15

246. For a detailed study of the book's reception see André Parreaux, *The Publication of the Monk: A Literary Event, 1796–1798* (Paris, 1960).

247. *Northanger Abbey* (1923 edn., ed. R. W. Chapman), p. 48. The novel, though first published in 1818, was begun in 1797.

248. See Quinlan, *op. cit.*, pp. 229–50, and Perrin, *op. cit.*, pp. 139–61

249. James Plumptre, *Four Discourses on the Stage* (Cambridge, 1809), p. 222

250. John Hayden, *The Romantic Reviewers 1802–1824* (1969), pp. 126–31

251. Quoted Kathleen Tillotson, *Novels of the Eighteen Forties* (Oxford, 1954), p. 54

252. I am indebted here and in some of what follows to the introductory chapter in Newman Ivey White's *Shelley and his Contemporary Critics* (Durham, N.C. 1938).

253. *Fashion and Other Poems* (1825), p. 23

254. See a parliamentary report quoted in the *Westminster Review* (Jan, 1833) XVIII, 42

255. See Quinlan, *op. cit.*, pp. 160–1

256. Margaret Dalziel, *op. cit.*, and Louis James, *Fiction for the Working Man 1830–1850* (1963)

257. Quoted Dalziel, *op. cit.*, p. 24

258. Quoted Oscar Maurer in 'My Squeamish Public', *Studies in Bibliography* (1959) XII, 34

259. I am indebted here to Tom Winnifrith, *The Brontës and their Background* (1973), especially ch. 7

260. (July 1857) LVIII, 487. The writer is reviewing Mrs Gaskell's *Life of Charlotte Brontë*.

261. *Works* XII, 237. For the moral attack on Fielding see *Works* VII, 582–4

262. *Trollope: A Commentary* (rev. edn. 1945), pp. 169–75
263. Aina Rubenius, *The Woman Question in Mrs Gaskell's Life and Works* (Upsala, 1950), p. 211; Gardner B. Taplin, *The Life of Elizabeth Barrett Browning* (1957), p. 312
264. Alethea Hayter, *Mrs Browning* (1962), p. 182
265. Quoted Rubenius, *op. cit.*, p. 214
266. *The Letters of Mrs. Gaskell*, ed. J. A. V. Chapple and Arthur Pollard (Manchester, 1966), pp. 221, 223
267. *National Review* (Jan. 1859) VIII, 164–7
268. Lionel Stevenson, *The Ordeal of George Meredith* (1954), p. 72
269. *National Review* (July 1860) CI, 217
270. Quoted the *Magdalen's Friend* (Nov. 1861) II, 330–1
271. F. W. Maitland, *The Life and Letters of Leslie Stephen* (1906), p. 276; R. A. Colby, 'The Librarian Rules the Roost: The Career of Charles Edward Mudie (1818–1890)', *Wilson Library Bulletin* (1952) XXVI, 624–5
272. *Miscellanies* (1889) III, 277
273. Tillotson, *op. cit.*, p. 64
274. See Richard Stang, *The Theory of the Novel in England 1850–1870* (1959), p. 196
275. *The Letters of Charles Dickens*, ed. Walter Dexter (1938) III, 510–11. It seems Dickens came to reconsider his opinion: see Mark Antony De Wolfe Howe, *Memories of a Hostess* (1923), p. 146
276. *Illustrated Times* (24 Nov. 1866), p. 331
277. This point has been well made by Clarence Decker, *The Victorian Conscience* (New York, 1952), p. 79
278. See, for example, the *St. James's Gazette* (1 Nov. 1888), p. 3
279. *Liverpool Mercury* (1 Nov. 1888), p. 5
280. *Yellow Book* (July 1894) II, 262
281. Percy Lubbock, *Mary Cholmondeley* (1928), p. 25. It is probable that Miss Broughton made this remark in the early years of this century, but it would have been equally true in the nineties.
282. *Westminster Gazette* (9 March 1895), p. 1
283. *Contemporary Review* (June 1895) LXVII, 762
284. Quoted in *Nineteenth-Century Opinion*, ed. Michael Goodwin (1951), p. 170
285. See Richard Findlater, *Banned! A Review of Theatrical Censorship in Britain* (1967), p. 92

286. Quoted Quinlan, *op. cit.*, p. 63
287. John Moir, *Female Tuition; or an Address to Mothers* (1784), p. 12
288. John Gregory, *A Father's Legacy to his Daughters* (1774), pp. 50–1, 31–2
289. Quinlan, *op. cit.*, p. 141
290. *The Letters of Elizabeth Barrett Browning*, ed. F. G. Kenyon (1897) II, 258; Vineta and Robert A. Colby, *The Equivocal Virtue: Mrs. Oliphant and the Victorian Literary Market Place* (1966), pp. 77–9; J. C. Furnas, *op. cit.*, pp. 87, 398; *The George Eliot Letters*, ed. Gordon S. Haight (New Haven, 1954–6) VI, 120–1 and *passim*.
291. Alaric Alfred Watts, *Alaric Watts* (1884) I, 85–6
292. Helmut Gernsheim; *Julia Margaret Cameron* (1948), p. 80
293. See, for example, Mrs Opie's *Tales of Real Life* (1813) III, 163; and Lady Blessington's *Strathern* (1845) I, 69
294. For the biographical significance of this poem see R. W. Rader, *op. cit.*, p. 29
295. The Thackeray *Letters* IV, 419
296. Frederick Page, *Patmore: A Study in Poetry* (Oxford, 1933), p. 142
297. Robert Bernard Martin, *The Dust of Combat: A Life of Charles Kingsley* (1960), p. 107
298. *Shirley* I, 54; *The Professor*, p. 84; *Villette* I, 265
299. *My Lyrical Life* (1889) II, 222–3
300. *The George Eliot Letters* IV, 103–4
301. 'The Limits of Realism in Fiction', reprinted in Gosse's *Questions at Issue* (1893), pp. 152–3. For an intriguing examination of the Madonna-heroine in Shaw's *Candida*, written in 1894, see Margery M. Morgan, *The Shavian Playground* (1972), ch. 4
302. *Works* XXXIV, 371
303. Cecil Woodham Smith, *Florence Nightingale* (1950), p. 93
304. Reprinted in Mrs Linton's *The Girl of the Period and Other Social Essays* (1883) I, 10, 90, 2–3
305. Joseph Hatton, *Christopher Kenrick* (1869), p. 136
306. Quoted Janet Dunbar, *The Early Victorian Woman* (1953), p. 172
307. *Works* XXVII, 431; cf. *ibid*, pp. 208, 211
308. Quoted J. A. and Olive Banks, *op. cit.*, p. 41
309. *The Nineteenth Century* (May 1892) XXXI, 819–20

310. Quoted Viola Klein, 'The Emancipation of Women' in *Ideas and Beliefs of the Victorians* (1949), p. 207. Cf. 'An Appeal against Female Suffrage' signed by about a hundred eminent women in *The Nineteenth Century* (June 1889) XXV, 781–8

311. *Op. cit.*, p. 49.

312. *New Review* (June 1894) X, 682

313. Quoted C. W. Cunnington, *Feminine Attitudes*, p. 291

314. II, 135. For Mrs Oliphant's objection see *Blackwood's* (Sept. 1867) CII, 274

315. This poem and the one that follows may be found in Ellis' *Sonnets with Folk Songs from the Spanish* (1925).

316. Ellis, *My Life*, pp. 68–70

317. There is a vivid account of a 'very pleasing performance' by Dodd in 1760 before a group of aristocrats and royals in the *Yale Edition of Horace Walpole's Correspondence*, ed. W. S. Lewis (1937–) IX, 273–4. See also Gerald Howson, *The Macaroni Parson: A Life of the Unfortunate Dr. Dodd* (1973), pp. 39–46

318. *Letters to a Young Lady* I, 257–8

319. *Considerations of the Causes and the Prevalence of Female Prostitution* (1812), p. 25. Cf. the denunciation of the prostitute's remorseless tricks and wiles in a poem published the previous year, 'Winter-Night Meditations', by the father of the Brontës, reprinted in *Brontëana*, ed. J. Horsfall Turner (1898), pp. 37–43

320. *Sketches by Boz*, p. 224

321. *Works* III, 643

322. *The Girlhood of Queen Victoria: a Selection from her Diaries 1832–40*, ed. Viscount Esher (1912) II, 144

323. The poem is quoted and discussed in *Autobiographical Notes of the Life of William Bell Scott*, ed. W. Minto (1892) I, 101–2, 135–52.

324. *Works* IV, 555

325. *Proverbs* 31: 28; *Ruth* III, 253; *Recommended to Mercy* II, 248

326. Deacon, *op. cit.*, p. 49

327. Philip Collins, *Dickens and Crime* (1962), p. 109

328. *Prostitution Considered*, p. 56

329. *Prostitution Considered* (1870 edn.), pp. 262–3

330. A brief sketch of this remarkable woman is given by Pearl, *op. cit.*, pp. 142–5

331. See, for example, the *Saturday Review* (9 July) VIII, 49; the *Press* (16 July), pp. 740–1; *John Bull* (18 July), p. 460

332. Michael R. Booth, *English Melodrama* (1965), pp. 127–8; Louis James, *op. cit.*, p. 100
333. *Leader* (2 April 1853) IV, 333
334. G. B. Shaw, *Advice to a Young Critic* (1956), pp. 36–7
335. *A Woman's Thoughts about Women*, p. 297
336. *The Fallen and their Associates* (1870), p. 10
337. *Cornhill Magazine* (Feb. 1874) XXIX, 203
338. *Daily Telegraph* (4 April 1889), p. 3; (27 March), p. 5
339. Philip Collins, *op. cit.*, p. 114
340. *The Works of Oscar Wilde*, ed. G. F. Maine (1948), p. 410

Bibliography

Bibliography

A COMPREHENSIVE BIBLIOGRAPHY would be both wearisome and pointless. A selective bibliography, on the other hand, would necessarily be arbitrary and misleading. I have decided therefore to recommend my footnotes as the most useful guide I can give to further reading, and to list here only those works which I have found relevant and of fairly general interest, *and* which do not appear anywhere in my citations. The reader may recall I listed the works to which I am most indebted in the preface.

Altick, Richard D., *The English Common Reader* (Chicago 1957)
Brightfield, Myron F., *Victorian England in its Novels 1840–1870* (Los Angeles 1968)
Brown, Ford K., *Fathers of the Victorians* (Cambridge 1961)
Fryer, Peter, *The Birth Controllers* (1965)
Laver, James, *The Age of Optimism* (1966)
McGregor, O. R., *Divorce in England* (1957)
Pearsall, Ronald, *The Worm in the Bud* (1969)
Stafford, Ann, *The Age of Consent* (1964)
Stevas, Norman St John, *Obscenity and the Law* (1956)
Taylor, Gordon Rattray, *The Angel Makers* (1958)
Thomas, Donald, *A Long Time Burning* (1969)

Index

Index